Down the Danube

Down the Danube

from the Black Forest to the Black Sea

Guy Arnold

CASSELL

First published in the UK 1989 by
Cassell Publishers Ltd,
Artillery House, Artillery Row
London SW1P 1RT

Distributed in the United States by
Sterling Publishing Co. Inc.
2 Park Avenue, New York, NY 10016

Distributed in Australia by
Capricorn Link (Australia) Pty Ltd
PO Box 665, Lane Cove, NSW 2066

British Library Cataloguing in Publication Data
Arnold, Guy
  Down the Danube : from the Black Forest to the Black
  sea.
  1. Europe. Danube River region. Description & travel
  I. Title
  914.96'04

ISBN 0-304-322474-4

Filmset in Linotron Times by
Input Typesetting Ltd, London

Printed in Great Britain by
Mackays of Chatham plc

Contents

Introduction

The Danube is one of the most used waterways in the world, an ancient European highway with beautiful cities and three splendid capitals–Vienna, Budapest and Belgrade–gracing its banks. Castles and monasteries sit along its crags. In prehistory it was a principal route into the heartland of Europe: some of the earliest movements of peoples, thousands of years before Christ, made their slow progressions from the Middle East up the Danube to populate the forest wastelands of central Europe. As both transport route and boundary, the river has been fought over through the centuries while Roman remains along its course signify its importance to that long-lasting empire of the ancient world.

Alexander the Great made an expedition through what is now Bulgaria to subjugate tribes which might otherwise have posed a threat to his campaign to conquer Asia. He reached the Danube (the Greek Ister) and decided to cross to demonstrate his power to the Getae and force their submission. But, as Arrian says, Alexander had a longing to cross to the other side. Four centuries later Trajan conquered the Getae and added Dacia (Rumania) to Rome's possessions. Many other military commanders have fought along the banks of this great river.

Having travelled mostly outside Europe–in Africa, Asia and the Americas–I felt it was time to turn my attention to Europe and explore its greatest river. I decided that the first 400 kilometres (248 miles) of the Danube, from the source at Donaueschingen to Regensburg where the barge traffic begins, should be covered on foot. This meant reducing my luggage to an absolute minimum so I purchased a light Austrian army rucksack from one of London's many military surplus stores and that, with a small shoulder bag for my camera, was all my luggage. Otherwise I made few plans. Instead, I decided simply to pursue the river, never trying to cover too much ground in any day and using whatever appeared to be the most

1

appropriate form of available transport. So I walked, begged lifts on the barges, took trains or buses between towns on the river's banks and, on occasion, used the passenger hydrofoils. And slowly, as I experienced its differing moods and watched its growing size, I came to understand that the Danube has a life of its own.

The nature of travel compels a writer to present cameos or snapshots of what he encounters: a scene in a small town, a bizarre conversation on a train, a startling face, an unexpected and unnerving encounter with customs officials. A sense of distance helps. Gradually as I approached the Black Sea along the Danube's 2,840 kilometres (1,765 miles), I saw the tiny glittering stream gradually transform itself into the huge roiling waterway which separates Rumania and Bulgaria.

Vienna, Budapest and Belgrade grace the river's banks, each with its own long history. Belgrade was once regarded as the forward post of Europe facing the Moslem Turks while the siege of Vienna in 1683 saw the climax of the Turkish threat to Christian Europe. Often in the course of its history the river has iced over. It did so during the fourth century, enabling the barbarians to swarm across it into the crumbling empire of Rome. It iced over again at Budapest in the winter of 1984–85 during one of Europe's coldest seasons in a generation.

The Danube drains an area of 777,000 square kilometres (300,000 square miles). It rises in the Black Forest of southern Germany and reaches the Black Sea at its delta in Rumania 2,840 kilometres (1,765 miles) further east. It is a silt-bearing river and each year extends its delta into the Black Sea. It is rarely blue and the further downstream one travels the more likely one is to find the Danube murky brown, for it receives a great deal of mud from its tributaries and waste from passing ships and barges. Pollution control ranks low in East European priorities and arguments about conservation surround the proposed dams in Austria and Hungary.

Organised tourism has killed the old art of travel. Everything is done for you: accommodation is laid on, coaches take you to your scheduled places of interest, guides take care of language problems. And, too often, when people travel by car the vehicle rules: the itinerary is determined by what is considered to be a comfortable day's drive. In a beer garden in West Germany I saw Americans turn to neighbouring Germans and ask for information in English. They did so without apology or hesitation, as though all the world ought to know their language. Seeing such behaviour one can comprehend why the rich English were so often disliked in the Europe of the nineteenth century.

It is both intriguing and exasperating to have to puzzle out customs which seem incomprehensible at first. Thus, in the early stages of my journey in southern Germany, when I was walking between small towns along the river, I did not understand the practice of the *Stammtisch*, the table reserved in a German *Gasthof* for use by its regular customers. At first I was only aware that certain tables had some special significance. Discovering the answers to such puzzles imbues travel with much of its excitement.

The football tragedy in Brussels (when 39 spectators, only one of them British, were killed as a result of riotous behaviour) occurred while I was on the trip. I am British, I deplore the sort of conduct that brought this particular tragedy about and so was not surprised or offended when an Austrian asked me: 'But why are British football fans so aggressive and brutal?' Why indeed? Yet I found his criticism of the British hard to take. Travel can give one a totally different perspective on one's own country.

One of my happiest 'cameos' from eastern Europe was the sight of a Hungarian Communist intellectual in a plush restaurant tucking into caviar as though it were the last food on earth. In the east European countries, apart from the fairly obvious presence of the military, the most conspicious signs of Communism which I encountered were: border searches for paper matter, in case subversive literature were being imported; red stars on the tops of buildings including churches; street names such as November 7 or Lenin; and statues to Marx, Engels or other Communist heroes which were unmistakable in the angular artistry which is a hallmark of socialist sculpture.

The Danube axis was used as a pathway into Europe from at least 5500 BC, as the ancient farming people of the Middle East, perhaps from overcrowded Sumer, sought new lands to settle. These early migrants either moved along the Mediterranean or followed the Danube and then the Rhine valley northwards, so that from the beginning of history the river has acted as a highway. Again and again invaders from Asia were to arrive upon the plains to the north of the river which sooner or later they sought to cross to reach the fertile, more civilised lands to the south.

Rome's influence upon the Danube and the river's influence upon Rome were both profound. During the reign of Augustus (27 BC–14 AD) the territories bordering the Danube from Switzerland to the Black Sea were annexed to the empire; under his successor, Tiberius (14–37 AD) a system of roadways was created to cover these Danube lands. For centuries the river acted as the frontier of Rome, as evidenced by the remains of forts and walls. In 104 AD Trajan built a great bridge (remains of which can still be seen) across the Danube below the Iron Gates to make possible his conquest of Dacia (Rumania). In both Yugoslavia and Rumania the emperor Trajan is celebrated in street names, while museums make much of the Roman

3

connection. Military camps on the river's banks developed into cities. The philosopher emperor, Marcus Aurelius (161–180), spent eight bitter winter campaigns on the frozen banks of the Danube facing the barbarians who threatened Rome. The severity of the final winter killed him. Septimus Severus (193–211) controlled twelve legions along the Danube – nearly half the empire's permanent regular army – when in 193 he made his bid for supreme power. But by the fourth century the Danube no longer held the barbarians at bay; they crossed it increasingly to ravage the provinces of the empire. In about 376, under the emperor Valens, a million Goths crossed the Danube to the south; this marked the real beginning of the collapse of the Western Empire.

The legend of the Nibelungs relates to Europe's two great rivers, the Rhine and the Danube: the Nibelungs followed the Danube to the court of King Etzel (Attila) and their destruction.

Napoleon's campaigns often brought him to the banks of the Danube. He had a good deal to say about the river. He wrote of his defeat at Aspern-Essling: 'It was not my fault that the Danube rose sixteen feet in one night. But for that, I should have finished off the Habsburgs once for all.' On another occasion in Vienna he contemplated ruling the world 'from this office on the Danube'. The river intrigued him as a symbol for the imagination. Speaking to Gourgaudon, one of his intimates, he said: 'It is like the Danube: at the source of the river one can cross it in a bound.'

War has touched the river so often that its effects are impossible to escape. There are many reminders of World War Two the length of the river. Central Europe has certainly had its share of sadness and the bravery of a superbly rebuilt Budapest, for example, cannot eradicate the political effects of a war that left Europe split down the middle. It may be possible to cross the Iron Curtain as a traveller, but the differences which divide the two sides remain profound.

Yet, coming from insular, isolated Britain my journey made me realise forcibly just how far the British remain apart from the main springs of European life. Despite their many antagonisms Germans, Austrians, Czechs, Hungarians, Yugoslavs, Rumanians and even Russians trading up the river see the Danube as a highway which belongs to them all. It is a great commercial road for the endless stream of barges as well as a storehouse of historical associations.

Chapter One

Munich

I began my journey in Munich. The city sits astride the River Isar and is many kilometres from the Danube. It is a beautiful city of wide streets and great squares with magnificent public buildings, splendid parks and a profusion of museums and galleries. The greatest cultural glory is the *Alte Pinakothek* gallery with its incredible collection of giant Rubens canvases and Dürers. My friend Ruth Schutz lives in Munich and she provided me with a *pied-à-terre* from which to organise my journey. But I did not begin in Munich for any of these reasons: I chose Munich because of Hitler.

For one of my generation it is almost impossible to think of Germany without also thinking of the Hitler war which changed the face of Europe and the politics of the world. I was to be reminded of this many times on my travels. My earliest political memories include snatches of Hitler's speeches broadcast over the BBC and then on Sunday 3 September 1939, the tired voice of Neville Chamberlain saying: 'That was the final note. No such undertaking was received by the time stipulated, and, consequently, this country is at war with Germany.'

War for a child in Croydon meant air-raid warnings, the haunting wail of the siren, bombs, collecting shrapnel in the garden in the early morning, Spitfires and Hurricanes flying low over the house on their way to the nearby airport, the blackout, rationing and the other excitements of that time. And, always, constant references to Hitler. Later came victory and the partition of Germany, the Cold War and a divided world. It was the age of the cinema and an endless stream of war films depicted stiff British upper lips or American heroes winning campaigns single-handed. But if those were my recollections how many more were there for battered Europe: for Germany herself or for occupied countries over which the invading Allied armies later fought their way into Hitler's Reich?

In Britain the name Munich is forever coupled with that of

Chamberlain and his policy of appeasement which was enshrined in the Munich Agreement of September 1938 that forced Czechoslovakia to cede Sudetenland to Germany. But if the name has such associations for the British what does it mean for Germans? The National Socialists had their beginnings here; Bavaria and Munich were the heartland of the movement. The city was the scene of the unsuccessful *Putsch* of 1923 which led to Hitler's imprisonment for treason. In prison he completed *Mein Kampf*. Hitler's early successes and failures were in Munich, the city which he loved above all others. As he wrote in *Mein Kampf* (1925):

'There was the heartfelt love which seized me for this city more than for any other place that I knew, almost from the first hour of my sojourn there. A *German* city . . . If today I am more attached to this city than to any other spot on earth in this world, it is partly due to the fact that it is and remains inseparably bound up with the development of my own life.'

Munich is one of the loveliest cities in Europe. It has been a city since 1253; it was largely destroyed by fire in 1327, then rebuilt. It suffered greatly in the Thirty Years' War (1618–48), was ravaged by plague and has undergone many changes of fortune since then. In our own time it became the centre of the Nazi movement and was devastated by Allied bombing which destroyed most of the old city. Since 1945 it has been so well restored that one has to search for evidence of war damage and today it is one of the principal tourist attractions of West Germany.

As I was to discover, my journey provided me with many reminders of World War Two. There were German reminders in the form of wargraves and monuments. Allied monuments and later, behind the Iron Curtain, exhibitions whose principal purpose was to keep alive memories of what had happened.

Forty years is a long time but World War Two has not receded into the past. I learnt some German viewpoints which startled by their ordinariness. There is an absolute sadness about war which has been commented upon many times. Historians reckon that the Thirty Years' War set Germany back in relation to the rest of Europe by two centuries. World War Two established divisions which will be with us into the foreseeable future. Sometimes I met German regrets: nostalgia for a Germany that had disappeared, for a Europe lost forever. And this had its counterpart in the eastern countries, where the order which Hitler would have imposed has been replaced by a Communist order. Part of the paraphernalia to sustain Communism relies upon a vivid and constant reminder of what Hitler stood for.

Munich's beer cellars were favourite meeting places for the Nazis and today their popularity remains as major tourist attractions. The *Ratskeller* beneath the townhall is famous, so I went there for lunch one day. I went early to ensure I could select a place to my liking and settled upon one of the large round tables which seat nine. It was then empty.

At this stage my German was minimal, although I had worked hard at books and tapes before leaving England. Carefully I decided what I wanted to eat and managed to give the waitress my order without a hitch. To my vast satisfaction I found I had sufficiently mastered the language to answer a query which she put to me, while managing to conceal the tiny extent of my total vocabulary. Then I sat back to watch the scene around me. The lunch hour was upon us and the *Ratskeller* was rapidly filling. For a while people went to smaller tables and I was left in isolation.

Then a family came to my table: a man, his wife and their teenage son. They ignored me to take three seats further round the table, leaving one space between the teenage son and me, the father sitting in the middle. The man was of diminutive stature with a crinkled old face, white short-cropped hair topping a small bullet-shaped head. He had a thin, obstinate mouth, ruddy complexion and pale blue eyes. His wife was much younger but also small; a little black-haired woman who was clearly the family manager. Their son, the child of a late marriage, was about 17: a large, raw-boned awkward youth who tried to maintain an air of detachment as though he were not with his parents at all.

The waitress serving our table was dumpy and plain, tired from a lifetime of dealing with ungrateful customers. She gave this family trio one look and asked abruptly what they wanted. Their order did not please her. 'Not possible,' she snapped but the man, lines of obstinacy forming round his small mouth, insisted and, in the end, with haughty reluctance she agreed. When she had gone the man looked at his wife and said: 'There, you see, we shall have it.' They had managed both to infuriate the waitress and earn her contempt. Indeed, at one stage while taking their order, she had looked across at me and raised her eyebrows.

They had ordered *Weisswurst*. This is a non-smoked white sausage which, tradition dictates, should be served only as a snack between midnight and midday, not as the main course for the midday meal; hence the irritation and contempt of the waitress. It said much for the man's obstinacy that he got his way. The waitress returned with a large tureen of steaming water in which reposed three double white sausages. She provided plates and brought the man a beer. Neither the wife nor the son had anything to drink.

The woman helped first her husband and then her son to their

7

sausages and the boy and his mother at once began eating. But the father wanted a roll of bread. There was a basket of rolls in front of them but it did not contain the variety he sought. He looked round in an effort to catch the eye of the waitress. She was not easily to be caught but in the end his persistence trapped her. He described the roll he wanted. She indicated the basket but he only shook his head. Reluctantly she went off to look, pouting her fury, to return after a perfunctory search to say none was available. An argument ensued: she was adamant, so was he.

How long this exchange might have lasted is difficult to say but at that moment another threesome approached the table. They looked at the family trio, then at me and the man asked me if they might sit there. Graciously I bowed assent. The waitress hastened to place menus in front of them, relieved to escape from the argument with her obstinate customer.

The newcomers, a middle-aged man and two women, were of the prosperous burgher class, the man's sense of his own importance clearly outstripping reality. His wife was a strong *Hausfrau* but their guest, whom they seated between them, was slightly older than her hosts, somewhat more distinguished in appearance, indeed almost aristocratic in that company.

The waitress, impressed by a difference in quality, fawned upon the newcomers. They took their time choosing and when the waitress finally turned to get their order the white-haired father opposite tried once more to engage her in the matter of rolls, but she tossed her head and ignored him. Not to be put off by such treatment he beckoned another waitress only to be informed that it was not her table. His wife and son, meanwhile, were halfway through their white sausages while his remained untouched, cooling upon his plate. Now he forked it up to return it to the still steaming tureen of water, muttered something to his wife and rose to go in search of the roll he deemed essential to his meal.

The *Ratskeller* is large with many ramifications: there are big interconnected rooms and a variety of different-sized alcoves to the sides. In my imagination I peopled these alcoves with Hitler's soldiers or Nazi officials in the uniforms of the 'Thousand Year Reich'. Instead, for the next five minutes I kept glimpsing the white-haired man in his search for the perfect roll, wandering between tables, peering into baskets to the astonishment of other diners, then again passing from sight.

By this time the second trio had become aware of their three neighbours–me they could not place–and looked with increasing disdain upon the woman and boy eating *Weisswurst*. At one point the man turned to me. I had a horror that he would ask me something which I could not understand and so force me to betray my lack of

German, but instead he gave me a little bow, an intimation that we were 'quality' as opposed to those peasants.

The waitress returned with their order. The man and his wife each had a plate of stew with a large dumpling while their guest had snails. The man also had a plate of salad. Their guest had a glass of white wine, the man a beer, his wife nothing. There was, I thought, a certain parsimonious element about their meal, an unwillingness to stretch things despite the guest they wished to impress.

And then the father returned clutching in his hand a long roll of a kind not present in the two baskets of bread upon our table. He held it up for all to see, his little bullet head gleaming from his search, a triumph of obstinacy fulfilled. He sat down and told his wife that he had been right all along. The two of them ignored their son who seemed pleased by this lack of attention and ate the last of his white sausage. The wife took her husband's sausages out of the bowl of no longer steaming water and placed them in front of him once more. But he was not yet ready to begin. He looked round for our waitress and as she came by he held up his roll in a gesture of victory: 'You see,' he said, 'there are such rolls.'

Once more the waitress tossed her head, a now familiar gesture, and walked angrily away. The aristocratic guest opposite took no notice; she was busy forking the last of her snails from its shell. But the wife looked across the table with a snort of contempt while her husband again looked towards me to give a second apologetic little inclination of his head to excuse the behaviour of the 'peasants' with whom we were obliged to share our table. I was smartly dressed on that occasion and the man had clearly assigned me to a category at least as exalted if not higher than that of his guest. I gave the barest of nods in acknowledgement, which increased my standing yet further. I was not to be upset by such loutish behaviour, his expression made plain.

My obstinate friend finished his roll and looked round, half expecting to get another, but his wife and son were now ready to go so he refrained. He had savoured his triumph. I was reminded of the English music hall song: 'You get no bread with one meat ball.' He, however, was the exception.

The waitress came to hover; she wanted to clear us away and make room for the next wave of diners. The burgher paid his bill, after checking each item with care, gave her a very small tip which he exactly calculated before her eyes and for which she was duly grateful and then the trio got to their feet to leave, the man remembering to give me a final bow. The peasants paid their bill, the man reminding the waitress that there *were* rolls of the kind he had wanted. He did not give her a tip. They too departed. The waitress looked at me but maintaining the pose of superiority which had stood me in such good stead throughout the meal I took a sip of my beer thereby indicating that I was not yet ready to depart. At once she left me alone.

I found this scene curiously reassuring. I could have witnessed something similar in England. But in Munich, in the *Ratskeller*, where my thoughts had been on Hitler and the Nazis singing the *Horst Wessel*, I had instead been treated to a comedy of manners; bourgeois Germans concerned with hierarchy on the one hand and Bavarian peasants betraying native obstinacy on the other, both characteristics of a Germany that long preceded and will long survive Hitler and everything he stood for.

Chapter Two

The Black Forest

I took the train from Munich to St Georgen halfway up the valley of the River Brigach. This and the Breg are the two tributaries which come together at Donaueschingen to form the Danube. Only upstream of Ulm, which sits astride the river, does the railway follow the Danube valley. I felt I was getting a preview of my river as at first just occasionally and then almost constantly we ran alongside it or crossed it by bridge. Names which meant nothing to me then–Ehingen or Riedlingen–were just stops on a seven-hour journey. But after Sigmaringen the valley closes in on the river: high crags and forest-covered hills crowded the train below as it slowly wound its way up one of the most spectacular stretches of the entire river. Here the Danube is small, sometimes blue-green as it reflects the forest above. It is not easy to imagine how fierce a torrent it must have once been to cut such a dramatic path through these crags, for when I caught sight of it from the train window it was no more than a gentle meandering stream, perhaps only 30 metres (90 ft) wide.

I watched a happy holiday trio across from me in the open-plan carriage. A man in his mid-fifties sat with his wife and sister: pleasant-faced, prosperous, middle-class Germans. As we wound up the Danube valley the man visibly relaxed: he was going on vacation. They became increasingly animated at the prospect of their approaching holiday. At one stop the man left the train to purchase something, followed by injunctions from his wife to be quick; he returned to his place just as the train moved out of the station. He had bought a box of 50 small cigars, a holiday indulgence. He went to the platform between the two carriages so that he could immediately have a smoke. It was the conscious act of a man unbending, putting aside the normal restraints which governed his life. He came back to talk happily, like a boy released from school, making what I suspect were not very good jokes at which the two women laughed dutifully.

Near Beuron, where the Danube looked glitteringly lovely under a brilliant sun and the rock crags broke through the high forest above us, the man across the way spread out a map on the seat beside him and proceeded to identify landmarks. I was also busy examining my map and he looked at me in friendly complicity. There were plenty of landmarks to identify. Here the Danube might be called the *Schloss* river: weird, Disney-like castles, perched high on rocky eminences without any obvious approach to them, looked down on the valley below. In the sunlight they belonged to a fairy landscape but in a storm backed by great clouds they would at once take on a grim quality as guardians of the valley, eyries of medieval barons.

The man stole occasional glances at me thereafter, inviting understanding. I smiled my agreement back at him and, happily, he returned to a study of his map. His pleasure at release was infectious and as his boisterousness grew, so too did that of his two companions. Ours was a brief, passing acquaintance; we never actually spoke.

By two o'clock when we arrived at St Georgen the day had clouded over. St Georgen is a small winter sports resort on the edge of the Black Forest. The town is halfway up the valley of the Brigach which I intended to explore first. A steep hill leads from the station to the town and, for the first time, I began to get the feel of my Austrian army pack. I tried three small guest houses in my search for a room—each was firmly closed—before I settled upon the Stag. It was the best place in town. I had at once, therefore, broken my resolution to save money on accommodation. But, I argued, it was pleasant to begin in comfort.

The Black Forest stretches for 160 kilometres (99 miles) from north to south and varies in width between 25 and 60 kilometres forming one of the most beautiful regions of Germany. Although once quite remote, it has now become one of the country's most popular holiday areas. I travelled out of season and did not encounter many tourists until I reached Ulm.

The western extremity of the Danube Basin lies in the Black Forest where the two streams, the Breg and the Brigach, rise. They unite in Donaueschingen to form the Danube. Donaueschingen lies on the eastern edge of the Black Forest and although that is officially where the river begins, there is argument as to its true source: the Brigach on which St Georgen lies; the Breg; or the castle park at Donaueschingen. For this reason I planned to make trips up both valleys. The Black Forest is a deceptive name; the area does not consist of solid forest but is broken up by open valleys and farm land.

When finally I set off to walk through the edge of the Black Forest from the valley of the Brigach I felt that my real journey had begun. It is true that I was not yet following the Danube itself but I was exploring one of its original tributaries. I like to be thorough and I was determined to explore both tributaries so that no one could later say I had not been to the true source of my river. It rained as a foretaste of the weather to come for much of my journey down the river.

It is easy to see how the Black Forest got its name. Even in bright sunshine it is dark and gloomy below the canopy of the tall pines and firs. When it rains the forest indeed becomes black. Curiously, the steady noise of rain on the trees has the effect of emphasising the silence that is so characteristic of the forest. Suddenly one comes out of the trees into one of the small rolling valleys to follow the undulating path before it disappears among the trees again. It is marvellous walking country.

The Germans in their thorough way have created the *Wanderweg* (a path for walkers and cyclists) and to enable the wanderer to follow the route of his choice these paths are each marked with different coloured arrows. From time to time along the forest paths one comes upon a board with various walks–9, 18 or 24 kilometres for example–marked upon it and each walk will have its own colour. At path junctions it is advisable to check that you are following the correct path marked by its appropriate coloured arrow–red, brown, yellow or blue; sometimes I would come upon an intersection where three or four coloured arrows pointed in different directions. They were immensely confusing.

I made a great circle, lost my no doubt correctly arrowed path several times but eventually followed the Brigach back down the valley to St Georgen. I was soaking wet, a good introduction to a long wet summer. The tiny stream of the Brigach which (like Napoleon on imagination) I could and did easily leap gave little promise of the mighty Danube to come. But I had made a beginning; I was coming to grips with my river.

Although, deliberately, I had made no plans, a journey such as mine sets its own pattern. On walking days I would arrive at my hotel in the late afternoon and if I had just arrived in a town for the first time, might spend an hour tramping round in search of a place that suited me. I would settle in, bath and change, then set off to explore the town. I usually spent the evening in the bar or restaurant where I could survey the local scene, write notes or read. I found that the bar of my *Gasthof* usually provided the best vantage-point from which to observe local customs. The evening after my first long tramp I watched an Anglo-German business deal in the making.

I was studying the menu when a middle-aged, formally dressed man came to sit at a nearby table. He ordered a beer and told the waitress he would eat later when his friend joined him. The hotel manager came to greet him with a certain deference and make sure

13

all was well. They shook hands, a constant German practice to which I was still unaccustomed. I assumed he was a local man of some importance or, maybe, just a good customer. Now he sat nursing his beer and I turned back to my book.

Then a large, youngish man, casual and relaxed in an open-necked shirt came to join him. The businessman rose and said 'Hello'. The newcomer replied with a broad Scots accent. The German, naturally, spoke English. They ordered food and talked of delivery dates. At first I thought it was run-of-the-mill business but changed my mind as I caught more of the conversation. They were concerned with some shipments of heavy machinery that were to come from Britain. The local man, the host, spoke in correct if slightly stilted, formal English; his guest sometimes spoke too fast to be clearly understood and had to repeat himself. The local businessman was dressed far more formally than anyone else in the dining room and clearly regarded their dinner as a business meeting. Not so the Scotsman, who had adopted the local custom; Germans like to change into their casual, *freizeit*, clothes at the end of the day. I suspect he had done so deliberately: each was playing for an advantage. When the host did not understand something–it could well have been because of the Scots accent–he would say '*bitte*' inquiringly, forgetting his correct English.

They were absorbed and so was I. The deal clearly had a long way to go. Phrases about motor types, generators and '80 power', meaningless to me, came across regularly. Then the Scot proposed: 'Let's talk delivery dates.' But at this point they were joined by a second Englishman–reserve battalions being thrown in. The German was slightly taken aback, clearly not expecting the newcomer, but he recovered his composure quickly enough while calling the waitress to order another drink.

It was an interesting scene and I spied upon it shamelessly. The two British businessmen would chat with each other about some point, often nothing whatever to do with the deal, and their German host would look on politely with a slightly lost expression, an eyebrow of inquiry raised. In any case he had different priorities; while his two guests chatted in their own tongue he ate his way stolidly through his food. Then the Scot asked about their programme for the next day and courteously, slowly, he took them through their forthcoming itinerary. Whatever the deal was about both sides wanted it.

The difference of approach between the German and his two British guests came across clearly, even though I could hear only snatches of their talk: half sentences or phrases. Their behaviour, their physical activities at that table, told me more. The German had the psychological advantage of speaking English while between them his two guests possessed no more than a *bitte* or two. But this also put an added strain upon him. He was correct: in both his dress and in his approach. *Ordnung*! The Germans love it or at least we British think they do. He ate first: get the meal out of the way then conduct the business talk, go over details, set the next day's programme. It is a matter of temperament. His difficulty lay in the fact that the two Britons did not operate in the same way. They began by being off-handedly casual; but not too off-hand and not too casual. It was a tactic, of course. They were both directors and St Georgen is hardly in the mainstream of German industrial towns so the prospective deal must have offered attractions. The two of them, as if by pre-arrangement, talked business, reverted to idle chat between them-selves, asked their host an inconsequential question and then returned to business. When finally their host asked what they would like to do afterwards–he had decided it was now time to relax–they plumped for a *Bierkeller* the Scot had discovered the night before. The manager came to hover, wanting his German customer to have all possible attention: what was good for him and his company was also good for St Georgen. When eventually they got up to leave (I had prolonged my meal indefinitely) I gave the edge in the deal, just, to the German.

One carries stereotypes through life. I certainly have my own picture of a typical German. The scene I had watched reminded me of an encounter of my own years before with another German in very different circumstances. Then I had been negotiating an aid deal for a newly independent African country. My host in Bonn was a senior civil servant. Clearly intrigued by my apparently varied background he asked what I had done before undertaking the particular job which brought me to Bonn. I told him. 'And before that?' he asked again. Once more I told him. His face registered an increasing bewilderment at the extent of my activities and experience and then, after careful thought, he declared: 'In Germany we would say, "You are not very seerious".'

From St Georgen I took the bus down the valley in steady rain to the little medieval town of Villingen. The town's history goes back 1,000 years. It possesses a charming twelfth-century minster and its medieval walls are intact. In the old townhall, which houses an exhibition of the town's history, a woman guide, on discovering I was English, insisted on showing me round. She had no knowledge of English and this forced me to practise my slowly improving German.

An open market flourished round the minster whose massive doors had copper figures in bas-relief. This region of Germany forms part of the Roman Catholic heartland of Europe. Inside the minster a series of paintings high on the walls depicted the Stations of the Cross. As I was to discover in many towns, though not in this particular case, a plain church exterior often hides the most gloriously decorated ceilings and ornate altars for which the Danube valley is famous.

I spent half a day wandering round Villingen and felt that I was beginning to distinguish some of the characteristics of the region: the thick accents, the distinctive grey suits with their green facings. I was also discovering how much more palatable was German beer in contrast to English beer.

I am not by temperament racist; nor am I one of those Englishmen who prefer to travel in ignorance, and so maintain a feeling of superiority to the rest of Europe. Such sensitivities make it difficult for me to discourse with confidence upon German characteristics. If I say that at this early stage of my journey I found the people of Germany's deep south in both their persons and steady approach to life to be slow and heavy I may be misunderstood. I am not saying they are dull. And if I comment upon the German love of order and precision, punctuality and punctiliousness, it's because these are all characteristics which I personally value. It is easy to fall into traps: British stereotypes of Germans are as well known as German stereotypes of the British. At this juncture I simply found that some preconceptions were actually confirmed.

Chapter Three

Donaueschingen

Donaueschingen lies on the Brigach just above its confluence with the Breg. An eighteenth-century *Schloss*, more palace than castle, its stucco peeling, its grounds half overgrown and tramped by sightseers, sits in the centre of the town, surrounded by a park. It is the former residence of the Fürstenburg family, last renovated between 1893 and 1896, and contains a famous library. A spring of clear water, walled and surrounded by a walkway, rises in the grounds of the *Schloss*. It is a graceful, charming starting point for Europe's grandest river. Underground its waters proceed to join those of the Brigach and Breg to form the Danube. This spring is the official source of the river: it is 2,840 kilometres (1,765 miles) from the mouth of the river on the Black Sea and 678 metres (2,224 ft) above sea level (Col. pl. 3).

Donaueschingen is a small pleasant town and though guide books list its chief functions as rail junction, brewing, metal and wood working its principal attraction is its possession of the Danube spring. The town lies on the eastern edge of the Black Forest in the deep south of Baden. Of all European rivers only the Volga is longer and drains a larger area; the Danube discharges a greater volume of water. The river passes through eight countries: in West Germany and Austria it is the Donau; in Czechoslovakia the Dunaj; in Hungary the Duna; in Yugoslavia and Bulgaria the Dunav; in Rumania the Dunarea; and in the USSR the Dunay.

It was a lovely evening when I visited the Danube spring. The limpid pool which is the source of the Danube is a traditional wishing well and visitors must look down upon it over the circular wall to make their wish like visitors to the tomb of Napoleon in Paris who are obliged to bow their heads as they look down upon the great man's final resting place. It is customary to throw a coin into the pool. I duly threw in a deutschmark but at that stage I had no idea how my journey would work out. I was not in search of anything in particular from the Danube. I simply wanted to make an old-fashioned progression along a much used, ancient highway. I was to walk along paths at the river's edge or roads that were near but by no means always in sight of the Danube; I would take buses and trains from one point on the river to another and travel in barges or passenger boats. At Donaueschingen the Black Sea was indeed remote.

After a day of rain the evening sun brought many visitors to the now glistening park. They wandered round the Danube spring and then they wandered over the park grounds in front of the castle's dignified though neglected façade. At some distance from the spring, apparently unconnected, the Brigach runs through the park grounds: an elegant, shallow, swift-flowing stream with thick trees overhanging its banks. I soon left the evening crowd of sightseers as I followed the Brigach through the woods until I came upon its junction with the Breg. This I still had to investigate before finally setting off for the Black Sea.

When I arrived at Donaueschingen from Villingen, I wandered for some time in search of a place to stay, determined on this occasion to begin my regime of economy by patronising a cheap inn. After a considerable search I settled upon a small unprepossessing hotel. The landlord was a fat, unkempt man, his wife an even larger, shapeless woman with heavy coarse features and a squint. My room though was cheap and I had my own shower.

The next day I intended to explore the Breg valley but when I rose from my breakfast table both the landlord and his wife who were drinking coffee at the big round *Stammtisch* also came to their feet: in courtesy at my departure? to receive my money? to support one another in this purpose? I believe they assumed that no one, and certainly not a foreigner such as I, would wish to remain a second day in their establishment. When I explained that I was going walking for the day they were amazed. Then they relaxed.

The stream of the Breg rises near the small Black Forest town of Furtwangen some 35 kilometres (22 miles) from Donaueschingen. Furtwangen is famous for its collection of historical clocks; it is cuckoo-clock country. There are those who dispute the source of the Danube and claim that the Breg represents the true beginning of the river. But a well-known German saying: '*Brigach und Breg bringen die Donau zuweg*', suggests that only when the two streams have joined does the Danube proper begin.

I did a lot of walking that day, at first through thick forest. Again it rained and again I was confused by the frequent, different coloured arrows marking the variety of walks. In mid-morning I found an inn where I stopped for a beer. The public rooms were deserted except for a bent, sour-looking woman setting the tables for lunch. She served me without greeting or comment and then returned to her work.

I often wonder what sets people talking. I must have sat there for 20 minutes over my beer and all the while she laid places on the tables around me. Then, when my beer was all but finished, I took out my map to study my way. The moment she saw the map she became almost voluble in her desire to talk. Was I on a walking tour? Yes! That day, I told her, I was following the course of the Breg, then I intended to pursue the Danube to the Black Sea. At that her ordinary, plain-to-ugly face which showed only lines and strain from a hard-working life became transformed by a sudden friendly smile. Just what significance such a journey held for her I shall never know. She was only just able to decipher my German. She sat on a chair at the next table patiently listening as I stuttered out my plans with inadequate vocabulary. She gave me directions for the rest of the day's walk, though these I hardly needed, and wished me a 'great' voyage to the Black Sea. Her interest was unfeigned and charming yet I had thought her sour and unfriendly.

Much later in the day in heavy rain I found an inn which might have been an advertisement for an older Germany, the Baden of pre-World War One. When I entered the main public room the noise of conversation came from one corner where the *Stammtisch* had a full complement of old men. Several of them had large walrus moustaches, one magnificent specimen was pure white like its owner's hair, while their accents were so thick that I would have had great difficulty understanding them even had my own German been far better. I asked for a dry white wine, local; what came was pleasant but sweet.

I was served by a woman even larger than the hostess at my hotel. She was aided by two huge men in their late twenties, obviously her sons. All three lacked shape but were of forbidding strength. One of these strong sons now made up a foursome with three of the old men who settled round a table behind mine. They were going to play cards. The game was *Schafkopf* (sheepshead), a game that was immensely popular the length of my journey to Ulm and beyond. It is played with great intensity for money, although betting on it is forbidden since its devotees are known to gamble away their wages at a sitting. This I learnt later. At that point I was surprised only at the intensity with which the foursome played, slapping cards down upon the table with gusto, especially when a card was to take the trick. I was to witness *Schafkopf* in inn after inn along my way: sometimes in the remoter places money was on the table, at others it was not in evidence. But always there would be the same intensity, the same banging down of cards, the same oblivion of players to those about them. I looked round as this game got underway and

19

one of the old men laughed happily at me; it was a vice which clearly brought great enjoyment to its devotees.

The *Stammtisch* of old men could have been lifted straight out of a Brueghel painting: the faces were weathered, the noses long and thin or bulbous and red, a triple chin would set off one head beside another on long withered, scrawny necks. Sometimes cunning peasant eyes wandered briefly over the stranger in their midst, but after an appraisal they left me in peace to drink my wine and returned to their habitual gossip. Calls for drinks were dealt with by the big proprietress or the other son. No money passed over, a note was merely made on a pad. My anglicised High German accent with half the words incorrect drew good-humoured laughter but otherwise they politely left me to my own devices. I spent an hour there before my bus arrived (on schedule to the minute) to take me back down the valley.

Now I felt ready for the real journey down the Danube: I had both Brigach and Breg behind me and from then on, as I walked, it would be beside the Danube.

Only the *Stammtisch* was occupied when I went for my supper that evening. I was given a small table to myself. Eight men sat round the table engaged in a heated argument. Like many such arguments among friends or acquaintances it did not at first appear to be serious. Irwin was the target of their attacks. He sat with his back to me: a big thickset man with long black hair and a bushy beard. His appearance was remarkably similar to illustrations of Ludwig III of Bavaria, as depicted on its postage stamps prior to World War One. Irwin's broad shoulders and massive back strained the fabric of his waistcoat. His complexion was a deep red-brown, the result of weather and drink in equal proportions. The argument grew fiercer.

They shouted at each other in a growing crescendo of sound and at a climax took time off to order fresh drinks. The landlady, usually passive of face, leant her great bare arms on the serving counter where she had taken up her position and made notes of the drinks they ordered on a pad. The composition of the table steadily changed. One would get up to leave and, as though by pre-arrangement, someone else would arrive almost at once to take the vacant place.

Irwin was on the defensive, at least as far as I could judge. He appeared to be under determined attack by all the others. When everyone shouted at once I could make little of what was said. But when reason or moderate quietness prevailed I was able to pick out elements of the argument. Irwin had failed them on a point of principle and no amount of reasoning on his part could alter this fact. Just what the principle was I never discovered.

20

A 'shouting' man sat on Irwin's left; he led the general attack. He lacked the index finger of his left hand and since he frequently doubled the two middle fingers into his palm he appeared to have a hand with but a small finger and thumb. This he frequently brandished aloft in the excitement of his arguments so that he seemed to be making the sign against the 'evil one'–in this case Irwin. The more excited he became, the higher his voice rose, his face became redder and his neck almost purple as it bulged over an old-fashioned, tightly secured shirt collar.

The landlord's wife ran that place and everyone knew it. Her husband came a long way second. Sometimes she stood behind the bar leaning her great fleshy arms upon it, eyeing her regulars, or casting a glance over the rest of the room. And although she passed me over without pause she always noted the state of my glass. Then her attention would return to the big table. She would throw in a remark, often when the argument was at its most furious, or she would bring drinks round to her customers and having distributed them stand behind one of the men, from which vantage-point she would address the others. Once, when someone left, she took his place while her husband occupied her station behind the bar, ready to deal with the drinks.

A quiet man sat on the left of the shouting man. He sipped his drink, nodded at the remarks of the others and only very occasionally made a point of his own. The landlord was behind the bar when the telephone rang. He answered and then caught the eye of the quiet man who shook his head from side to side. The landlord said: 'No, your husband left five minutes ago.' He replaced the receiver and the whole table laughed as at an old, much-loved joke. Ten minutes later, apologetically, the quiet man got up and left.

The composition of the table continued to change though never with abruptness. All this time Irwin had muttered replies to the others. But the shouting man had clearly won the day, though whether by the force of his arguments coupled with the apparently general disapproval of Irwin's lack of principles or simply because no one wished to take him on I was unable to tell. I suspect the latter reason to have been the decisive one. With an astonishing phlegm, Irwin had put up with shouting directed at his face from no more than a foot away but finally, after a more than usually vitriolic performance from the shouting man, Irwin had had enough. He came to his feet, the great spread of his back matched by his girth and huge tree-trunk thighs though he was no more than five foot six in height. He crammed a small leather porkpie hat on his head, muttered a perfunctory '*grüss Gott!*' to the rest of the table, ignored the shouting man, and stomped out. The rest shook their heads: 'Irwin, Irwin.' It had certainly been an entertainment.

I had walked between 30 and 40 kilometres (18–25 miles) that day in a burst of starter's enthusiasm–an abrupt change of physical activity from my usual London life–and suddenly I felt tired and stiff. In any case, Irwin's departure had taken the liveliness from the *Stammtisch* and the others showed signs of leaving. The cook's boy cleaned glasses behind the bar counter and then left, the landlord flicked his braces and went to fiddle at the dishes, his wife joined him and the shouting man at last fell silent. I felt so stiff when I got up that all I wanted was to get to my bed. At the bar the landlord picked up his pad with my reckoning on it. I said, 'Can you add it to my account for the morning?' Landlord and wife exchanged glances but I was too tired to attach any significance to this. Then he smiled. 'Yes, of course.' I went to bed.

At breakfast the next morning I examined my map, checking the next stage of my journey while the landlord looked across with interest. When I went to the bar to settle my account he asked whether I was making a journey so I told him. He became quite animated. 'I cannot speak English,' he said as I stumbled with my German and he smiled a wary, obsequious smile. He made suggestions about my proposed route; I inquired about a particular place I wanted to visit and he studied my map with care and then produced a brochure which included a section in English about my next destination. I thanked him; he seemed far more friendly than hitherto. Then he said 'Your bill' and pushed the pad across the counter to me. It was, I saw at once, ten marks more than it ought to have been. It doesn't pay in such a small place to be grand as I had been the night before, telling him to add my evening meal and drinks to the account. I recalled the look which had passed between landlord and wife and understood its meaning. Perhaps they had added Irwin's account to mine for, certainly, he had not paid anything when he stomped out. I looked up at the landlord to find his cunning, calculating eyes upon me, trying to gauge what I would do.

He had made a point of telling me he did not speak English: I foresaw that in any argument my German would be inadequate and his understanding would promptly dwindle to nil. He waited. And then I smiled. I looked into his wary little eyes and smiled with amusement, indeed an enjoyment he could not understand. I paid in full without demur. He was astonished. But he did not know of the small place I had reserved for him, even then, in my forthcoming book.

Chapter Four

Beuron

From Donaueschingen to Tuttlingen the Danube, still a small stream, flows through flat farmland, giving little promise of excitement to come. Then, between Tuttlingen and Sigmaringen, the river passes through one of the most beautiful, scenically dramatic stretches of its entire length, cutting through the high rocks of a spectacular gorge. It is as though a giant had taken hold of the two outer edges of the plateau and simply pulled it apart to create a fissure—jagged and haphazard, like the corresponding contours of a jigsaw puzzle which a child has completed and then split down the middle. The Danube passes through this fissure, a stream whose playful gentleness belies the force which cut such a path through the rocks aeons ago. Through this gorge the drama is supplied by the high crags, the castles and follies which crown them, the forest which clings to every available rock and comes down to invade the valley while the Danube, in an astonishing reversal of roles, shallow and twinkling, rippling over its stony bed, smiles up in the sunlight at its creation almost as if to say: 'I made this valley, I may be small here but what power is mine!'

Beuron is one of those enchanting lost places that even tourists cannot spoil. Here the high gorge closes in on the Danube, forest covers the hills to either side and frequent stark outcrops of rock form dramatic crags. The Benedictine monastery at Beuron dates from 1077; it remains the focus of life in the small town where there is also a corresponding establishment for nuns. The monks were originally attracted to the site because the gorge widens enough to permit an open meadow where they could support themselves by farming. The monastery has long been a centre of learning and acquired fame by fostering the Gregorian chant (Col. pl. 2).

Beuron's other activity is tourism. There are two hotels, a guest-house run by nuns and another guesthouse by the station. I obtained a room in the second hotel which was run by two elderly ladies. I spent the following day walking the hills on either side of the gorge.

I passed a morning high in the forest and encountered one buck, one fox, eight squirrels and two woodcutters. These latter had a huge power-driven saw, a truck with trailer and were in the process of removing many tons of cut logs. At one point I came out of the woods to see across a high meadow an extraordinary dreamland *Schloss* rising up in the distance. It grew out of a backdrop of steep green hills and surrounding forest, its turrets and towers piled indiscriminately upon the walls or each other. There was no sign of life, no road leading to it, no indication that this was the centre of local authority or that it had any connection with Beuron in the valley below. It was just there. I sat for a long while at the edge of the woods to absorb this *Schloss*: inscrutable, secret, part of an old Germany which has grown up over the centuries along the hills and crags which cradle the Danube.

Later, sitting outside Beuron's principle hostelry over a mid-morning beer I watched tourists, including a spattering of foreigners, as they meandered round the outside of the monastery (there was no admittance to the public) or made their way to the chapel. Then I witnessed a scene that I had thought was only to be found within the pages of an English novel. Two middle-aged ladies walked past me. They wore tweeds, walked firmly with consciously straight backs and peered at buildings they passed, pointing out archaeological details to one another. Yet, clearly, they were searching for something in particular. They saw a monk on the other side of the road and one made as if to question him, then thought better of it. They had come to a stop on the corner within three yards of the table where I sat drinking my beer but they ignored me. Instead, one said to her companion: 'Do you think there is another cafe down this road?' Her companion considered for a moment, then replied: 'I do not know, my dear, but we can try. You can never tell where you will find anything in these little German towns.' Then they headed down the hill towards the station.

Perhaps five minutes had passed when a slightly flustered lady came along the road. She peered into the hotel and then asked me in German whether I had seen two English ladies. I indicated the station road and, greatly relieved, she trotted after them but not without the faintest raising of her eyebrows to suggest the difficulties that went with looking after foreigners. I nodded sympathetically. Later I met the three of them at the entrance to the monastery chapel; their guide gave me a friendly smile.

The monastery chapel has one of the splendid baroque interiors which are to be found all along the Danube (Col. pl. 1). Someone was playing the organ which peeled out high above the empty nave. I sat for half an hour relaxing, enjoying the music, the painted roof and the glittering splendour of the ornate gilt altar. Visitors kept coming in to look but almost without exception they took no more than a cursory glance at the ceiling. They would walk round the chapel in that familiar manner which tourists adopt as they chalk up one more of the sights on their list. Then they would leave. Those who were Catholics crossed themselves and bobbed in perfunctory style in the aisle but few took time to examine the beauty of the chapel.

I went walking again that afternoon, this time in the forest on the other side of the valley. I had to cross the Danube by means of an old, covered wooden bridge and, looking back at the meadow as I rose into the hills, I tried to visualise the monks of medieval days, beside the shelter of their monastery, tilling this gentle sunlit corner of the rugged gorge. I was again astonished that the small river flowing beneath the bridge had been able to cut such a chasm through the landscape. The water, though, was swift. It was a marvellously hot day. When I returned to Beuron, having completed a great circle in the hills, an influx of sightseers had filled the car park with vehicles while groups paraded along the main street to view the monastery and chapel or in search of refreshment. I found a table outside a shop where I had a glass of tea and an ice cream. An elderly couple asked to share my table. The woman made polite conversation and on discovering that I was English with only limited German at my command she articulated slowly and carefully. She did not speak English, which pleased me. All too frequently in my encounters Germans would say, as though it were part of the natural order of things: 'But of course I speak English.'

She inquired about my walks and both she and her husband expressed great interest when I said I had seen some wildlife. She wanted to know what animals I had encountered. The deer she accepted as normal. When I was obliged to resort to my pocket dictionary for names, she nodded approvingly at my enterprise: an Englishman endeavouring to speak German! She was surprised at my fox but at the mention of squirrels she was dismissive: 'Those little creatures with tails,' she said, as though they did not qualify. She gave the impression that nothing less than bears or boars would satisfy her.

My hotel appeared to be completely deserted except for me. After an excellent dinner of venison, served by the ancient bowed lady who seemed to do just about everything in that establishment, I went for a stroll. I found myself following the Stations of the Cross up a hill. For me, Beuron was altogether too holy with its profusion of crosses, Marys and monasteries. I descended a path through thick woods until I came to a grotto. This was shrouded in gloom with trees rising up to 45 metres (150 ft) above me. An altar had been carved out of the rocks and a bright blue-robed Mary painted in a niche above it. The path ran between this altar with a bubbling spring in front of it and a small dark wooden shelter which with its few benches, formed a tiny chapel. Beyond the grotto a dramatic path went off to one side through high rocks with trees towering far above them while the path I had followed rose sharply again towards distant sunlight. I pursued this path upwards to emerge into rolling open fields illumined by the softness of the evening sun. Ahead of me, high up and fantastic, was the *Schloss* of the morning, detached and mysterious as ever: tall, eerie, isolated–a picture-book castle of turrets and towers. It only required a thunderstorm to provide the perfect setting for a Dracula film. I climbed into a bird tower and from this vantage-point watched the rays of the setting sun pick out the yellows and golds of the castle walls.

By the time I came back to the grotto it was nearly dark, at least down there among the trees and rocks. Several candles had been lit and placed near the feet of the depiction of Mary. The spring provided a constant flow of ice-cold drinking water and, using the chained metal mug, I took several long draughts. Only when I had finished did I realise that in the near darkness I had an audience: two woman sat silent on benches in the little shelter. To me that place was creepy with superstition. It did not belong to any God–Christian, Roman or otherwise–but to earlier pagan deities. Pan and his pipes should have inhabited that grotto, not Mary and her candles. Perhaps he did. As I turned round from drinking the water the two women, black silhouettes in the gloom, crossed themselves. Possibly the same thought had occurred to them.

Chapter Five

SIGMARINGEN

The walk from Beuron to Sigmaringen was one of the most enchanting of any I made along the upper reaches of the Danube. The weather was perfect and the first stretch of the valley was both picturesque and dramatic before it opened out into flatter, more placid country approaching Sigmaringen.

At breakfast that morning, as was my invariable custom, I asked for a second pot of coffee. The old lady who served me took ill-concealed delight in prolonging the business of producing this second pot. She did not take her time in order to incommode me, but to keep waiting a noisy family of four who were not residents but had come in for breakfast from outside. They irritated her! This was a pleasant beginning to a day full of similar amusing vignettes. The coffee was superb.

I found that I walked an exact five kilometres (3 miles) an hour, a pace that with pack I could maintain all day long. This was an encouraging revelation of my state of fitness coming from a sedentary life in London. For the first 17 kilometres (10 miles), until I reached a convenient inn for a rest and beer, I was almost always in sight of the Danube. Sometimes the river was below me down a steep tree-covered bank. Once I was trapped when my path came to a dead end and I was forced to retrace my steps to cross the river by a rickety wooden bridge designed to hold one person at a time. At that point the river had become quite wide but I was deceiving myself–farther on it resumed its small, stream-like quality. It was taunting me: I still had more than 2,700 kilometres (1,678 miles) to go.

About halfway on this walk the gorge widened into a broad valley and I looked back at another *Schloss* perched precariously on a crag, guarding the mouth of the gorge. How it came to be up there was a mystery, although there probably existed a quite ordinary road which approached it over the hills from the rear. There was a

27

Wanderweg along this stretch of the river. I always made a point of greeting those I met, a gesture to show I was not the reserved Englishman of German imagination but a putatively gregarious, hearty walker! It didn't do me much good. Sometimes, it is true, I received an equally pleasant friendly response yet at others I was rewarded with a stare of amazement at such temerity or a startled, hasty reply as though I had done something unusual.

I had to leave the riverside when I got nearer to Sigmaringen but before doing so was rewarded with a perfect picture. I left the path to walk through the woods to the riverbank and, from under the boughs of an overhanging tree across swift, urgent waters, looked at yet another *Schloss*. Smaller than the fairy-tale castles on the crags, this was squat and turretless, rising square and grey on an isolated eminence of its own, a very private castle surrounded by a thick foliage of trees, enjoying its own quiet bend of the Danube.

I approached Sigmaringen in the extreme heat of the late afternoon. For several miles and from different angles, sometimes losing sight of it altogether, I watched the mass of the Sigmaringen castle, turreted, jumbled, absurd, rising above the approaching town which snuggles beneath it. It was Saturday and since the coming Monday was a public holiday and Sigmaringen is a recognised tourist attraction the town was crowded and the inns were full.

There was a fair on the outskirts of the town. I visited this, had an ice, inspected the stalls and took photographs, by which time I was in need of stronger refreshment. Sigmaringen is dominated by its eighteenth/nineteenth-century castle. This picture-book affair of castellated turrets was formerly the glory of the Sigmaringen-Hohenzollerns. Now it is a museum. I found a restaurant for supper and, like everywhere else in town that weekend, it soon became crowded.

Of all the towns along this early stretch of the Danube, Sigmaringen in particular remains in my memory. I did little except wander the old town, visit the castle, eat, drink and observe; and yet vignettes crowded upon me. The Danube had grown by then–not much, yet it was appreciably bigger than the stream passing through the monks' meadow at Beuron. The Hohenzollerns were just one of the aristocratic families who chose to site their castles overlooking the Danube.

In the restaurant where I had supper I betrayed myself over the soup. The embarrassments of life are often absurd. I was beginning to congratulate myself upon my improving German and so ventured to ask my waitress about the contents of the soup of the day. She did not know. In her turn she asked the head waitress the same question across the crowded restaurant. The latter reeled off what I presumed were the soup's ingredients but my German was inadequate to enable me to grasp them all, certainly not when given at such speed, and my consequent blank face revealed my lack of understanding. Another foreigner in their midst!

As I ate my meal I witnessed a scene which demonstrated how easily and how often the subject of race can arise. The table near to mine was long, capable of seating three a side and one at each end: it was designed to accommodate more than one party or a number of individual diners. It was free when I began my meal; then a fat, choleric little man took his seat at one end, gave an abrupt order without consulting the menu, was rapidly served and set to work systematically eating his way through a plate piled high with stolid-looking food.

Then an American party came in: a man, his wife and their son, a boy of about sixteen. They had Bronx accents, looked and sounded Jewish and at the same time acted all-American. They spoke loudly and assumed that English (American-style) would automatically be understood. It was not. They took the three seats at the opposite end of the table from the solitary German. They demanded instant service in English. The boy's voice was a high-pitched nasal whine, while the mother seemed very much the matriarch. The father on the other hand was, I suspect, an essentially shy man. He made gestures of compensation for the behaviour of his family by a sort of quietness that the staff of the restaurant, all of whom became involved, mistook for meekness. So they despised him and looked to the mother. This suited her as I suspect it had done throughout their married life. The first waitress did not understand English. She fetched a second one who had a mere smattering of English. At this the mother turned to the husband and said, 'I *ask* you honey.' Then the head waitress came over; she did have some English and asked for their order. They wanted to change money. The manager now appeared on the scene. He could not, or would not, change travel-ler's cheques and clearly wished to see them leave.

The fat little man at the other end of their table had at first ignored them; he was too busy eating. But gradually he became conscious of the fuss and looked up to examine them between mouthfuls. He did not like them: they were Americans, they were also Jews, and they could not speak the language—three marks against them. More-over, they had the effect of making him feel both antagonistic and guilty—antagonistic because of the fuss they created and because they were American; guilty because they were Jews. Remarkably yet clearly these conflicting emotions passed across his features. The family, particularly the mother and son who modelled his behaviour upon hers, wished to make a point or rather several points: about the service; about what they could not get; and about the fact that everyone did not respond to them in English. In the end they had

29

three Pepsis, three creamy looking cakes and three ice-creams. The German, still busily munching, took time off to look up when this sticky array was placed before them. Later, loudly, they left. The waitress who had served them looked relieved and made some remark to her colleague at which nearby customers laughed.

Such an incident might appear irrelevant to a journey down the Danube and, of course, could occur anywhere. Yet though I said I had no particular object when making my journey that was not entirely correct. People were my object: people and the river. What differentiates the people who live along the Danube's great valley? The Germans, whose many attributes I was logging on my way, suffer still from regret and guilt about the War. This Jewish family, which was also American, had underscored these German sensitivities.

By this stage of my journey I had noticed the German fondness for physical fitness. Everywhere I came upon aspects of this health craze. In town after town the two most regular and prominent notices were likely to be those which pointed to the sports centre and those indicating the whereabouts of the hospital, the first presumably often providing custom for the second. There were signs for *Trimm Dich*, the craze for various forms of exercise matched in Britain by the Apple studios. *Trimm Dich* appeared to be going on everywhere. On my walks I met determined, labouring cyclists, and hearty perspiring trampers; on the river I saw muscled canoeists; in fields by summer camps youths being organised for collective sports; and on a huge rockface, halfway between Beuron and Sigmaringen, rock climbers. The climbers spread all over the rock, connected by ropes, clinging to the surface like spiders and watched from below by telescope. But if Germans appreciate fitness, they also appreciate beer and the *Gasthof*, the *Biergarten* or the restaurant were all busy places.

Towards sunset I took a stroll along the river opposite the castle. That astonishing building was reflected perfectly in the still, mirror-like waters of the Danube. I sat on a riverside bench to relax. The seat I had chosen was near a big tree, under which sat two tramps. They were middle-aged, strongly built men with leathery, weather-beaten faces, red and coarsened by constant exposure to the elements yet open and shrewd-featured. Their clothes were a mixture of leather for endurance and oddments and they had identical pork-pie hats with feathers stuck in the sides. One sat on the grass, the other sprawled on a bench. Spread out around them was an assortment of gear–small packs and bags of varying descriptions–which carried their entire wealth. They had eyed me as I walked past but appeared to take little further interest. They were drinking, passing between them a bottle of an indeterminate liquor, possibly meths, and chatting amiably together.

I sat watching the reflection of the castle in the water and idly enjoying the cool that follows a long hot day. But of course it had been a mistake to seat myself so close to the gentlemen of the road. It was simply a question of when they would make their move, nothing else. I took a photograph: no action. I took another: still no move. I felt relieved; perhaps my suspicions were unfounded. I got up to go; one of the tramps was beside me.

'We are wanderers like you,' he said. 'Tomorrow we go to Riedlingen and we need 11 Deutschmarks to help us get there.'

'Please speak slowly, I only have a little German,' I answered.

He nodded at this and with the consideration and natural courtesy of his timeless calling began again–for his benefit. 'I understand,' and he now spoke with the slow, careful exaggeration one might employ when addressing a small and not too bright child.

'We are two wanderers,' and he paused, 'tomorrow–we–go–to Reidlingen. We *need*,' and he pantomimed the number with his fingers, 'eleven marks–to–get there.'

He waited patiently for this information to sink in. When my continued silence suggested I might not be prepared to provide such a sum he lowered his demand.

'Never mind,' he said, 'one or two will do.'

He had the eternal tramp's face: weathered and humorous, sly yet open, with a quality of ready expectancy for anything. His friend, still sprawled on the bench under the tree, raised his pork-pie hat at me encouragingly.

'I also go to Riedlingen tomorrow,' I said, 'as a wanderer. I shall walk.' I pointed to my feet to make certain he had understood.

At this gesture he looked horrified; had his line of begging come to nothing? In such circumstances there is always a moment of uncertainty: the request had been made and absorbed, my response had yet to come. The tramp was patient. I put my hand in my pocket and pulled out some loose coins. As luck had it a five-mark piece lay on top.

'That will do nicely,' he said and I gave it to him.

With this unexpectedly large coin, certainly more than he had anticipated, he thanked me courteously and retreated to the bench and his friend. The latter gave me a cheerful salute.

In my hotel that evening I secured a corner seat that would enable me to survey the whole bar and most of the dining room. The restaurant was busy with late diners. The work of serving was shared by a morose waiter who never smiled and a petite bouncing little waitress who did most of the work. She kept her back very straight, wore her jet black hair in a bob and allowed her two firm breasts to bounce their way across the room before her. She had a pointed nose and small pointed chin to match.

At a nearby table sat a large, comfortable-looking man. He told the waiter he was waiting for someone and would eat later. He was not in fact comfortable but tense and uncertain. He drank quickly. When I took out my map to study my next day's walk he asked if he too might examine it. He ordered another drink. Then he was joined by a handsome, pouting young man. He fussed and ordered food for them both while the young man made a point of looking bored. But the older man was well-off and the young man wanted money. It was sad: the waiter knew; the waitress knew; other diners knew.

A party of late diners came to the table on the other side of me. Their host sat at the head of the table facing towards me with a couple on either side of him. He quickly noted my interest in all that happened. I was in fact scribbling notes to cover my day while I observed the scene round me. He was an observant man but he chose to make his remark just as there occurred one of those curious, unexpected silences which sometimes descend upon public, even crowded, rooms. As everyone ceased talking and both waitress and waiter were momentarily still he said to his table: 'The stranger is studying the locale,' and his group turned as one to look at me. I bowed; he grinned.

The Hohenzollern family traces its origins back to the ninth century. In 1576 the main, Swabian line of the Hohenzollerns was divided into the Hechingen and Sigmaringen branches, both of which were to continue unbroken until 1849 when the family came under the control of Prussia. The actual Hohenzollern territory consisted of an enclave in Württemberg which stretched south-east from the Black Forest and was watered by the Neckar and Danube rivers. Sigmaringen was its capital until the land was ceded to Prussia in 1849. The proposal to make Prince Leopold of Hohenzollern-Sigmaringen King of Spain sparked off the Franco-Prussian War of 1870.

Another Sigmaringen prince, Charles, became King of Rumania in 1881 while the main Hohenzollern line provided the newly united Germany with its rulers until the abdication of Kaiser Wilhelm II who fled to Holland in 1918 at the end of World War One. The Hohenzollerns were to continue to reign in Rumania–a troubled line in a troubled country–until the reconstructed (Communist-controlled) government forced Michael to abdicate in 1947. The curious ornate Schloss at Sigmaringen would have been equally at home rising above a forest in Transylvania and somehow it was fitting that the family should end its monarchical pretensions in that country (Col. pl. 5).

Sigmaringen Castle is now a museum. It houses a valuable art collection, many relics and family portraits, reputedly the largest private collection of weapons on the Continent as well as numerous hunting trophies. Like most of Europe's ruling families, an insatiable desire to slaughter and then stuff or otherwise display animal trophies seems to have been an essential part of Hohenzollern psychology judging by the rows of specimens displayed on the castle walls.

The castle opened to the public at nine in the morning. On the first stroke of the hour the little wicket beside the main entrance shot up and the ticket salesman was in place waiting for the tourists. A party of us was shown round. Our group comprised pretty teenage girls, a middle-aged couple and myself. Our guide was a young woman, hardly older than the teenagers, perhaps a student doing the job part-time. She was nervous but had learnt her lines. From stateroom to stateroom she led us, firmly detailing the history of the Hohenzollerns. Some castles look as though they might once have been lived in; this did not.

The guide engaged us with the compelling glance of the school prefect. In each room she took up a central position–by a particular piece of furniture, the mantleshelf, under the main picture or on a convenient dais–where she would wait for us to gather round before delivering the appropriate lecture for the room. No one asked her a single question. I should have liked to do so but felt my command of the language insufficient for the occasion. So each time she addressed us we stood silent. The girls would giggle together as we moved from one room to the next but they behaved impeccably when our guide delivered her set piece. Then they stood grave and silent. They did this partly out of sympathy for one of their own age who, clearly, was at the outset of her possibly temporary castle-guiding career, and partly from German discipline.

Chapter Six

Riedlingen to Ulm

My walk from Sigmaringen to Riedlingen proved a baffling affair. First I could not find the correct route out of Sigmaringen. Then I got lost high up in woodland paths, though from time to time I glimpsed the valley road, and sometimes flashes of the Danube, far below me. Later again, walking beside a now placid and certainly larger Danube, I came upon a holiday stretch of river. People were out in force using a variety of coloured dinghies, swimming and then returning up the green bank to a little town of red, orange and yellow tents. Yet just round a bend in the river away from this vivid, noisy scene my path rose steeply until I found myself out of sight though not sound of the holidaymakers, some 20 metres (65 ft) above the water, glimpsing great fish idling just below its surface. Then I had to scramble out of the meadow across a railway embankment to find my road again.

By this time I had established a rhythm to my day. I liked to get in a good three hours walk, about 15 kilometres (9 miles), before my first halt which, preferably, I made at an inn for a beer. I had discovered that large baroque churches were worth investigating; though on the outside they might look plain, almost drab, inside they would delight with their splendour of paintings and great gilt decorated altars. Sometimes I took lunch at an inn, at others I bought a roll, cheese and an apple to eat on my way. Once I had reached my destination and found a place to stay I would set off to explore the town.

Riedlingen is a pretty town of picturesque old streets, an attractive fourteenth-century church and a fifteenth-century townhall. A stork's nest was perched conveniently on a chimney in the centre of town, the stork posing elegantly for tourist cameras. Among the town's modest places of entertainment was the City Pub and a thriving Italian ice cream parlour.

At Riedlingen the Danube is still a small river; in the centre of town it runs over a pretty weir to form a pool below (Col. pl. 6). This proved to be a popular place for practising canoeists and I watched earnest but by no means expert performers sporting in the evening sun. The elegant sixteenth-century buildings overlooking the river were bathed in a whole spectrum of beautiful pastel shades by the setting sun. I became accustomed to the spectacle of Germans busy at some healthy physical exercise, but I always experienced a secret pleasure when I saw they were not very good. At Riedlingen the canoeists obliged me in this respect.

My inn (yet another Stag) was not especially clean, the shower was defective, the service slow, my breakfast egg the next morning hard-boiled and cold. What had happened, I wondered, to Germany's much vaunted cleanliness and efficiency? But, I reflected, I was still in Baden-Württemberg, the Danube had a long way to go before it became a commercial highway and only from Ulm, the first city of note along the river, had navigation ever been possible. Anyway, I like a bit of inefficiency on my travels–especially in a country with a contrary reputation. It makes me feel better.

The landlord kept his position behind the bar and leaned across this to talk with his cronies at the *Stammtisch*. His nose had been flattened by an accident many years before and part had also eroded away. His thick accent was beyond me; in his turn he realised that I, too, presented a baffling language problem so after the first exchange he was careful to ensure that the woman who did most of the waiting attended to my needs. As always the *Stammtisch* was the centre of activity and most of its *habitués* as well as the landlord himself appeared old enough to have fought in the War. Half of them were permanent fixtures, one only periodically waking to drink from his huge beer mug before lapsing into slumber again.

When I settled my bill the next morning several of the *Stammtisch* regulars were already in place. They were intrigued by my Austrian army pack and one pointed it out to the landlord. He leant across the bar to peer down at it and his eyes gleamed with an unmistakable nostalgia. He scrutinised me with a quite different regard: old comrades in arms–or rather old enemies? He now developed an interest in my business so I told him of the journey I was making and in return he made a special effort to speak slowly so that I might understand his accent, an effort his friends found vastly amusing. One of them asked whether I had been a soldier, meaning of course in World War Two. Their interest in that topic was plain and once more on my trip the War had cropped up.

It is strange how you can walk beside a river for many miles looking for change yet finding little. Then, quite suddenly, the river has grown, is swifter, appears deeper. I might lose sight of the river for a few miles only to find that this had happened when I came back to it. This was my experience when I reached Ehingen. Almost by stealth the Danube had become wide and deep enough to bear traffic–at least a launch or two–yet, obstinately, the river was deserted and I didn't even see a canoeist. But I did have an odd encounter at Ehingen. The Danube lies quite a distance from the centre of town so once settled in my hotel I went for a walk along its banks.

The river was high and fast flowing though still without any sign of life on it. Quite suddenly in my walk I came upon two women who appeared to be gathering herbs or berries. They had a large, beautiful Alsatian with them so ought to have felt secure (I doubt that I look dangerous) yet on my approach they exhibited every sign of extreme nervousness. Only when I reached them, as I thought simply to pass, did I realise that they were in a corner, cut off from any retreat by a small deep stream that joined the river at this point. I had trapped them at the confluence of the stream with the Danube. I also was trapped and would have to go back unless the stream could be crossed. I asked them whether there was a bridge. They were extraordinarily relieved to hear my foreign accent. There was a small plank bridge nearby which they pointed out to me. I thanked them and headed back along the stream for some forty metres to the bridge. When I had crossed this I returned along the other bank of the stream to the path beside the Danube. There was no sign of the two women or the Alsatian which had watched me silently at our meeting. What they had been doing or why they had been so nervous at my approach I cannot imagine.

Ulm sits on the left bank of the Danube in Baden-Württemberg while across the river in Bavaria is Neu-Ulm. Up to Ulm the Danube remains a small river but here at its confluence with the River Iller it becomes navigable, a fact which contributed to the growth of the city, the first of any consequence along the river. Downstream from Ulm the Danube flows through Bavaria.

The city has had a long and turbulent history; it reached its greatest glory and importance in the fifteenth century. At that time its merchants had raised it to greater importance than Vienna. Its beginnings were in the ninth century when it became a centre for the Carolingian sovereigns, but in 1134 it was destroyed by the Guelf Duke, Henry the Proud. It was rebuilt by the Hohenstaufens and in 1164 was granted a municipal charter by Frederick Barbarossa. A century later, in 1274, it became a free imperial city.

Ulm's strategic position at the beginning of the navigable Danube contributed to its initial growth as a commercial river port and industrial town. Special flat barges designed to carry 100 tons could be used downstream of Ulm, although the river still has an average depth of just one metre (3.5 ft) and is no more than 70 metres (230 ft) wide. Nowadays the river traffic begins much further downstream at Regensburg. Ulm also sits astride a number of important overland routes: to the Rhine and Holland; to Switzerland, Italy and the Tirol; and to the east. It is a modern road and rail centre with the railway from the Netherlands and France passing through the city on the route of the old Orient Express to the Balkans.

Ulm has the distinction of producing one of the earliest democratic constitutions of Europe. In 1397 its guilds of merchants and craftsmen obtained a constitution which brought to an end disputes with the city's patricians. This achievement is still celebrated every year. Ulm played a leading role in the disastrous Thirty Years' War which devastated Germany in the first half of the seventeenth century. In 1618, at the outbreak of these religious hostilities, Ulm was a free imperial city which then owned a whole province. It became part of the Protestant Evangelical Union and in 1620 was the site for the Treaty of Ulm, under which the two sides agreed to respect the neutrality of the opposing princes, but only in Germany and without prejudice to action elsewhere–of this there was to be plenty. In 1647 the Armistice of Ulm signalled the end of the grim struggle and three years later in 1650 thanksgiving services were held in the city and the surrounding villages to celebrate an end to the suffering. A special prayer to mark the occasion began: 'We thank you, Dear Lord, that you have given us peace after years of suffering turmoil and war.' But Ulm's long involvement in the war led to a decline which continued through the eighteenth century when Ulm suffered further as a result of the French wars and the War of Austrian Succession.

Ulm was the site of one of Napoleon's greatest triumphs, the surrender in 1805 of General Mack and an Austrian army, virtually without a shot being fired. Until August of that year Napoleon had been sitting at Boulogne preparing to invade England. But when the Austrians and Russians renewed hostilities he marched his huge army across Europe in six weeks to force the supine and inert Mack into surrender. At Boulogne Napoleon said of his intended march: 'If the enemy [the Austrian army] comes to meet me, I will destroy him before he has regained the Danube; if he waits for me, I will surprise him between Augsburg and Ulm.' And surprise him he did.

Napoleon had an astonishing memory for detail. At Boulogne he dictated the order of march for his army across the Continent to the Danube. Later, on his way to Paris when 200,000 men were on the march, he came upon a troop of soldiers who had lost their way. He asked them their regiment, whence they had set out and then from memory told them their line of march and where their battalion was to spend the night.

37

And so his forces closed in on Ulm and the Austrians. Marshal Lannes just prevented the Austrians cutting the bridge across the Danube at Donauwörth while 6,000 Austrian troops were taken at Memmingen. On 20 October 1805, General Mack marched his troops out of Ulm to pile their arms and surrender. So it came about that Napoleon, who was about to go on to his greatest victory at Auster-litz, was able first to chalk up this astonishing triumph at Ulm. The history books seem unable to agree upon the number who surren-dered under Mack: 30,000, 33,000, 36,000, 42,000, 50,000 and even 60,000 have been cited while one source suggests that the remainder of his army of 70,000 was unaccounted for after the surrender. This bloodless victory elicited from a soldier in the ranks one of those apocryphal remarks: 'The Emperor had found a new way of waging war; he makes use of our legs instead of our bayonets.'

Only six years afterwards in 1811 Albrecht Ludwig Berblinger, known to posterity as the 'Flying Tailor of Ulm', made one of the earliest attempts to fly. Watched by a crowd of 10,000 he jumped off the Eagle Bastion of the city walls with home-made wings strapped to his arms. He plummeted straight into the Danube. Later his wife sold the wings to an umbrella-maker.

Ulm recovered some of its importance in the nineteenth century. Today it is a thriving commercial/industrial city of 100,000 people: the economic and cultural centre of Upper Württemberg. Its position as a centre of communications made it a major target for Allied bombing in World War Two and it was badly damaged. It is the birthplace of Albert Einstein.

Much of the old city remains, including part of the fifteenth-century walls along the Danube. Ulm Cathedral is Germany's largest Gothic church after Cologne. Building commenced in 1377 and it was designed to hold twice the then population of the city. Its spire at 161 metres (528 ft) is the highest of any church in the world. The building was finally completed, after six centuries, in 1890.

Rain pursued me down the Danube for much of the summer. I arrived at Ulm in the rain and got steadily wetter as I sought a place to stay. Ulm prices were considerably higher than those I had previously encountered. I turned down two hotels as over-expensive before settling upon a third. This was run by a prim, proper little woman and turned out to be more expensive than the others I had rejected.

I detected a certain smugness in Ulm's citizens who seemed full of their history and commercial importance. I saw several black people in Ulm, for the first time on my trip. As I have spent a good deal of my life travelling in Africa and writing about its people, I was curious whenever I encountered black people on my journey.

Later, especially in the east European countries, I was more than once to meet solitary Africans, usually students whose language problems and cultural differences led them to feel isolated and lonely. Here in Ulm I had already met one African from Kenya and we had talked together happily for half an hour; he was delighted to find someone who knew his country.

There is an attractive riverside walk in Ulm: first beneath the old walls, then along a meadow. By now the river has been swollen by the Iller and is broader, swifter and at last fully capable of carrying heavy traffic. I saw quite a large tourist launch with a sign offering trips downriver but it was deserted and still there was nothing actually moving on the Danube. It was as though the river were consciously holding back, maintaining its still pristine idyllic character before commerce really begins at Regensburg. Looking back towards the city over the thick green trees I could see only the great spire of the cathedral, a brown jagged-edged knife rising out of a sea of green. From Donaueschingen to Ulm, about 145 kilometres (90 miles) the Danube had passed through some of the loveliest scenery of its German course.

In the late afternoon I found a small café in an alleyway which had been converted into a pedestrian precinct. I sat at an outside table under a large round shade not to escape the summer sun but in case the threatening skies let down yet more rain. I had a coffee and wrote up my notes. A large, comfortable, overdressed woman then occupied the only other pavement table. She ordered an enormous multiple ice cream covered with fruit and hot sauce. She nodded to me and greeted several passers-by, all male, with an assurance that was less than matched by their timid responses. One smart burgher whom she greeted felt obliged to say something in reply and told her he had just been to the chemist round the corner. 'Ah yes,' she replied, 'they are the best.' This remark he clearly did not appreciate.

Then three small boys idled past. They were scruffy, bored, ready for mischief. She addressed them, told them to wait, then heaved herself up and disappeared into the café. The boys looked at each other in calculation, wondering whether they would not do better to idle off but then she reappeared with three ice-cream cornets which she distributed to their astonished delight. Clasping this unexpected largesse they hurried away in case a mistake had been made. The lady explained: 'Boys, I like children,' and shrugged. She said something else which I failed to decipher. She was demonstrating a heart of gold; my reply made her realise that I was a foreigner. Shortly after this exchange she went into the café and I forgot about her. Later, however, when I went inside to pay for my coffee, I discovered her sitting at the bar eating a large steak and chips.

Halfway through my breakfast the following morning the landlady placed the bill in front of me. It was larger than I had anticipated. Then, as usual, I asked for another coffee. She made a fuss getting this and when I went to settle my bill demanded an additional three marks for the extra coffee. This I regarded as mean; it was the only occasion when I was charged for a second breakfast coffee.

Chapter Seven

The Danube and War

From Ulm to Regensburg the Danube has been fought over since earliest times and the names of towns and cities–Ulm, Donauwörth, Ingolstadt, Höchstädt and Regensburg (the ancient Castra Regina of the Romans)–are a roll call of battle honours. The river here has become wider, more difficult to cross, an obstacle in warfare so that the bridging of it, when this occurred, brought strategic importance and prosperity to the Danube towns. Yet often such considerations seem to have little relevance nowadays. Frequently I found myself in a small medieval town whose modern preoccupations, perhaps with its tourist potential, made it oblivious of an earlier, more important role.

But the river knew. Near the elegant little medieval town of Günzburg the Danube flows swift. It was high, swollen by the incessant rains, and I sat on its banks where it curves through woods out of sight of the town, an energetic river now, gathering momentum for the great passage ahead of it. There can be little the river has not witnessed in its timeless passage. Violence and warfare may occur along its banks, commanders with their armies search for crossing points or pitch their tents, towns grow to prosperity beside it and then decline but, always silent, constantly flowing, the Danube can testify to these events. No Danube and no towns, no concern with strategic crossing points and no battles.

I arrived at Günzburg, predictably enough, in the rain. I found an inn in the wide open main street which is enclosed by gates at either end. That evening the *Stammtisch* was lively and at a neighbouring table four men were engrossed playing the ubiquitous *Schafkopf*. As usual they played fast, slapping their cards down on the table in quick succession like a never-ending ragged volley. They were playing for money. I was watching them idly when two elderly American couples entered the dining room. They had no German and looked surprised,

indeed naively frustrated, when they were not automatically understood. They sat near the card players.

One of the Americans, bald like a withered Yul Brynner, had a
small pointed nose and pale blue eyes which peered through rimless,
hexagonal-shaped glasses. He couldn't take his eyes from the card
players. He ignored the talk of his three companions as he turned
awkwardly in his seat to watch what happened behind him. Then he
stood up and moved to the table better to watch the game. Finally,
addressing no one in particular, he asked: 'What game is this you
are playing?' No answer–*slap slap slap*. Unabashed he turned to his
own table.'Say, this must be serious.' He moved closer to the card
players. They, as usual, were absorbed, slapping the cards down,
concerned only with what would appear next. They ignored the
inquisitive American. He peered at the cards on the table. 'Why,
these are different.' No one took any notice. He turned to the other
American man at his table. 'They are not using ordinary cards, it
must be some special game.' He turned back to the players. 'Is this
a special game?' he asked. 'A German game?' The player nearest
him, over whose shoulder he had conducted his investigations,
looked up irritated, disturbed in his concentration, but then he took
in the curious shrunken appearance of the bald American. It was as
if he said to himself: 'the poor man cannot help himself.' He had
been on the point of saying something but instead shrugged before
pointedly turning his back again.

For the next half hour the American hovered like a diminutive
vulture, trying to see their hands, making comments to his own table.
The forbearance of the four players was truly amazing. When the
waiter came to take their dinner order his wife called to see what
he wanted but he said: 'You order honey,' and continued his vigil by
the card players. Another card game, meanwhile, had been started at
a table somewhat further away and for a moment I thought he would
move across to that but his wife now called him. 'Elmer,' she said,
'the food is ready.' Like a reluctant child he went to take his seat,
though not without backward glances at the cards.

In order to reach my bedroom I had to pass through a hall which
had been converted into a television room. I do not much like
television and the room was crowded, but on impulse I took the only
vacant seat just as the news came on. The programme was devoted
to the Brussels football disaster of that summer when, following
riotous behaviour by British fans, a barrier collapsed and 39 people
were killed. As a blow-by-blow account of what had taken place was
reported on the small screen the comments in the room became
increasingly acid about the brutal British. I agreed fully with the
various censures which I heard expressed and yet found I resented

them. It is extraordinarily difficult to be objective and extremely easy to be nationalist. I found myself thinking: how can these Germans talk like this about the British? World War Two reared its head again and subconsciously I had reverted to childhood wartime judgements of the Germans: they were the brutal enemy, we were fighting for justice. What you learn early in life you do not forget. Yet it seems that little has changed; in medieval days the brutality of the English soldiery was a byword on the Continent.

Some people appear to have grown old without ever enjoying youth. This thought had come to me as I watched the two American men of the evening before. Both had faintly puckish wrinkle-skinned faces, scrawny necks and features fixed in later middle age as though they had been born that way, while their wives were dull and plain. And yet it is remarkable how a character can change according to circumstances. When the four of them came into the dining room the next morning they greeted me politely, ordered their breakfast without any of the irritating loudness of the previous evening and then talked together as old friends. Elmer was telling them of his youth; he had started work in a garage in California, aged fourteen. I caught only snatches of what he said but it had been a hard life and only now could he afford to come on a holiday to Europe.

The first part of my walk from Günzburg to Dillingen was through woods away from the river. When this happened I played a game as part of my lonely walk: spot the Danube. I would try to guess when I should next see the river: round an obvious bend, down a steep bank through trees or over the hill? Would it appear nearby or farther away than I expected? I often guessed incorrectly, for the Danube played an elusive game with me. I was more than once reminded of the current German concern with conservation. I came upon anthills beside the woodland path with notices asking the public to leave them in peace: '*Lasst uns bitte in Ruhe*' or '*Lasst uns endlich in Ruhe.*' Then I came out of the woods and was surprised that a clear day had turned to mist until I distinguished the giant chimneys of a power station belching their white smoke across the countryside into the woods and the ants.

In this part of Germany I came upon reminders of NATO and a different confrontation. In Britain it is easy to forget how close West Germany lies to the countries of the Warsaw Pact. I saw military convoys, the occasional barracks, military helicopters and fighter planes on exercises swooping low over the countryside.

From Ulm to Regensburg the Danube had acted as a strategic axis since ancient times. It was fortified as the Roman frontier and Marcus Aurelius spent a third of his reign sitting at Regensburg to watch over the threatening barbarians. The same stretch of river was fought over throughout the Thirty Years War. Marlborough and Eugène fought here, as did Napoleon a century later. In World War Two its cities were the targets of repeated Allied bombing. Yet despite this history of warfare, the Danube towns have retained their character; medieval features, walls and castles blend with the modern to display an architectural variety covering many centuries.

The Italian influence is strong here, a phenomenon that followed the German economic miracle of the 1960s when many Italians came seeking work. These immigrants have established their *ristorantes* and *pizzerias* and ice cream parlours: *Eis Bomba*! I found such establishments provided a welcome change of diet from the more stolid German fare and, judging by their popularity, so did the Germans. But residence in the new land and familiarity with German eating must eventually have had its effect, for I found Italian food often took on a stolid quality, a heaviness of pizza that would have been absent in Italy.

I went for supper to the Pizza Romana, a popular restaurant which soon filled. At an adjoining table a mother and her son shared a glass of wine. I quite often encountered this curious German practice of two people sharing a single glass of wine or beer. In hot weather, in a beer garden, a couple might share one of the huge *maas* (litre) steins of beer. This is understandable since the beer can quickly become warm and sometimes it is not possible to order anything smaller. Sharing a glass of wine, however, seemed to me an excessive economy although waiters appeared to regard the practice as normal. The young man took a sip of wine and passed the glass to his mother. She in turn drank and then placed the glass between them in the middle of the table.

When the restaurant was full a man with two children asked to share my table. He saw the small dictionary I had beside my plate and inquired politely where I came from. Of course he spoke good English. He was a schoolteacher and he and his family had spent the previous summer as guests of a Scottish family. His hosts were to visit him later in the year and so, he explained, his children wished to practise their English. After a shy beginning they did so but I wanted to practise my German. I was constantly frustrated in my desire to speak German because so many Germans speak such good English.

I do not recall how we arrived at the subject, but I asked him how many states made up the Federal Republic. 'Eleven,' he answered and then, like any schoolmaster, listed them for me. But he could only remember ten, which deeply embarrassed him as though he had failed in front of his class. 'Now Germany is so small,' he said in explanation of a mere 11 states. It was a typical reference to the partition of Germany; I had heard a number. In this case it was casual enough yet, for all that, tinged with regret for a world that had passed and tinged also with antagonism towards the Communists who had ensured that the division lasted. I think he wished to tell me that he was a good, democratic German.

The little town of Höchstädt has a long history. Herman of Luxembourg defeated Frederick Hohenstaufen here in 1081. But later–from 1138 to 1254–the Hohenstaufens provided a line of Holy Roman Emperors. The Austrians were defeated here in 1703 by the French General Villars and again in 1800 by Moreau. But for the British, Höchstädt's fame is its connection with the Battle of Blenheim. It is a British speciality to distort foreign names. A short distance downstream from Höchstädt, also on the left bank of the Danube, is the little village of Blindheim, which for Marlborough and his men became Blenheim.

I almost missed the village of Blindheim. I was walking some distance from the river and though at the back of my mind I had registered that the battle of Blenheim had been fought nearby I had forgotten that the name would be different. As a rule there is not much to see at an old battle site; here the land is flat and rather uninteresting. The French advancing from Augsburg had crossed the Danube to its northern bank to take up their position to the west of the marshy stream, the Nebelbach, which flows into the Danube at this point. Their army (French and Bavarian) stretched from Blindheim to another little village, Lutzingen, but they only meant to cut off Marlborough's supplies, not to give battle. Yet before the end of the day the Danube had witnessed one of the bloodiest battles ever fought along its banks.

The Battle of Blenheim is known on the Continent as the Battle of Höchstädt. It was Marlborough's greatest victory though equal honours should go to Prince Eugène of Savoy. The English and Austrian forces defeated the French and Bavarians whose losses (30,000 dead, wounded and missing) were two and a half times greater than those of the English and Austrians. Earlier in the year Marlborough was stationed in the Netherlands; had his design to link up with Prince Eugène on the Danube been known in either the Netherlands or England he would have been stopped. Keeping close counsel, however, the Duke made forays down the Rhine against the French and then suddenly at the end of May began a series of forced marches across Germany to the Danube. He covered between 12 and fourteen miles a day, a pace which was almost precisely matched a century later by Napoleon's army when, in 1805, it too made forced marches from Boulogne to Ulm.

From Dillingen to Donauwörth was a long walk through farm

country. Signs along the way representing the farming interest complained how EEC policy was ruining the farmers. I saw women hoeing in the fields, a sight that I have not come across in Britain since the land girls did such work during and just after the war. The Danube had recently flooded, which was hardly surprising in view of the endless rains. I was forced to make a detour on the outskirts of Donauwörth to bypass a flooded road and so found myself clambering up an embankment over a railway and down the other side onto a busy main road. I arrived just as a police car passed. They slowed at sight of me, decided I was harmless and drove on. Later that afternoon I listened to two old men arguing fiercely in a café about the Danube's worst floods of the century. One of them insisted that the present floods were the worst he could recall.

Donauwörth is an ancient town with settlements that date from the Stone Age. It became an important centre for the Romans. The town lies at the confluence of the Wörnitz and Danube and originally was built on an island in the Wörnitz. When the Danube was bridged here, Donauwörth grew in economic and strategic value to become the largest Danube port in Swabia, noted for salt. It was made an imperial town in 1301. It reached its greatest splendour at the beginning of the sixteenth century when the Emperor Maximilian I (1459–1519) attended celebrations in the town to honour the birth of his grandson, the future Charles V.

In 1608 when the Emperor Rudolf II mortgaged Donauwörth to Maximilian I (1756–1825), Duke of Bavaria, he unwittingly provided one of the primary causes of the Thirty Years' War. The problem was sparked off by Catholic and Protestant rivalry: the Catholic monastery constantly challenged the decisions of the Protestant town coucil. Maximilian was a champion of the Counter-Reformation and, following riots in 1606, the emperor asked him to intervene in the affairs of Donauwörth; the Duke did so by creating a Catholic majority on the council. The emperor authorised Maximilian to occupy the town until he could pay him for restoring order. The Affair of Donauwörth, as it became known, helped inflame the bitter rivalries and resentments which culminated in the war that lasted from 1618–48. There was hostile reaction in Protestant Germany to Maximilian's intervention and the Affair of Donauwörth remained a *cause célèbre* while the town continued to be of strategic and symbolic importance until the end of the war. King Gustavus Adolphus invested it and laid waste the surrounding country in 1632, shortly before he met his death at Lützen. In 1634, Ferdinand of Hungary crossed the river here to advance to his victory at Nördlingen. In 1645 Donauwörth was the focal point of Bavarian resistance to the French and Swedes under Enghien and Turenne. Marlborough fought the bloody battle of Donauwörther Schellenberg in July 1704 shortly before going on to his far greater victory at Blenheim. And in 1805 Soult defeated the Austrians here as his corps manoeuvred to cut off Mack at Ulm. The town's importance as a road and rail junction and bridge across the Danube attracted heavy Allied bombing in April 1945 just before the end of World War Two.

Despite the bombing, much of the old town remains. It is particularly pretty under the walls along the Wörnitz. The Gothic church with its six and a half ton bell, the *Pummerin*, is famous. Not far away is the Benedictine Abbey, the focus of Catholic opposition to the town council in 1606.

By and large the locale of a restaurant, as my friend in Sigmaringen had remarked, is as good a place as any in which to observe people. I did have my disappointments: not in any absolute sense for I witnessed many amusing scenes, but rather in finding German actors to people my dramas. One evening in Donauwörth, for example, I found myself next to a couple whom at first I took to be Germans. They turned out to be a South African businessman and an extremely dumb English blonde. He worked hard to try and impress her with his knowledge of German wines and food–he persuaded her to have snails. But she was heavy-going. She was pretty in the style made famous by Diana Dors, but stupid. The man was being too clever by half and snails defeated her both as to taste and as to handling. He ordered an expensive wine but I think she would have preferred a Pepsi. It was a familiar scene and they both had the same end in mind: he was paying.

I saw many young and beautiful Germans, classic Aryan types, but I often wondered what happens to them in middle age. Many elderly Germans lack both form and looks. They are too heavy and they tend to large protuberant stomachs, though these are often less fat than muscle which has gone to seed.

I watched a group of four middle-aged, heavy-built Germans at a nearby table. One of the men was fat and jolly: he wished to clink glasses with his companions and toast whatever occasion they were supposedly out to celebrate. But his wife took him in hand; she had no time for such foolishness. At first she busied herself passing round the neatly wrapped bundles of cutlery which had been piled at the end of the table in their napkins. Then she arranged each person's place to her satisfaction, fiddling with the table until the food came. She deflated the others with her embarrassed organising so that the jolly man felt obliged to eat without being jolly.

There were some charming walks around Donauwörth. In a little park I found another reminder of World War Two: a simple monument to German War dead: 'Let Them Rest in Peace 1939–45.'

The bookshops, however, were full of war books brought out by calculating publishers to coincide with the fortieth anniversary of the War's end.

Chapter Eight

Ingolstadt and
Munich Again

Rennertshofen at midday on a Sunday seemed peculiarly deserted. The broad main street was sealed off by an arched gate at either end, the townhall stood in the middle but at first I could see no sign of an inn. Then I discovered a Stag hotel round a corner. Its main room had a superb collection of trophies on its walls: a huge boar's head, a fox, a bear skin, a large lynx-like cat, stoats and deer–though whether these were all the result of local hunting is another matter.

The centre of the room was occupied by a large *Stammtisch* whose full complement was engaged in a permanent though good-humoured shouting match. The accents were thick. At another table a young man sat on his own reading a newspaper but chatted with his friend the waitress whenever she passed. His clear ambition was to be admitted to the *Stammtisch* which he eyed with the longing of an outsider. How or when one qualified for that honour I never discovered. At a third table three boys and a girl played a ferocious game of cards with a great deal of table slapping, in imitation of their more practised elders. The Stag was clearly the hub of Sunday activity in Rennertshofen.

The walk that day was a long one, and often I was in high rolling meadowland with the river snaking below me in and out of sight. Gradually yet perceptibly it was now becoming larger. At Neuburg, though no more than 45 metres (50 yd) wide, the river was swift flowing, swollen by the recent rains. Neuburg lies on the south bank along a concave curve of river and the old town and castle sit on a hill rising dramatically above the Danube waters. Here town and river belong to each other: Neuburg is one of a dozen such towns which long ago grew to importance because of its position in relation to the river; and the Danube, still small but hinting at grandeur to come, is enhanced by the strong, imposing buildings which rise above it.

I had walked 37 kilometres (23 miles) and felt stiff, but after a shower I set off, refreshed, to explore the town. Its old municipal buildings, which were heavy with civic pride, offered little to the Sunday visitor. After a supper consisting mainly of asparagus, a speciality of the region, I found a seedy pub in which to study the locale. The *Stammtisch* was full. A German friend had suggested that I should try to sit at a *Stammtisch*–at least if one were half empty and some opportunity presented itself. I doubt if such an intrusion would in fact have been welcome and in any case I never saw an appropriate opportunity to try. I cannot recall seeing a *Stammtisch* that was not fully active.

Neuburg possesses ancient fortifications and a number of fine old buildings. In the political manoeuvring which foreshadowed the Thirty Years' War the Count of Neuburg became a Catholic. More important, towards the end of the century, the fortunes of the ruling Wittelsbach family were immensely improved when the Emperor, Leopold I, took Eleanor-Magdalene of Pfalz-Neuburg as his third wife. A Neuburg regiment served in defence of Vienna during the siege by the Ottoman Turks in 1683. And Eleanor's father, Philip William, Count of Pfalz-Neuburg, rose rapidly as a result of his daughter's marriage to become the Elector Palatine. His elevation ushered in the town's period of greatest power and influence.

Ingolstadt, in the middle of Bavaria, lies at the centre of the strategically vital stretch of Danube between Ulm and Regensburg (Col. pl. 7). In 1363 the Danube was diverted to pass the town while 30 years later the town became the seat of the Dukes of Bavaria. When the Thirty Years' War began, Ingolstadt had become an important fortress and trading centre and was a focus of the Counter-Reformation. In the period 1570–1640 its university was one of the few in Germany which admitted plebeians, a high proportion of whom became Catholic priests. After the battle on the banks of the Lech in 1632 the great Tilly, then mortally wounded, retired to Ingolstadt where he died of his wounds. Reputedly he died with the word 'Regensburg' on his lips: he was thinking of the key place from which to defend the Danube against the advance of Gustavus Aldolphus. And Maximilian, to his credit, deserted his capital, Munich, and went to defend Regensburg, allowing Gustavus to take Munich. Marlborough besieged Ingolstadt in 1704 but it declined in importance after 1800 when its university was removed and the fortifications were dismantled.

Here the Danube has again widened noticeably. Perhaps I was lucky that on my trip there was so much rain. It meant that almost everywhere the river was full so that it looked deeper, swifter, more impressive than would have been the case in a dry hot summer.

Here where the waters pass the famous thirteenth-century Ingolstadt *Schloss* the Danube has become a river of strong currents, though to my constant surprise I still saw no boats upon it, not even the earnest canoeists I had come to expect.

Today Ingolstadt has two castles dating from the thirteenth and fifteenth centuries, some lovely churches and its famous towers, including the seven turreted gateway, as well as a few remains of its ancient walls. It is a bustling place of commercial and industrial prosperity as well as tourist attraction.

I decided to break my journey at Ingolstadt and make a brief visit to Munich before continuing to Regensburg and the barges. While waiting for a train I went for a drink in a pub near the station. It was an ordinary establishment but I happened to witness an interesting set scene there, German-style, concerned with football. Eleven civilian soccer players were seated at one table, eleven soldiers at another. The latter burst out laughing at the sight of my Austrian army pack which clearly evoked familiar activities. One or two individuals sat at other tables and about six men sat at the *Stammtisch*. The two soccer teams called across to one another; they had played a game earlier in the day, apparently part of a club series.

The host now came forward to act as master of ceremonies. The walls of his establishment were adorned with football pennants as well as other trophies. He called for silence and the captain of the civilian team made a short speech and then handed a pennant to the captain of the soldier's team. After drinking and talking for a while the host called upon the captain of the soldier's team, who was also a military captain, to take the floor. He gave an equally polite speech and then presented to the other team a plate with the regimental insignia upon it. There were cheers all round. Some of the civilian team went to sit with the soldiers and some of the soldiers went to sit with the civilians. It was most polite. The two team captains then presented their trophies to the host to add to his wall decorations. In view of recent behaviour by British soccer fans in Brussels I felt I should keep my national identity to myself.

The open-air food market in Munich is a lively place. All round the square are food stalls but the middle is taken up with tables which can seat perhaps 600 people. There are stalls selling sandwiches and kiosks selling beer. One queues to purchase a beer and then searches for a seat. At lunchtime on a summer's day the market is packed and one may be obliged to wander among the tables for some time in search of a seat.

Grasping a large stein of beer and weaving my way between crowded tables I eventually found a single place at a table with an Italian family: a man, his wife, their teenage daughter and a woman friend. They were happy for me to sit there; they thought I was German. They were on holiday and the man kept getting up to take photographs of the crowded scene or of his family. He took one of me just as I raised the big stein to my lips, presumably so that back home he could show a typical German drinking beer. We got into conversation and I then discovered that they were Argentinians, although of Italian extraction. They were intrigued to find that I was not German after all but British. Their holiday tour was to include Germany, Italy and France–but not Britain.

'Why not?' I asked.

'The Falklands,' they said. 'Of course.'

The girl had competent school English which she was happy to exercise and she acted as our interpreter. The father then spoke.

'The Argentinian people are good people. It is the military who cause the trouble.' This was by way of a tentative opening statement, a feeler.

'Yes indeed,' I agreed, 'the military are a nuisance just about everywhere.' And we took a good draught of beer as we considered this general truth about the world's military.

'Naturally we would like to go to England,' he continued, 'but at present it is difficult: there are still no proper relations.'

We discussed the absurdity of national behaviour and then for a time spoke of other things. I asked what he did; he was some kind of engineer. He asked what I did. We surveyed the bustling scene round us. It was a friendly, casual encounter of a kind one can have anywhere. But I knew that he had something on his mind and eventually, after a slightly hesitant family colloquy, his daughter smiled and said in her correct careful English:

'My father ask, do you like *the* Thatcher?'

'Certainly not,' I replied.

'Ah,' said the father, 'you are *laborista*?'

My politics are difficult enough for me to quantify let alone explain to a foreigner through an interpreting daughter, so I simply said: 'I am not especially *laborista* but I do not like *the* Thatcher.' General relief all round.

No one can claim to have got the feel of Munich without a visit to one of its beer gardens. One of the largest and most famous was close to my friend Ruth's flat. It was a huge place, seating maybe 700 people, and proved an excellent locale. I went there one Saturday at noon. It was not especially busy but I still had to wait 15 minutes before a waiter came to serve me. He was an interesting study, that waiter. He was tall and thickset with a developing stomach and possessed of a waiter's quick-footed waddle, his shoulders rolling as he balanced half a dozen large steins of beer in one hand and a tray of food at shoulder level in the other. He had the priceless professional advantage of a mouth full of silver-plated teeth; in consequence he only had to withdraw his lips to reveal those shining accoutrements and at once he would be flashing a silver smile, even if his thoughts were of quite another kind. He also wore thick-lensed glasses through which his eyes bulged at you. Their thickness prevented an accurate assessment of the feelings that might otherwise have been detected in the eyes above the flashing teeth. A silver cord attached to the legs of his glasses ran behind his head so that he would not lose them as he bustled about the beer garden. He was used to smiling. Or, more accurately, to flashing those teeth. He took his time. He told customers to wait or ignored them altogether. He plonked a great tray of food on my table in order to distribute its contents to people elsewhere. He made jokes. When he had forgotten for whom he had brought an order he would stand in the middle of his serving area and call out with authoritarian anger to discover who was waiting for whatever he had on offer. When customers who had been waiting a long time complained that they were thirsty he would, with a great sweep of his arm, indicate all the other seated people and disdain to offer any other explanation. He made off-the-cuff remarks. And when customers laughed at these sallies delivered with a deadpan expression or uttered fiercely as though blaming them for being there at all, he would allow his lips to retract, once more revealing his silver teeth. His smile was mechanical and, despite the distortion of the thick lenses, I do not believe those smiles ever reached his eyes. He had been working there for years. The beer garden was his stage and the customers his audience; it was for them to respond to him, not the other way round.

I had made the break to visit Munich because I needed to contact London as well as to check arrangements about the barges at Regensburg. I was there only a few days, yet I found myself fretting to get back to my river. By then my walking routine had grown upon me as had my daily search for a route close to the Danube–not always as easy as one might suppose for such an important river. I wanted once more to be trekking into little towns in the late afternoon to search for a suitable hostelry and I was anxious to plot the deepening size of the Danube since from Ingolstadt to Regensburg it again passes through dramatic scenery. I was now keen to experience a change of action and travel by barge. So I felt relief when I found myself in a train heading back to Ingolstadt and the Danube once more.

Chapter Nine

Neustadt to Regensburg

Neustadt, halfway between Ingolstadt and Regensburg, is an unpretentious little town. It has nothing much of historic significance to show and there is no particular reason for tourists to stop there, except that it is on the way to somewhere more important. It is the better for that. I found a small hotel and having settled in walked several kilometres to the river where I sat on the bank reading and watching canoeists and other sportsmen whom the fine weather had brought out in considerable numbers.

As though to make up for the absence of any craft upon the river between Neuburg and Ingolstadt the Danube that afternoon seemed crowded. A dramatic bridge crossed the river and from the bank, through its arches, I watched distant sportsmen in an inflatable dinghy. They were a good distance from me on the far side of the river and idly I took out my camera for a picture. To my astonishment, by the time I had it in focus the dinghy swept past me on my side of the river not more than 4 metres (13 ft) from the bank, its occupants helpless in the grip of a strong swift current. Then they were gone. Others were also busy on the water. A couple came to the bank close to my position and in typical English fashion I thought how very unfriendly of them to crowd me, but they only wanted to inflate another rubber dinghy and take to the water.

The hotel was cheap, had no pretensions and served excellent food. The waitress thought I was German which pleased me: my accent appeared to be improving. Each time I ordered a drink she made a mark on my beermat which was my tally to be settled on departure. It is a civilised custom but I found myself wondering how it would work in a crowded English pub.

For much of the distance between Neustadt and Weltenburg I walked along the flood barrage. Often I was in sight of the river but sometimes it was masked by thick trees along its banks. At one point I cut through these woods to watch the river's waters gather their strength for the Weltenburg Gorge ahead, but my contemplation was cut short by swarms of vicious mosquitoes from the damp undergrowth. A sign on the opposite bank showed the Black Sea to be 2,488 kilometres (1,546 miles) distant.

This was Roman country: traces of fortifications and settlements are to be found all along this stretch of river until Regensburg. Weltenburg provides a dramatic setting for a monastery and the ancient Benedictine foundation dates back to 600. The town, which has been developed as a tourist centre, possesses an eighteenth-century baroque church. Passenger boats come upstream to Weltenburg from Kelheim through the Donaudurchbruch Gorge and the Danube narrows spectacularly here as it passes through the gorge whose cliff sides sometimes tower 120 metres (400 ft) above the river. I took the passenger boat to Kelheim–once more in rain–and actually travelled upon the Danube for the first time. I was strangely enough becoming increasingly attached to the rain. Pictures in guide books invariably show the river under brilliant sunshine, which enhances the scenic beauty of the countryside and bolsters the myth of a blue Danube. But the river's power becomes apparent in the rain when the surface rises to meet you in response to the gloom and wet from above.

The Donaudurchbruch Gorge would be exciting in any weather. Sheer rocks crowd the water's edge and the river narrows in a spectacular cleft which concentrates the water's energies. When heavy clouds descend to make the gorge grey and gloomy and the rain beats down on the surface of the water the gorge becomes a wild passage. How much wilder must it have been all those centuries ago when the Benedictine monks first established their monastery at its head. Here, for the first time, it is possible to sense the real force of the Danube as its waters concentrate to surge through their spectacular gorge.

Kelheim is the old ducal town of the Wittelsbach family and much of the centre retains its medieval character (Col. pl. 8). Here the Altmühl joins the Danube. But Kelheim is overlooked by the great rotunda of the *Befreiungshalle* (the Liberation Hall) high above the town on the Michelsberg hill. The *Befreiungshalle* can be seen as one approaches Kelheim through the gorge from Weltenburg; it can also be seen from the centre of the town rising above the trees high on its hill, standing in solitary grandeur.

The Altmühl Canal, now under construction, will complete the series of waterways connecting the Danube and the Rhine, so that by the 1990s commercial traffic will be able to pass from the North Sea through central Europe to the Black Sea for the first time.

My boat reached Kelheim in pouring rain. The town was full and by the time I had found accommodation I was drenched. That evening my hotel was a busy place but I secured a convenient corner seat in the main room. The *Stammtisch* was in happy mood and the host found time to join in when a seat became vacant. But hardly had he sat down when another 'regular' arrived. He wanted his place at the *Stammtisch* and when he saw all the seats occupied he pouted in an unashamed sulk. He was aged about 50. The host at once relinquished his seat to the newcomer. There was a second *Stammtisch* at which a game of cards was in progress, while an entire side room had been given over to chess; members of a club played each other against clocks. By nine o'clock three games of *Schafkopf* were being played: the betting was brisk. Its prohibition clearly made little difference.

The *Befreiungshalle* was built to commemorate the war of liberation (1813–15) against Napoleon, when Bavaria changed sides to join the ultimately victorious allies and so keep all the advantages which the state had won from Napoleon. The hall is a huge rotunda of yellow sandstone approached through thick trees up the steep hill which stands behind the town. This dramatic edifice was begun in 1842 by Lugwig I but not completed until 1863, by which time Ludwig had long abdicated (1848) in favour of his son Maximilian II. It is vast, decorated both inside and out with a series of forbidding allegorical females. The interior consists of a huge circular marble hall with 34 winged victories standing between panels round the sides. On each panel are named the battles and victories of the struggle. High up round the balcony a series of marble shields displays the names of Prussian generals such as Gneisenau and Blücher. The building was modelled upon the tomb of Theodoric at Ravenna. Its marble grandeur, its glorification of the military and its sheer scale–Wagnerian and awe-inspiring–epitomises that Teutonic spirit which at its best produced unification under Bismarck and at the other extreme the excesses of Hitler.

The first time I visited the *Befreiungshalle* was in the late afternoon when the rain had finally stopped. Crowds of tourists had come by bus and car and some, like me, had even walked up the steep hill. The hall was impressive, awesome. But I visited it a second time that evening when its gates were shut and no one else was in sight. Then it was extraordinarily peaceful. It is an amazing monument to find anywhere, alone on the top of its hill, about two thirds the size of London's Albert Hall. The yellow sandstone gleamed in the evening sunlight, turning the rotunda into a giant wedding cake.

Below in the deep gorge, framed in the thick trees of the forested hillside, I watched another of the tourist boats coming from Weltenburg, a small white dot in the distance, while racing in the foreground 120 metres (400 ft) below were three tiny speedboats leaving miniature wakes behind them. Through another window of trees, this time looking downstream, lay the town of Kelheim, grey and smoky under the heavy clouds, with the River Altmühl curving beyond to join the Danube.

The Bavarian royal house in the nineteenth century was a strange mixture. In 1818 Maximilian I, who had switched sides at the end of the Napoleonic Wars, presented his people with a constitution which went some way to providing them with political freedom, while maintaining royal rights. He was a reformer and much loved. His son Ludwig I, who succeeded him in 1825, made Munich a centre of art and culture. However, Ludwig became increasingly reactionary and was forced to abdicate in favour of his son, Maximilian II. Ludwig II succeeded his father in 1864 but was declared insane in 1886 and committed suicide shortly afterwards. His brother Otto then became king but he too suffered from insanity and so his uncle, Luitpold, was made regent.

Kelheim to Regensburg was to be my last walk in Germany. I was not interested in hitching but a car stopped as I left Kelheim and the driver offered me a lift. He only took me five kilometres (3 miles) out of Kelheim but it was a friendly gesture to put me on the Regensburg road. I had a long riverside walk that day and for some reason all my encounters with people, other walkers for example, turned out to be gruff. They were unfriendly, not me. Thus when I sat beside a weir to eat an apple a car drew up and a couple got out their fishing tackle. I greeted them politely but they barely answered me, angry perhaps to find their fishing ground invaded by a stranger–and a foreign stranger at that. Cyclists whom I now greeted as a matter of principle stared ahead to cycle straight past me. In the *Gasthof* where I stopped for a lunchtime beer the young man who served me verged on the rude because I did not also want to eat. And in the little village shop where I purchased a roll and cheese the woman behind the counter was equally abrupt. It was, I suppose, everyone's off-day. I could see no reason for such gruffness in a country where, normally, formal politeness far surpassed that to be found in Britain.

I arrived in Regensburg with a limp. I thought I had strained a muscle in my foot. None the less I wandered round the old city for an hour before settling upon a hotel: it was a Friday so I had the weekend before me. On the Monday I would seek out the offices of the DDGS (the First Danube Steamship Company), which had promised to allow me to travel from Regensburg to Vienna by barge.

My foot became unbearably painful and I wondered whether I had broken a small bone. In fact I was suffering a sudden onset of crippling rheumatism, the result of walking long distances in shoes which had been soaked by the incessant rains.

57

Regensburg is situated on the northernmost point of the Danube (Col. pl. 9). The river is joined here by three tributaries from the north: the Laaber, the Naab and the Regen. The city of Regensburg is one of the oldest in Germany: old and elegant, it is a place of substance and one can easily become lost in its medieval streets and winding lanes. The great gothic cathedral and the ancient stone bridge across the Danube–the oldest bridge in Germany–are its two most impressive attractions but it is also a centre of culture and art, renowned for its music and Bavarian hospitality. Regensburg claims to possess Germany's oldest restaurant, the 'Historic Sausage Kitchen' on the bank of the river by the stone bridge. There one can sit at a long table under awnings to drink beer and eat one of the various sausage dishes on offer. I visited this 'kitchen' more than once and on one occasion seated myself at the end of an otherwise empty table which could accommodate four a side. After a while a couple approached and went to sit at the end away from me. Politely they inquired whether that end of the table was free–it clearly was–and only when I agreed did they take their seats. Germans, I found, practise a formal courtesy rarely encountered in Britain.

I bought a ticket for a concert of chamber music; I regard that concert as a landmark in my German journey. In Britain I had long before built up a picture of musical Germany in which the smallest town would offer regular concerts of the highest standard, but in this I had been disappointed. In all the towns in which I stayed, from Donaueschingen to Regensburg, only in Ulm was there music available. *Die Fledermaus* was being performed but was sold out, as I was twice told with great emphasis. Elsewhere I had always found that while a concert might have taken place the week before my arrival or that one was due to be performed two weeks after my departure there was nothing available during my stay. Now, however, Regensburg offered me a concert of Bach and Vivaldi. The concert was by no means sold out and the hall was maybe two-thirds full. It was a relaxing occasion but I had forgotten my foot, even though I had limped all the way to the concert hall. At the end, when I got up to leave, I put my weight upon it without thinking and the pain was so great that I doubled up before struggling to an upright position again. Courteously a young man and his girl friend who were following me out came to either side to offer assistance. This mortified me: not their concern but because they imagined that I required help.

There is a lot of history to Regensburg. The city's medieval buildings, cathedral, churches and towers as well as the old river front have that well-worn, blended appearance which only comes with great age. The original Celtic settlement was named Radasbona, hence the English Ratisbon. Its position on the northernmost bend of the Danube gave it strategic significance in Roman times, like a redoubt on the long frontier facing the increasingly aggressive and confident barbarians. The Romans converted the Celtic settlement into a fortress which became the Emperor Marcus Aurelius' headquarters as, winter after winter, he faced the ever-increasing hostility of the barbarians. In 179 the Emperor turned the older foundation into Castra Regina: Regensburg is a corruption of that name.

The city became the first capital of the Bavarian dukes whose tribes migrated into the area in the sixth century. It was made a bishopric in 739 and the seat of the Carolingians in 788. By medieval times Regensburg had become one of the great cities of Europe and for a while it rivalled Vienna. When, in the thirteenth century, it became an imperial city, Regensburg was the wealthiest and most populous city of southern Germany, the principal Danube crossing for traffic from northern Europe to the Brenner Pass and Venice. Albrecht Altdorfer (c. 1480–1538) was one of its burghers, and fragments of his imperial bath frescoes are now in the municipal museum. The city suffered a decline in the fourteenth century when Augsburg and Nurnberg rose to prominence.

During the Reformation the new term 'Interim' was first used, when the two sides in the religious conflict sought a peace formula. The first Interim Agreement was concluded in 1541 at Regensburg. In the seventeenth century the gothic *Rathaus* (townhall) became the site for the Reichstag meetings of the Empire. These became known as the 'everlasting parliament' and were to continue from 1663 to 1806, when the Holy Roman Empire (once described as neither holy nor Roman nor an empire) was finally abolished by Napoleon.

Goethe described the city's situation as enchanting; its nearby vineyards have been cultivated since Roman times. It was captured in 1809 by Napoleon and became part of an expanded Bavaria the following year. Despite heavy bombing during World War Two, the old part of the city miraculously escaped almost unscathed.

Perhaps its greatest glory, the architectural miracle of its time, is the twelfth-century Stone Bridge erected between 1135 and 1146. This crosses the Danube at its most northerly curve. It is 310 metres (339 yd) long and 7 metres (23 ft) wide. Hans Sachs, the sixteenth-century writer who was the model for Wagner's *Meistersinger von Nürnberg*, said 400 years after its construction that the bridge had no equal in Germany. Today Regensburg is a busy port at the head of commercial navigation down the Danube. It was the starting point for my barge journey.

Chapter Ten

The Barges

The Danube is not a wild untamed river passing through little known territory but an ancient European highway, and one way to capture the essence of the river is to chug along it in a barge. Barges of many nations ply the Danube from the Black Sea to Regensburg, which is in the heart of Germany and very nearly at the centre of Europe. Sometimes barges go singly, driven by their own power, but as a rule they are linked together, side by side: a pair, a unit of four, or six barges in three pairs are pushed or pulled by powerful tugs. There is a camaraderie about river life comparable to that between seafaring men. The confines are more narrow, the visions limited to the river banks of the countries through which, year after year, the same journey is made. I spoke with a number of crewmen from the barges as well as my two captains and none had ever worked at sea. Their life was the river which they had come to know and love. Some had left it to try their hands at other occupations: 'But it draws you back,' one told me. And the Danube–turgid, glassy, polluted and brown, choppy and swirling or smooth and gentle but hardly ever Strauss's blue–laps the banks of eight lands.

I had wanted to travel the Danube by barge ever since reading John Buchan's *Greenmantle* when I was about 14. In his fast moving, carelessly researched book Buchan, irritatingly, is not sufficiently obvious in his inaccuracies for these to be pinpointed. The hero, Richard Hannay, on the run in the Black Forest, comes out to the Danube to find barges on the river at a point that would extend the forest at least 160 kilometres (100 miles) farther east than it ever reached. Later he manages to move his barges from the Austrian border to Vienna in a long afternoon. But the story is vintage Buchan for all that, and he captures the romance of the barges.

I had obtained permission as a writer to travel on the barges, though not without considerable difficulty. The DDGS (the First Danube

Steamship Company) has been sailing the river with passenger steamers and barges since its foundation in 1829. It is the oldest, best-known company on the Danube. I found its Danube handbooks invaluable: they map the river, 50-kilometre (30-mile) stretches to a page, and pinpoint all the places of interest, towns, castles, monasteries, gorges and islands, giving their distance from the Delta.

On the Monday morning Regensburg lived up to its name. A steady downpour of rain cloaked the city in dreary grey and by the time I had limped to the DDGS offices on the riverfront I was soaked. They were expecting me sometime in June. Normally the company never takes passengers on its barges. I had already signed an indemnity for the company in advance, exonerating it of blame should I fall overboard or suffer any other mishap while travelling on its barges. The company had only reluctantly agreed to my request after considerable correspondence; my friend Ruth Schutz in Munich had acted as my agent in this matter. I was, therefore, uncertain as to my reception and wondered whether they would regard me simply as a nuisance. By the time I reached the DDGS offices after a wet and painful limp from my hotel (I had failed to find a taxi), I was myself uncertain of temper. I need not have worried.

In the Director's office I gave the secretary my name and added 'the writer from London'. She appeared quite excited at this and went at once into the inner office into which she invited me a moment later. Herr Schmidt could not have been kinder. Neither he nor his secretary spoke any English so I had to stretch my German. We talked of my journey that far, he asked when I would like to go by barge, provided me with information about the company and then got onto his intercom to the docks.

A barge was about to take on a load and would set off down the Danube that afternoon. He asked if that would suit me. It was ideal. So he made arrangements with the captain while I signed more forms. Herr Schmidt said he would telephone through to the company offices in Linz to warn them of my coming, since my barge would end its journey there. Then he took me back to my hotel to collect my baggage and we drove to the docks (Col. pl. 10).

There are two Regensburgs: the old, tightly clustered medieval city of winding streets with its cathedral and merchant towers; and the expanding modern commercial town with high-rise blocks of flats and the docks. This is the starting point for traffic down the river, the farthest inland that the barges come to deliver their cargoes. Docks are exciting places with their great cranes weirdly drooped like birds of prey above the cargo vessels, engines shunting trucks along the quayside, constant noise and activity. And always, there is the sense of impending departure, the lure of distant places which are as yet only names.

61

I was to travel on the *Rosenburg*. At the quayside we looked down at least 6 metres (20 ft) to the bridge of the barge from which Captain Schwebel peered before he came up to greet us. He must have been near 60, a short thick-set grey-haired man, slow of speech, relaxed and friendly. Herr Schmidt introduced me and then they spoke of the cargo. I was not sure what to do about food. On the ordinary barges, as opposed to the big tugs which carried larger numbers, each crew member provides his own food which he cooks for himself. However, the captain insisted that I was his guest, though later I saw a package of extra supplies brought on board, probably the gift of Herr Schmidt. The captain now called a young member of the crew who came back with us to the car to carry my pack on board. I was quite capable of doing that for myself but all seamen, even of barges, assume that landlubbers are likely to fall off gangways or do something else equally stupid. In any case I was being given VIP treatment. I noticed the director slipped a pack of cigarettes to the crewman as payment for this simple service: passengers and how to treat them, I felt, were a new experience all round.

I thanked Herr Schmidt for his help and spontaneous kindness and was escorted below by the captain. Here I found another member of the crew clearing his belongings from a cabin for my benefit. It was then eleven o'clock and we were not due to depart until three that afternoon. I had time on my hands so I wandered round the docks, though never far from my barge. When Herr Schmidt had accompanied me to the barge, a rugged docker wearing a balaclava and generally making himself useful on the quayside securing ropes had knuckled his forehead to the Director who had spoken a civil word to him. He was a thick-muscled working dwarf with a black seamed face weathered by a lifetime of dockside coal dust. He ignored me as a stranger who clearly did not know what to do with himself. It had stopped raining but the lowering sky was heavy with promise of water to come.

The captain hailed me from his bridge and as soon as I had joined him he started the engine and began to manoeuvre the barge into the middle of the dock pool. He invited me to share the bridge with him for the journey. We moved to the other side of the docks where we were secured to a second barge which we were to tow.

Our cargo consisted of coaldust, and the loading was both dirty and noisy as the crane moved back and forth along its rails swinging its huge clamp-bucket over the bays to discharge its coal, the barge shuddering and displacing water with the impact of each new load. The barge was 90 metres (295 ft) long and carried a normal load of 1,100 to 1,200 tonnes, though it could take considerably more.

The rain came down in torrents again and with a certain dour pleasure Captain Schwebel told me that the name of the town meant rain, so it was merely living up to its reputation. When the loading was completed he invited me to have lunch with him. We went below to the small mess where he prepared our meal. Captain Schwebel prided himself upon his cooking. I drank a beer. He broke four eggs into the frying pan, then asked if they were sufficient or whether I would prefer six. Four would do, I replied. He cut slices from a side of fat bacon and added a variety of spices. When this healthy plateful was ready he placed it before me, serving himself with a more modest portion. In the meantime he had opened a bottle of red Austrian wine which we shared, but though he plied me generously with this he drank sparingly himself for he was on duty.

Captain Schwebel had spent 28 years of his life on the Danube and spoke of the river with deep affection. On the bridge he had at first appeared dour and reserved with little to say but this I judged had been from shyness with a foreigner who had but indifferent German. Later in the mess he relaxed to become expansive. He was of Hungarian origin though he had taken German citizenship three decades earlier. Now he was approaching retirement. I found his accent difficult to understand but once I had asked him to repeat remarks a few times he became increasingly friendly and talkative. Then he would forget the limited extent of my German to speak faster and faster as he warmed to a theme until he recollected, smiled, and slowed his pace again.

There was a crew of three. The number two who had cleared out his cabin for me was Austrian. He was fat and jolly in a slow sort of way and told me he spoke English, although this turned out to be a good deal more limited than my German. He was not a regular crew member but worked for the company on standby. Petrovic Bogosor, the engineer, who always worked on the *Rosenburg*, was a Yugoslav. At first he seemed to have no conversation of any kind. He came into the mess while we were having lunch and stood with his back to the stove waiting for water to boil. Then he made coffee for the three of us but remained standing to drink his, silent. The captain clearly regarded this as normal and spoke only with me. Petrovic's one contribution to our discussion was an occasional affirmation of something the captain said, usually with a slow nod of his square flat-topped head. The final member of the crew, also an Austrian, was the young man who had carried my pack on board. They were an oddly assorted quartet. The silences of the Yugoslav provided a source of amusement for the others, who spoke as though he were elsewhere while he remained standing like a sentinel. He did not appear to resent jokes at his expense.

Each member of the crew had his personal locker for food as well as a shelf in the refrigerator; they cooked their own meals when they had time off to do so. There was a plentiful supply of beer, and at various times I was offered a drink by different crew members. I think the beer was communal though I never found out for certain. That evening, though, the youngest crewman asked permission of the captain before helping himself to a beer. When our meal was finished the captain asked me if I should like to take a rest: he would call me before we departed. He wanted me out of the way. After the considerable quantities of beer, wine and food which I had consumed I found no difficulty in sleeping at once. I woke with a start at the captain's knock on my door and went up onto the bridge to watch our departure.

The sky was black with clouds and the rain lashed against the cabin superstructure. Two of the crew, in heavy yellow sou'westers, were sweeping coaldust from the runways of the hold covers before, one by one, they rolled these into place over the piled cargo of coal. We were only loaded to three-quarters capacity although both barges were well down in the water. Slowly, against the driving rain, we manoeuvred into the centre of the pool to proceed gently towards the river.

The captain held the barge idling while he waited for permission to set off downriver. There was no discernible break in the clouds and the rain beat down on the roof of the bridge while great drops danced upon the flat covers of the holds. Permission to depart crackled over the intercom, the captain sounded a long satisfying blast on the barge's horn, the engine revved into life and we were off. I sat on a leather-covered bench seat which ran from side to side at the rear of the bridge cabin. The captain sat at his wheel on a high swivel chair whose smooth rollers allowed him to change his position at will. We nosed our way out of the dock into the Danube.

Kilometre signs along the banks give the distance from the Black Sea and as we set off from Regensburg a sign showed that we still had 2,373 kilometres (1,475 miles) to go, so that from Donaueschingen to Regensburg I had covered 467 kilometres (290 miles). Since I had walked a great part of this I felt more than satisfied, although I had only covered a fraction of the total distance. I timed the barge between kilometre posts to find we were making a downstream speed of 15 kilometres (9 miles) an hour. The captain confirmed this but said that a barge coming upriver against the current with a full load might only manage four or five kilometres an hour.

I was fascinated watching the captain swing the wheel. There was a time lag between his actions on the bridge (for example, a turn to port), and the response of the barge's prow 90 metres (98yds) ahead of us. A change of direction of the prow did not synchronise with the turning of the wheel: the response came a measurable time after the captain had completed his turn of the wheel. Thus he would twirl the wheel furiously to starboard but by the time the prow of the barge had also begun to swing to starboard he would be busily turning the wheel to port again. When he had executed a particularly vigorous turn in one direction I tried to guess the moment when the prow would follow but I always got it wrong. Sometimes at a tricky passage, before the barge had begun to respond to one turn of the wheel, the captain was already turning it the opposite way. On bends in the river he appeared constantly to be turning the wheel in a contrary direction to that which the prow of the barge was taking.

We passed through some narrow channels marked by buoys, often close in to the bank. We met barges coming upstream at less than half our speed; some appeared to be hardly moving as they struggled against the strong currents. Most of the time, however, we had the river to ourselves. By evening the rain had stopped and we chugged along through flat meadow country with a lightly clouded blue sky above, the sun periodically breaking through to make the water dazzle and sparkle.

The Austrian mate joined us on the bridge. Periodically he would take a turn at the wheel while Schwebel would move his chair to the side to offer advice about the tricky channels. As yet the Danube was still only a modest-sized river although constantly winding and turning, its channels switching from bank to bank.

Schwebel's accent was far from easy to understand; he made funny long vowel sounds and German remained very much a second language for him. When he said something I could not understand I was never sure whether this was due to my limited German or his accent. The mate spent half his time on the bridge. When the captain was at the wheel he sat on the leather-covered bench seat with me. I was content to be silent until one or other of them spoke. The captain, too, sat for long spells without saying anything. Then he would make a comment and on cue the mate would reply, usually at greater length. Sometimes he talked to me about Austria. He pointed out landmarks which we passed and, long before Passau, told me it possessed the largest organ in the world. He had worked on the river for nine years; before that he had been a wood salesman. He enjoyed making jokes about the Germans, especially their beer-drinking habits. 'They all have big stomachs,' he said, emphasising the point by patting his own by no means diminutive one. Then he moved on to the German taste for *sauerkraut* which led him to describe them as *krauts*, a term he employed with a certain derisive contempt. In his slow way he was something of a lad.

We passed through a number of locks to drop about nine metres (30 ft) each time. Even from the bridge we had to peer up sharply by the time the lock waters had dropped their full extent. Our two barges, side by side, fitted neatly into the locks to leave no more than 60–90 cm (2–3 ft) of space at the sides. The engines had great power and this became apparent when we manoeuvred in the locks: then, hardly moving at all, I could feel the surge of the motors which vibrated the whole barge as they throbbed beneath us.

Although we appeared to have the river to ourselves for most of the time this was deceptive, and the locks especially made me aware of other river traffic. We would reach a lock only to wait while another barge went through ahead of us. Then, by the time we entered the lock yet another barge and sometimes two or three, would have come up to wait behind us. The river might appear peaceful but plenty of traffic was using it.

We made good speed after the first lock, positively consuming kilometres, while the sun made its first appearance of the day. Occasionally we passed villages and once a great barge, or rather four barges joined together, loaded with containers inched past us on their way upstream while we slowed almost to a halt.

From time to time the intercom crackled and the captain, who knew all the voices which came over it like old friends, would relay his position according to the last kilometre post we had passed. Once, in response to an inquiry, he replied: 'We are 2,351 kilometres up the Danube,' then, vastly pleased with himself, he turned to smile at me.

By late evening the river was glassy smooth. Rising above the reeds, herons flapped their great wings as they gathered momentum and took off, tucking in their long necks. We passed the village of Bogen with its 1,200-year-old church perched on a high hill overlooking the river. By then we were 2,310 kilometres (1,435 miles) from the Black Sea. At dusk we reversed to moor at the side of the river for the night.

The crew gathered in the mess to relax over their supper and have a drink before turning in. We were to be off again at four thirty in the morning. On this occasion even the taciturn Yugoslav made a few contributions to the conversation. Captain Schwebel turned out to be a great talker: politics and cooking were his two interests. He would look at me from under his drooping lids to size up my reaction after he had made one of his pronouncements.

'Everything,' he said, 'depends upon the two superpowers: they have both managed to unite polyglot mixtures of people.' He made it sound as though this had been achieved by sleight of hand and was not quite decent. He hankered for a union.

'A united Europe?' I asked.

'No, no!' That was not what he meant. He dismissed France, was contemptuous of Italy and thought the Scandinavians were too remote. What he meant was Germany, Austria, Hungary and Britain.

'That combination would be unbeatable.' He said this slowly with emphasis, eyeing me as he did so and waiting for my reaction.

It was clearly a favourite theme of his. I was not certain whether the inclusion of Britain in this 'Greater Europe' was a courtesy to me or a necessary part of the whole. I asked why, if such a union were possible, we should not go for a united Europe. That he brushed aside: 'It might come one day,' he said with airy disbelief, 'but not for a hundred years.'

Up to that point my trip along the Danube had already brought home to me just how isolated Britain remains in relation to the rest of Europe. I make this statement with personal conviction, though it is by no means easy to prove. In one sense it was simply that Europe cannot indulge in our form of insularity. Thus, in the railway station at Ulm I saw trains departing for Bucharest or Paris, a simple yet telling intimation of the unity of the continent which the barrier of the Channel removes from British psychology. Yet, far more important than any physical sign of that kind was the sense of a great mass, of continuity. The countryside changed, the people changed and yet there was no barrier. The farther down the Danube I travelled the more conscious I became of this sense of interlocking cultures.

I wondered whether Germans, Austrians, Czechs, Hungarians or Yugoslavs in this part of central Europe ever thought of Britain as belonging to the continent. I doubted it. At least, I thought, even despite their individual nationalism Europeans do think of themselves as Europeans, as part of a greater whole, while the British remain obstinately cocooned in their island mentality. I put this thought to the captain. His response was to decry the very idea of unity along the Danube.

'We all distrust each other too much,' he said. Then he returned to his idea of Germany (he meant a united Germany), Austria, Hungary and Britain in a special union of their own. He was bitterly anti-Communist. 'Hitler was right about the Communists,' he said.

When we got into our serious political discussion the youngest member of the crew got bored and went to bed. The first mate was only partly interested but the Yugoslav, Petrovic, came to life. Captain Schwebel, meanwhile, had opened a bottle of white wine to share with me. When he spoke of commerce along the river or the value of river traffic or anything to do with money, Captain Schwebel's right hand would rise unconsciously and he would rub his index finger and thumb together in the universal sign for value. He described for my benefit, but not he said for publication, some of the smuggling practices which went on along the river.

His brand of politics I had come across before. His other interest was cooking. He was married with two children, a boy and a girl now grown up; both of them, he informed me, could speak English. Then, like a chef giving a lecture, he described how he cooked some of his favourite dishes and concluded each description with another of his finger gestures. This time he placed his fingers and thumb together on his lips to explode them outwards as he kissed them. '*Geschmackvoll*,' he would say or sometimes just '*Geschmack*'.

The sudden roar of the engine coming to life woke me in the early hours of the morning. I went up onto the bridge in grey half-light as we nosed our way back into the channel to head downstream again. I sat silent on the bridge with the captain. It was unbelievably peaceful. We disturbed many herons as we chugged along in the first light of day. They kept pace with us for a while then, without visible effort, flapped lazily ahead and across our prow to settle on the opposite bank of the river or to soar upwards for a longer flight to distant trees.

The Isar, which flows swiftly through Munich, joins the Danube at Deggendorf. Here I saw Russian barges for the first time. A solitary heron, neck and head pointed to the sky, stood sentinel on a small island of reeds at the confluence of the two rivers and disdained to be disturbed by our passing. At Deggendorf we were 2,280 kilometres (1,417 miles) from the Black Sea.

Chapter Eleven

Passau to Linz

Our barge journey took us through hilly wooded country to the oldest lock in Germany, where we dropped about seven and a half metres (25 ft), and then on to Passau. With the town on either bank we reversed in mid-stream to face up river before docking. It was a skilful manoeuvre and I said so to the captain. He replied that it was normal but was pleased at the compliment. Passau is on the Austrian border and we waited for German and Austrian control officials to come aboard.

The Rivers Inn and Ilz join the Danube at Passau which was described by Alexander von Humboldt as one of the world's seven most beautifully situated towns. There has been a town here since Roman times. In the Middle Ages Passau became a thriving river port. The river bank is lined with old buildings painted in a variety of pastel shades and framed by green woods on the hills behind: The effect is both beautiful and dramatic. The full elegance of the colours was not apparent for it was raining.

Captain Schwebel and I sat chatting in the mess while we waited for the border officials. He had my passport and those of his crew as well as the barge manifesto. I watched the officials come along the quayside together: a dapper, elderly Austrian in his field grey uniform, white hair peeping from beneath his cap, and a giant German in green uniform who was at least six foot six inches tall.

The captain was clearly an old friend of theirs. They looked at me with interest. Captain Schwebel explained that I was a passenger, an English writer travelling with special permission from the company. This increased their interest, though in different ways. The Austrian's reaction reminded me of a phrase from a novel by Buchan, who was a dreadful snob: 'Desperately respectful in the presence of the gentry.' From the moment the captain revealed my role he regarded me with polite awe. On the other hand the German cross-examined me. What kind of books did I write? How many had

I had published? Who were my publishers? Was this to be a travel guide or an account of my journey? Or something else? He was politely relentless. Clearly intrigued by my presence on the barge he was determined to explore my credentials and did so with Teutonic thoroughness. He was very courteous and since my papers were in order and I was on the barge with the company's permission he had no professional reason for his questioning, it was simply personal interest. I was, I imagine, the only such traveller to have come his way.

He continued his interrogation. Would there be a German edition of my book? Had I ever had a best seller? Alas, not yet, but hopefully the Danube would make up for that deficiency, I replied. We laughed at that. The captain brought out four glasses and some white wine. The German proposed success to my book. Then a new thought occurred to him. What of the east European countries? How would they view my desire to write a book? I explained that I had decided to pass through east Europe simply as a tourist. This decision was the result of my Bulgarian experience in London. I had approached the Bulgarian Tourist Agency and told them of my plans. They had been friendly enough but referred my proposal back to Sofia: no visa had been forthcoming.

All three–the German, the Austrian and particularly Captain Schwebel–nodded their emphatic understanding at this revelation which reinforced their own views of the Communist countries. Now they insisted that under no circumstances should I reveal my intention to write a book, otherwise I would have trouble with all the authorities once I had passed from Austria into eastern Europe. They were unanimous and emphatic. Each then proferred examples of east European intransigence: they will not believe you; they are too suspicious; they will take you for a spy; you will be endlessly delayed. They examined the cargo manifest, the captain recharged our glasses and courteously, for the second time, the German customs officer proposed a toast to my forthcoming book. He hoped it would have a German edition. I thanked him; I hoped so too. Then they departed and we were free to continue our way. In all my years of travelling and encounters with border officials, this exchange was indeed a rare and pleasant one.

We set off at once. The captain wanted to reach Linz that evening. From Passau the Danube flows 375 km (233 miles) through Austria; it is a lovely stretch of river. Wood-covered hills rise steeply from the river's banks to be crowned by medieval castles or monasteries. Two of the most famous of these are the vast Benedictine Abbey of Melk, one of the world's greatest baroque buildings, and the ruins of Dürnstein Castle where, on his way home from the third Crusade in 1193, Richard I was imprisoned by the Emperor Henry VI and held to ransom. The minstrel Blondel supposedly located the king here.

The sun appeared for a short while after Passau and I sat in the prow of the barge. This was a different experience. Without the height of the bridge I obtained a new perspective of the river as I watched the two barge prows, flat and wide, surging over the calm waters. We passed through a long stretch of river with forest-covered hills crowding the water's edge. A large passenger craft of the DDGS came up steadily behind us and, as it passed, the passengers inspected our barge and me with interest so I took a photograph. Sometimes the woods receded, giving way to open fields, villages or small towns. Occasionally a little village nestled dramatically in a valley between high forest, the pastel colours of its buildings contrasting sharply with the deep green of the trees behind. About 75 metres (80 yds) behind me, a dark silhouette on the bridge, Captain Schwebel looked ahead at a scene he must have passed thousands of times during his 28 years on the Danube. A monotonous life I thought, and yet a river is never the same. Now it was placid: the waters high from the rains, its surface sparkling and changing shades under the evening sunlight. But the Danube, as I was learning, has many moods.

About an hour beyond Passau a kilometre post showed that we were 2,216 kilometres (1,377 miles) from the Black Sea. Back on the bridge the captain showed a sudden increase of interest in my affairs. The interrogation by the German customs officer had released his inhibitions. He insisted that I should obtain a copy of his favourite book, *Goldmarsh* by the Hungarian Jokaji Mor. I confess to not having heard of either author or title.

The captain liked a late lunch so, leaving the mate at the wheel, the two of us retired to the mess which we had to ourselves. This time he made schnitzels and we drank white wine. He nursed a single glass of wine and explained that on duty he kept to very strict limits. He made up for this, however, by the way he pressed me to take more wine and, later, schnapps. We had another far-ranging conversation, though its subject matter was mainly a repeat of the day before. He was a great admirer of Austria and first we spoke of the country through which we were passing. Then we returned to the subject of food or, rather, Captain Schwebel did. He described a succession of his favourite dishes and I was treated to more *geschmackvolls*. 'I am the cook of our house,' he said with pride. He did not just describe a dish; he gave a blow-by-blow account of how he would prepare it –salt, cayenne pepper, sliced onions–once more he was instructing a class of young chefs. Then, the description finished and the dish 'placed' before me, his face would light up and placing his fingers and thumb in a now familiar gesture to his mouth he would kiss them and withdraw his hand to splay its members outwards in an explosive star: '*geschmackvoll!*'

We returned to politics which we had reserved by mutual consent for the end of the meal. I again suggested that the Danube, which acted as a highway through so many countries, also possessed many political possibilities as a unifying link. The captain dismissed so extravagant an idea with a gesture, brushing it aside as a hopelessly inaccurate reading of the central European character. 'European unity,' he repeated, 'is impossible. Not in a hundred years.' He had made the same point the previous day. In my heart I agreed; there are few signs of real European unity even if there is greater understanding to be found on the Continent than exists between Britain and the rest of Europe. Aware of the differences between the British and the people of the Continent, I often had difficulty in putting a finger on just what these were. Language facility or lack of it is undoubtedly one, yet more complex and almost impossible to quantify is what might be termed acceptance: the peoples of Europe regard each other as belonging together even as they decry one another's national faults. To the British, on the other hand, they are all Europeans while we remain British outsiders. Sometimes I found myself surprised, despite such observations, that the farther I travelled down the Danube the less Britain meant to the people I met. I should not have been surprised. With equal facility my captain once more dismissed the Latins and made plain that he had little time for the Americans despite their power which he certainly admired in an abstract way. He hated and despised the Russians. I began to feel that if I were to spend a month on that barge we would have the same conversation every day. And so we returned to his favourite theme: a special union of Germany, Austria and Hungary with (an Aryan?) Britain tagged on.

We came to rest in a lock. He said that Hitler had been right about the Communists. 'If only Britain and the United States had understood this we would be living in a different world today.' He made the statement as though everything else Hitler had stood for somehow did not matter.

The captain was about 60 and even as we travelled down the Danube Europe was celebrating 40 years of peace after the devastation of the World War 2. Yet little had changed in his thinking from the ideas that had informed his youth. The cataclysm of defeat in war, contrary to belief, does not persuade people that they have been wrong; for most of them it merely demonstrates that they were not strong enough to win. Captain Schwebel was bitter that his country, Hungary, was Communist but he ignored the part she played in the years leading up to 1939 or her declaration of war against the USSR in 1941.

I found it strange how persistently the name of Hitler popped up along the Danube. Scratch and he was there: the memory, an action of the war, a political reminiscence and sooner or later someone would say he had been misunderstood or his policies might have worked if. . . . Forty years after the holocaust in which he drenched Europe with blood, his ideas still found many admirers.

We reached Linz at six o'clock. The town lies on a wide sweep of the Danube; it is the third city of Austria, an industrial and commercial centre dominated by its huge steelworks. I had hoped to repay the captain's hospitality by taking him out for a drink, but he excused himself. He lived 30 kilometres (18.6 miles) away and his wife would be expecting him (no doubt to cook the evening meal!). This was also the case with the mate. Both said goodbye and departed soon after we docked. I was to sleep on the barge. In the morning a representative of the company was to come aboard and I would discover from him when another barge could take me to Vienna.

The crew had been remarkably friendly in their different ways and, as I thought, their mixture of nationalities reinforced *my* theory, rather than Captain Schwebel's, about the Danube acting as a European link.

Everyone had disappeared and I wandered about the barge now moored in the deserted docks. I had a beer and then retired to my cabin to write some notes. I had not been there long when I heard the powerful motors of a tug come alongside. A few moments later someone came on board calling to know if anyone was about. No one replied so I went out and was promptly asked if the barge could be moved to the quay to be unloaded: the unloading was to be done first thing in the morning, I was told. The man was astonished to discover that I was only a passenger. Personally I did not mind if the barge was moved, but was hardly in a position to grant permission. He shrugged: men hitched us to the tug, others came aboard to unhitch us from the dockside. They were an efficient lot and soon we were being towed rapidly through the dock pool to another nearby quay. One of the crew from the tug was an old friend of Captain Schwebel and stayed aboard the barge to talk with me. He, too, was a Hungarian exile, a Magyar, and we spoke of Kossuth.

They left me in the barge at the dockside where coal was offloaded for the steel works. Once the sound of their tug had died away silence descended upon the docks again, although across the pool a huge wide chimney belched a fearsome cloud of smoke into the darkening evening sky. Petrovic Bogosor now appeared: he took out two beers for us and sat back to talk. He had been in his cabin when the tug came but avoided taking any responsibility and had left me to deal with them. He invited me to share supper with him

73

and cut up slices of ham and raw onion which we ate with brown bread. After supper he went ashore to find the youngest crew member who had gone for a drink and would now be unaware of the barge's new location.

They had told me the coal would be unloaded first thing in the morning: I had not realised just how literal this statement would prove to be, for it was only two o'clock when a dull booming thud made the barge shudder from end to end and nearly tumbled me out of my bunk. Vague cranking noises had preceded this, though only half penetrating my sleep. Now they were off-loading the coal.

I put everything down to experience; some experiences I regard as strictly once-only affairs. Lying in a Danube barge at two in the morning while its cargo is off-loaded can be unnerving. The huge crane bucket, wide open, was dropped at speed so that its teeth bit deep into the pile of coal in whichever hold was being emptied. The jaws would then close and the bucket with its full load be jerked up. It descended with a thud to rock the barge; when it lifted the barge surged with relief. When a pile of coaldust had been all but removed the bucket teeth would scrape along the iron deck of the hold, adding a screeching sound to the general commotion. As soon as one hold was empty men moved the covers back and the operation was repeated in the next hold. They started in the hold farthest from the bridge and sleeping quarters to move in towards me. They finished, finally, at about four in the morning. I then fell into a deep sleep.

Petrovic was about when I emerged at half past six; he offered me breakfast. The night's banging had given me a headache and I asked only for coffee which he obligingly made. 'Something to go with it?' he inquired, 'Rum?' 'No thanks,' I replied. 'Ah, I know,' he said, and disappeared to return with a bottle of twelve-year-old Chivas Regal. He poured me a generous tot and a smaller one for himself. We drank this. He promptly refilled my glass. He held his glass up in the gesture of a toast and I downed my second glass. He filled me up again. After three whiskies I felt better. Then he brought out the ham, onions and brown bread and we had breakfast. We drank beer with the ham, then more whisky. Petrovic became expansive. His children were grown up and, like the captain's, spoke English. He had worked on the Danube for many years and, like so many others, had come to love it.

I tried to imagine a life spent on a barge, much of it in the case of Petrovic down in the engine room. There is a steady rhythm to such a life but a rhythm that will be broken by the vagaries of the river, the different destinations for the cargo, the changing weather. Yet whenever we passed through a lock, an exciting experience for me, the crew treated the break in our steady progression downstream as a mechanical event. It is, however, never possible to get 'inside' someone else's life or truly imagine what you can only see from the outside as an observer.

We sat talking for two hours and, alone with me, Petrovic was a different character from the shy, awkward man whom the rest of the crew teased over his silences. He did most of the talking as though he had been bottled up for a long time. Really he only wanted to talk about his family and his job, although he did ask me about my life and wished me luck with the book. He lived on the Yugoslav border with Rumania in a small town I was later to pass through on my journey. He shied away from any discussion of Yugoslav politics, though he had been quite prepared to speak of more general political matters with the captain and me the day before. When the docks around us began to come to life he excused himself to clean the engines. He insisted that I should drink more whisky at my leisure.

The tug of the night before came alongside at half past eight to bring an agent of the DDGS who told me I was expected. He would take me into town. Petrovic came to say goodbye and at the last moment the young Austrian, shaking off the effects of an unmistakable hangover, also appeared to shake hands and wish me a good journey.

In the Linz offices of the DDGS I sat with another director of the company who gave me coffee and Bulgarian brandy while he arranged my passage on another barge which was to depart for Vienna that afternoon. I signed more indemnities. I had the middle of the day free to explore the town. So I limped into Linz–my foot was still troubling me–and had a haircut. Linz declared ecstatically for Hitler at the time of the *Anschluss* (The union of Austria and Germany,1938). He had, after all, been to school there. I limped in and out of churches, watched the trams go by and had a satisfying lunch with an excellent wine before returning to the offices of the DDGS.

Chapter Twelve

To Vienna

The DDGS were under no obligation to do anything for me; in fact the company was extremely kind. That afternoon I was taken to the docks, this time to join a large tug that was to push six barges to Vienna and beyond. These squat, powerful tugs become part of a barge once attached to it. The bridge can be raised and lowered about 3 metres (10 ft) though this I only discovered when we reached the first lock after Linz. I arrived at the dockside just in time to see my tug being hitched to its waiting barges. I was waved aboard, across a line of barges, to the tug where a member of the crew showed me to a cabin. Here I dumped my pack. On this occasion I would have to share the cabin with someone else. Back on deck I watched as the tug manoeuvred its six barges to mid-stream and then we set off at once for Vienna.

The crew numbered 13 and the bridge was an altogether more imposing affair than that on the *Rosenburg*. The captain, too, was a more formal man than the Hungarian. Once we were heading downstream he called me to join him on the bridge. Almost at once we came to a lock. Coffee was brought to us and I now settled down to watch the passing landscape from an enviable height above the water. From Linz onwards the Danube is a major river, wide and deep enough for the barges to travel without risk throughout the night, something Captain Schwebel had not been able to do on the journey from Regensburg to Linz. The passing scenery was always hilly, often forest-covered, yet gentle too: attractive tourist country rather than harsh or untamed.

The captain, courteous and friendly, employed a more correct German than had Schwebel and, curiously, this made conversation more difficult for me. Schwebel had appreciated my problems as a foreigner speaking German and we had understood each other without difficulty in a rough-and-ready fashion. Now I was obliged to repeat myself more often: '*bitte*,' the Captain would say as he failed to understand, so that I must begin again. With Schwebel I had supplemented words with gestures or facial expressions, at which we had both laughed. Now I tackled grammar.

Once it has become a major highway the Danube takes on a certain magisterial grandeur. I felt this sense of grandeur as I sat up on the bridge with six long, heavy, flat barges coupled in their pairs ahead and below me as they forged their way through the water. Hemmed in by the steep forest-covered banks that rose on either side, the river had taken on a new purpose, determined to move towards its distant goal. When a string of barges laboured upstream, the throb of their tug's powerful engines hardly moving them, the full force of the waters became apparent.

The panorama of the changing countryside unfolded endlessly as if we were progressing slowly along a great motorway. The rains had highlighted a rich spectrum of greens: the deep dark shade of the forests interspersed with lighter yellow-greens of the open country-side set off by azure skies peering between scudding white clouds. Villages and towns broke the pattern with slate and red roofs capping the pastel shades of the walls; or a ruined castle stood grey and grim on its crag. The river, too, changed constantly. When the sun shone it would sparkle, Strauss's blue fighting to get out; but when the clouds came overhead the waters reverted to surly sluggishness, a preferred darkness of mood which suits the river's ancient history. Villages and towns, their church towers or gables vying with each other for the skyline, gave way to flat meadows which were succeeded in turn by dramatic gorges, each passing in review as though the country were on parade for a general's inspection.

For most of the Danube's passage through Austria the scenery is beautiful and dramatic. The locks between Linz and Vienna have tamed a stretch of river which once must have been far wilder so that now, in middle age, the Danube has become a confident matron discharging her duty to the lands through which she passes; severe, needed by her charges (the endless strings of barges), secure in her role. The channels which these large groups of barges have to nego-tiate are often narrow, though the marking buoys convey a sense of long familiarity. The locks, which can handle six barges at a time and lower them with smooth efficiency, have weathered to become part of the river. The kilometre posts along the banks with inter-vening markers every 200 metres (656 ft) serve to emphasise how the river has turned into a highway. Some time after Linz I saw that we were 2,230 kilometres (1,386 miles) from the Black Sea. I had been on my journey for a long time but had not yet covered a quarter of the distance.

When I got the chance to talk with members of the crew I asked whether they had always worked on the barges. None had ever been to sea and some had spent their working lives on the river. Those I questioned were not especially articulate about the river or their lives on it. They might say, almost resentful at a foolish question, that it is there, I work on it and my livelihood depends upon these barges. It was simply a part of their lives. They took it for granted but held it in affection at the same time. They knew how it could change. A dramatic gorge, green with lush vegetation and trees to the water's edge, would become forbidding in the cold grey of winter when the same trees would droop heavy with snow and the water would swirl glassy with cold. These men knew the river's every curve, which town or village would spring to sight round the next bend, what story attached to the crumbling castle ruins high on the skyline. They had stored up snatches of history about the Abbey of Melk or the age of a church perched on a hill–not the learned stuff of books but a vivid anecdote that was probably historically incorrect yet part of a long and much-loved tradition. And when the throbbing engine changed gear and the tug slowed its pace, they knew by the sound which tricky bend or narrow channel was to be negotiated. Talking to them about the Danube made me think of a townsman telling a farm labourer how he admired the countryside. To such people the country is simply there, accepted as the background to their lives, and the Danube provides the same background for those who work upon it as it snakes its way across half Europe.

All ships have a life of their own and this tug with its bustling crew and heavy cargo had its own battle to fight with the river. It needed all its power not just to push the weight of the barges but to combat the river's many traps and defiant currents. As it cuts through the hilly Austrian landscape the Danube assumes a new strength and becomes a surging force steadily yet remorselessly moving towards the distant Black Sea.

The captain and I took supper together and politely he questioned me about my trip, although I found him a remote man in comparison to Schwebel; he may well have thought the same of me. Then we returned to the bridge where I sat until dusk.

I was alone in the mess writing when the engineer appeared. He was a huge, bearlike man of about 60, an Austrian, wearing the amiable expression of an amateur sports captain. He had come to seek me out and had brought some coloured photographs of the tug and its barges to show me. At his insistence I selected one as a souvenir and then he invited me to inspect the engine room below.

The engine was a 2,200 hp diesel but all I could see were dials and buttons, for the engine itself was entirely sealed. I have no mechanical aptitude of any kind yet take a certain perverse pleasure in being shown things mechanical. Over the years I have developed my 'listening' expression of bemused awe as I look on intelligently while performance and capabilities are explained to me. I only needed to ask one or two simple questions and the engineer was away, discoursing happily for minutes on end. He was immensely proud of his engines which he had spent a lifetime servicing. His kind are to be found manning engines the world over: friendly, talkative when he needed the release, yet ready to retire strategically into the oil and noise of his engine room, whenever he felt threatened or wished to escape outside pressures. Now, near the end of his career, he exuded the relaxed confidence of a man at home in his environment: engines were his life–Danube barge engines.

He obviously felt more at ease and relaxed in the private world of his engine room than anywhere else and his appearance above in the mess had been in the nature of an emergence. When we had exhausted the topic of engines I knew, instinctively, what was coming next. The slight pause as he eyed me, trying to gauge how I would respond, told me as though he had announced the topic in advance, that he wished to discuss Brussels and football.

'How do you explain the Brussels affair?' he asked, a tentative note creeping into his voice.

'The brutal British?' I responded.

'Yes,' and he nodded his agreement. 'Why are the British so aggressive and brutal about their football?' he continued.

Why indeed! I had no answer to his question and said so. He proceeded to suggest a few reasons of his own. Only when we entered the small area of the control panels, which was sealed off by a glass partition from the rest of the engine room, could we speak reasonably above the steady throb of the engines. I drank the coffee he had prepared for me while he continued ferreting at British football. 'We are not like that on the Continent' he said. This was too sweeping a generalisation for me although recent British behaviour–and not just at Brussels–gave point to his remark. He was, I think, trying to equate soccer violence with British national decline, a subject that gives rise to much speculation in Europe as it does elsewhere. I dislike nationalism yet as he rambled on in his slow German my subconscious nationalist reflexes began to work so that I had to check my resentment at some of his statements, not least because they were manifestly accurate.

The Brussels football tragedy kept cropping up so that I became weary of references to it. Yet these taught me much about Britain. The event itself was a tangible manifestation of unpleasant British behaviour and it was as though Europeans, tired of an endless diet of British remoteness and superiority–an apartness from the European continent to which, supposedly, we belong–were happy at last to find a concrete example of our everyday unpleasantness. They could not leave the subject alone.

From Linz eastwards the barges journey through the night and we were to reach Vienna at five the next morning. This was unfortunate for me since from Linz to Vienna the Danube is renowned both for its picturesque beauty and the many historical buildings to be seen adorning its crags and skyline. But one cannot have everything and I was to experience a barge night passage instead of these sights.

I went back to the bridge where the captain and another officer sat on swivel seats before the controls; the radar circle with its ever-moving hand gave off a faint, almost phosphorescent light and the captain's pipe glowed when he drew upon it but otherwise we were in darkness. It was an eerie sensation for me to be moving at a quite respectable speed high above the dark waters of the river. We were then passing through a dramatic part of the landscape with forest-covered hills closing in on the river, their black silhouettes framing a dark clear sky, but one without benefit of either stars or moon. Sometimes we passed a small riverside town or village, by then reduced to only a few midnight lights; at others we could see the mass of a castle or monastery making an extra dark projection against the trees of the skyline. We passed Melk Abbey in this darkness. There was no talking. The throb of the engines was steady and deep; the rush of displaced water and sometimes the sound of our wash lapping the near bank, the only accompaniments of our passage. Then we would round a bend in the river perhaps to glimpse more lights from another village or town ahead of us.

Finally I said goodnight to the captain and retired to my cabin. I never met its other occupant. I slept well, lulled by the steady throb of the powerful engines and awoke to the hoot of tugs. Through my porthole I saw a grey wet dawn: we were approaching Vienna. It was still only five o'clock when we docked; I shaved and packed my rucksack. In the mess one of the officers told me they were to remain there for two hours before resuming their journey. The company had been emphatic that they could not take me beyond Vienna through any of the Communist countries. The cook provided me with a lone breakfast while outside the rain came down with a steady, dreary persistence. I asked the only officer who appeared to be up to present my compliments and thanks to the captain, who was then sleeping after his night on the bridge. I shouldered my pack and stepped out into the Vienna wet, negotiated my way across another barge and onto the shore. Many people have visited Vienna but few visitors have arrived as I did that morning on a river barge.

Chapter Thirteen

Vienna

It is curious that Vienna, which is always associated with the Danube, has turned its back upon the great river on whose banks it has grown. The grand city of the Habsburgs faces northwest away from the Danube. Consequently, when I left my barge to walk into the city I made the mistake of crossing the bridge to the wrong side of the river, by the complex of ugly grey buildings which make up UNIDO (the United Nations Industrial Development Organisation), before I realised that I was heading away from the city. At least this huge UN addition to Vienna, by courtesy of its best-known postwar figure Kurt Waldheim, is an attempt to bring Vienna back to the river–although it does not work aesthetically whatever else it achieves.

Every other city the length of the Danube is proud of the river upon whose banks it stands: they bestride it magnificently like Budapest or look down upon it from secure eminences like Bratislava and they are grander because of the association. Only Vienna, perhaps in its heyday too proud to owe anything to the mighty river, deliberately turned away to face northwards towards the Christian Europe to which it belonged rather than south and east towards the Turks and Islam. Indeed, from Vienna eastwards the land and people change dramatically and the Danube, too, undergoes another transformation: it flows wider, faster, deeper as it forges its way into the Balkans.

My mistake in direction hardly mattered for it was still only six in the morning, so I trudged back to find a small workmen's bar where I spent an hour drinking coffee. No one bothered me. The regular customers came for their morning aperitifs–white wine or brandy–before they set off again, grudgingly, into the rain. Eventually I, too, headed into the city along a bleak wide street, part of a drab peeling Vienna which tourists avoid, all that Europe's splendid nineteenth-century capital could spare for its river. The gigantic wheel of the Prater funfair, made famous in *The Third Man*, lurks in this part of the city, south of the railway station. The result of this geographical divorce of city from river was to make my stay in Vienna an interlude before I travelled eastwards again.

Vienna was full: tourists, Americans, Japanese, high prices! I tried hotel after hotel or *pension* but none had a vacancy. It was many years since I had last been in Vienna and after a while I found myself going round in circles. I needed a coffee and settled upon a sleazy bar where I was ignored but being wet and tired, I did not mind. Behind the bar was a startlingly beautiful girl. She was talking across it disdainfully to a male hanger-on. She became increasingly bored with his conversation so she decided to notice me and languidly came to see what I wanted. Reluctantly the admirer left. Another young woman had been an amused spectator of their exchange and now the young lady from behind the bar went over to speak with her friend and they compared notes about young men until her hanger-on reappeared and she felt obliged to return to him.

Eventually I found a room in a *pension* just off St Stephen's Square; it occupied the second floor of a gloomy eighteenth-century apartment building, was very central and commensurately expensive.

Today Vienna is equipped for tourists yet it is a sad city and in one sense the tourists make it so. At the height of the season the city centre becomes a frenetic crush: tourists in groups, tourists following guides, tourists debouching from coaches, tourists alone or in pairs. Everything is designed to make them comfortable–they are, after all, the lifeblood of Vienna–and to trap them. Prices are high, almost every other shop displays the insignia of Visa, Access, American Express and Diners Club so as to induce the visitor to spend more than he can reasonably afford. Waiters and waitresses are brusque and bored, functionaries at the Opera treat those seeking tickets with overweening arrogance. Yet take away the tourists and UNIDO and the city would collapse back into its nineteenth-century empty shell.

Vienna is also a city of nostalgia. It lives on its past, the fading grandeur of the days when it was the capital of the Austro-Hungarian Empire, but since the end of World War Two and the withdrawal of the Four-Power Occupation the plastic credit card has become the symbol of this once glorious city. What, one might ask, could Vienna do without its tourists? At least Venice can sink gracefully into the sea. Everywhere I went tourists were seriously enjoying themselves: on foot, shepherded in groups or looking self-conscious in the city's famous two-horse fiacres. Every second person was a foreigner: American, British, French, Scandinavian, Italian, Japanese or German. And the sight of all these tourists has turned the famous Viennese charm into a fixed mask of flashing teeth–for those prepared to spend money. The smile is one of calculation.

The grandiose *Ringstrasse*, following the line of the old city walls, still acts as the limit of the inner city. Its huge heavy buildings are a mixture of different styles but share the common attributes of being oversized and over-decorated. I sat on the terrace of Sacher's Hotel round the corner from the Café Mozart to drink coffee and watch an endless stream of tourists pass in front of me, as though on parade.

Vienna has much to offer (Col. pl. 11). There are the palaces of the Habsburgs whose line supplied from 1483 to 1806 every Holy Roman Emperor save one. There are about 100 museums and galleries: the *Kunsthistorisches* Museum possesses one of the world's great collections of Brueghels, Rubens, Rembrandts and Dürers. And of course there is music, wine and food.

Since my room was close to St Stephen's Cathedral every excursion I made was outwards from the centre. The *Kärntnerstrasse* lead from the Cathedral to the Opera and is a pedestrian precinct which has also become a sort of beggars' way during the season. This is an improvement from the days of the *Anschluss*, when middle-aged professional Jews supervised by jeering Nazi thugs were forced to scrub its pavements. I passed along it often during my stay. One evening in particular everyone was on display: some were old friends, others were new to me. A demonstration of Kurds was watched by an equal number of policemen as they chanted slogans, held aloft their banners and generally seemed cheerful. The hopelessness of their cause and the remoteness of any support for it in this city seemed to make any other mood pointless, although occasionally a sort of *de rigueur* spasm of anger broke through and the chanting increased by two or three decibels. A charming Turk in a tattered fez and dirty pantaloons played endlessly upon a little piping whistle. He was always there. Another attraction was a long parchment scroll which had been unwound across the pavement: it stretched for at least 30m (99 ft) and had been weighted down with stones. There was always a line of people on either side, reading it right way up or upside down, and I never got close enough to see what it was about. Near the Opera a young man, three parts Chinese, sang Verdi arias with determination if no great skill. He amused the passers-by in this city of music, though his talents clearly lay in other directions. A young trio on flute, bass and violin played Haydn; a boy on his own played the violin; a hippie group displayed themselves as one of their number sang songs made famous by Joan Baez in the 1960s. Other assorted beggars took up their positions between these more flamboyant performers. One old man, unshaven and wearing an ancient tatty hat, yodelled in a high falsetto and commanded an appreciative audience while another, dressed as a Roman lictor, wandered up and down handing out tracts. Since the majority of the crowds jostling along the *Kärntnerstrasse* were on holiday and the performers were not offensive no doubt they did well enough. A woman who played the guitar thanked her contributors in impeccable upper-class English.

The wine scandal was just breaking, yet only when Austrian wines doctored with diethylene-glycol were banned in Germany did the Austrian authorities finally admit what they must long have known. And, of much greater long-term importance, the 'Green Party' supporters from different parts of the world were also making life difficult for the government with regard to a different matter: the planned construction of the dam at Hainburg. Eventually the plan was shelved since downriver from Vienna is one of Europe's last great riverine woodland areas. In what someone termed 'the scandal of the century' it was revealed that Austria already produces more power than she can either use or sell, so that the dam story became wrapped in government obduracy and corruption. Like Hamlet's King, Vienna 'may smile, and smile, and be a villain.'

One morning I decided to visit the Spanish Riding School, or to give it its full name, the Imperial Spanish Riding School of Vienna, one of the city's foremost attractions. A large queue had already formed round the square when I arrived but, though I hate queues, I decided to shuffle round for half an hour since I had allotted space in my timetable for this activity. The sun was out and the queue interesting. Periodically guides or doormen came to our stretch of queue to ask whether there were any groups. 'Yes,' came the reply from one bright youngster, 'We are a group.' But Austrian officials have no sense of humour.

Immediately in front of me an irritating Frenchman held forth with amusement about the people, the queue, the Austrians and the general tone of Vienna to his sophisticated girlfriend. She, I suspect, was more intelligent than he and allowed him to prattle on. Behind me a large talkative woman from Dallas told some young Americans about her group which was touring Europe by bus to give concerts, including spirituals. Hers was an all-embracing friendly, folksy voice with religious overtones. I think the entire queue was made up of foreigners. From time to time groups entered the square through an archway following a guiding umbrella.

The Lippizaner stallions which perform in the Spanish Riding School epitomise all that Vienna has ceased to be. After queuing one filters up stone steps into a gallery to gaze down upon these splendid creatures being put through their ritual but utterly pointless paces. The horses are beautifully groomed, their riders elegantly dressed in eighteenth-century uniforms. Grooms equipped with long-handled, tip-up shovel buckets move across the sawdust to remove the droppings. The horses–greys, some dappled–endlessly circle the arena, weaving and crossing each other's paths to the periodic bursts of polite clapping which follow the more intricately executed manoeuvres, while the huge galleried Riding School suitably muffles the chatter of the hundreds of spectators so that it sounds no more than a general murmur. It is a beautiful ritual reminiscent of long-vanished courts of grace. It also symbolises nostalgic dead Vienna. The whole city has become a museum and possibly nothing empha-sises this more than the futile prancing of the Lippizaner horses, an act frozen in times past.

Back in my *pension* I had to move to another room. A variation on 'musical rooms' took place in that establishment. On my arrival I had been told the room was only available for one night, but since I wanted to stay longer I asked them to fit me in somewhere else the next day. This they did. But the same shift took place the following day, and then the one after that, and not just with me. As far as I could tell any guest who stayed there for more than a day took part in this curious shuffle. I had just completed another room switch when, at the desk, I found an American guest who had done the same thing attempting to explain that his wife had had more to drink in their previous room than charged on the bill. Each room was equipped with a small bar and guests signed for what they took. The proprietess, though, could not follow his attempt to be honest. She had no knowledge of English but at my appearance called upon me to translate. 'This gentleman,' she said, 'speaks good German.' That was untrue by any stretch of imagination but, to quote Clint Eastwood, her remark 'made my day.'

Sitting in cafés watching the locale was my favourite occupation the length of the Danube. In Vienna I frequented an unglamorous yet lively little café where the clientele provided me with a variety of interesting subjects for study.

I watched as a mixed company, visitors and locals, also examined each other with curiosity. An elderly Bavarian couple occupied a strategic table on the opposite side of the room from me. She was a big woman with receding hair and a habitually grim expression, while her husband possessed a thin hatchet face redeemed by a humorous mouth and sharp amused eyes. They were commenting to each other upon the rest of the company; the attempts of a group of English tourists to speak German gave them special satisfaction. A young Italian couple had constant recourse to their dictionary and received marks for trying. But a quartet of French women, as was to be expected, employed only French. The grim-looking Bavarian woman's face was transformed as she smiled at her husband's covert remarks. She wore a traditional grey costume trimmed with green.

85

The noisy English group departed, to be replaced by an English couple who were so genteel and murmured so softly to one another that strain as we might none of us could hear anything they said.

On my last night, having failed to get a ticket to the Opera, I went to a Strauss concert. I am fond of the light elegance of Strauss and Lehár and if one is to enjoy Strauss, Vienna must surely be the place to do so. It was the Wiener-Hofburg Orchestra and the concert was one of a summer series. I had secured an excellent seat in the side balcony just above the stalls near the orchestra, an ideal vantage-point from which to survey the house as well as the players. Most of the audience were tourists, American accents were omnipresent and there was a conspicuous sprinkling of Japanese.

That concert was a disgrace: not the playing, which was adequate, but the manner in which it was performed. If the intention were to convert Strauss lovers into Strauss haters it would have been hard to find a better formula. There are many forms of vulgarity and the concert was designed to titillate emotions unrelated to music. The house was packed and the lights stayed up although there was a fractional dimming in a gesture of theatricality. The audience was middle-aged, or elderly, and sentimental. The music was cheapened by the antics of the orchestra whose members did not simply play music but acted as though they believed the tourists incapable of appreciating good music at all. The players clearly held the opinion that their audience, comprising mostly tourists, felt duty-bound, here in this 'city of music', to sit through at least one concert. The orchestra had decided that Strauss and Lehár required to be light-ened to such a level of banal frippery that even an uninterested audience would be able to get through the evening. It was an insult. At one point an outsize *Playboy* magazine was produced on stage, its double-spread pin-up waved at the stalls to assist everyone's limited appreciation of light music. One singer was a young Japanese woman and, though she was reasonably accomplished, I suspect her real purpose was to demonstrate to the Japanese contingent that, like their industrial conquest of the West, their musical and cultural conquest was not far behind. Members of that bizarre audience constantly nodded to one another as they recognised a melody. If a famous Vienna orchestra feels it has to flash *Playboy* at its audience to stimulate appreciation of Strauss the time has surely come for it to disband.

My first visit to Vienna had been 30 years earlier when the city was under joint Allied military occupation. Then it was the city of Graham Greene's *Third Man*. I was a very junior national service subaltern on leave and stayed at Sacher's Hotel for the princely sum of four shillings and two pence (old English currency) a night, by courtesy of the British army–for Sacher's was then reserved for British officers. I did everything: opera, theatre, museums, concerts and drinking the new wines of Grinzing. Vienna had been magic. This time, older and if no wiser at least better travelled, I found the city smug, corrupt and money-grabbing. On my first visit Vienna lacked any sense of security: it was an occupied city with the memory of defeat still fresh in everyone's mind. The present had seemed precarious: the future uncertain. Yet it had been enchanting, living from day to day on borrowed time. Now nostalgia has settled like a plague upon the city and on a grand scale Vienna resembles a nineteenth-century false-fronted American western town waiting for the boom to pass it by.

Chapter Fourteen

A Czech Interlude

The journey from Vienna to Bratislava takes an hour by hydrofoil and the Danube passes through thickly wooded land with hills rising up into the distance. Here the Danube is a big river and its deep, turgid waters lap the forest edges on both banks. Just before Bratislava the river becomes the boundary between Czechoslovakia and Hungary. Spurs of the Carpathian Mountains from the northeast and the Alps from the southwest create a defile in which the river, now only 120m (400ft) above sea level, narrows to no more than 275 metres (300yd) in width. This is the stretch of Danube where the disputed Hainburg Dam was to have been constructed.

The setting of Bratislava is dramatic. On the left bank rises the grim citadel crowned by its square fortress, a reminder that this was one the Magyar capital, the Pressburg of an earlier age. A spectacular modern bridge links the two banks of the Danube: on the one side is the old city whose thriving commercial/industrial sector spreads out beneath the citadel, while a vast sprawling forest of apparently endless high-rise apartment blocks occupies the other bank. Parts of the old city beneath the citadel appear to be crumbling but the rest thrives, and the river reflects its bustling activity. Bratislava is a major rail junction and busy Danube port.

Tourists from Vienna come on day trips to Bratislava and I arrived on one of these regular hydrofoils. I was last in line to go through customs. Nearly everyone else from the hydrofoil was a day tripper and they quickly passed through, although one Czech woman ahead of me fared badly: every scrap of paper in her possession was carefully checked and her baggage turned out on the counter to be rummaged through by two officials who finally confiscated the two Austrian newspapers she had brought back with her. The same officials were surprised at my British passport which was collectively examined. What really interested them was my mode of entry into the country once they realised I had not just come for the day. They were friendly enough but scrutinised all papers with care. I collect paper on a trip–old tickets, maps, brochures, programmes–and these had added considerably to my otherwise modest, pared-down luggage. My current notebook was in my pocket, my other completed notebooks I had sent to London from Vienna. The customs officials were looking for subversive literature.

At a wayside café whose tables spread across a wide pavement I offloaded my pack and had a glass of wine. Two old men at the next table chatted over their morning aperitif but I was more interested in the scene opposite, where two roads converged to create a triangle of grass and benches. A dozen teenage boys and girls occupied the benches and were chatting animatedly, periodically bursting into laughter at a sally from one of their number, when a prophetic oddly dressed woman came to stand in front of them to deliver a harangue. What she shouted at them I have no idea; what intrigued me was the manner in which the teenagers dealt with her unwanted attentions. After a short while, as though in response to a signal, they rose as one and moved away, leaving the woman to shout at two empty benches. In need of an audience she turned to follow them. But one young man from the group came back to remonstrate courteously with her. After a minute she shrugged, looked crestfallen, then drifted away. The teenagers who had watched this remonstrance by their companion now returned to their seats and resumed their conversation.

I found a hotel of the second rank. The woman receptionist was severe with me; she demanded my passport as though certain that I would otherwise leave without paying. Yet later, when I asked her advice about the sights to visit, she relaxed and became more friendly. She supplied me with a map and even expressed the hope that I would have a pleasant stay in the country.

Bratislava is the former Hungarian city of Pressburg (Col. pl. 12). Situated on the Danube near the meeting point of Austria, Czechoslovakia and Hungary it has a long history of strategic and cultural importance. Formerly the Roman town of Posonium, it became a Hungarian city in the tenth century and was the capital of Hungary from 1541 to 1784. During this period several of Hungary's kings were crowned in its cathedral. After a resounding victory at Austerlitz, Napoleon dictated the Treaty of Pressburg in 1805 and consolidated his gains at the expense of both Austria and Prussia; in the process taking some of the last remaining lands from the Habsburgs. The most impressive of the old city's historic buildings is the grim square castle (now a museum) which rises as a bleak fortress, high above the river.

I spent my time in Bratislava sightseeing. One of my most vivid first impressions was the quietness of the people, although this might have been because I arrived on Sunday. Later the gypsies were anything but quiet.

The palace on the citadel was an impressive building but much of the old city appeared to be crumbling into gentle decay. The palace has been turned into a museum but I cannot say it was very exciting although one section consisted of a photographic display depicting the Nazi occupation. This concentrated upon the doings of Reinhard Heydrich who was appointed Reich 'Protector' of Czechoslovakia in 1941. The cruelty of his regime became notorious and his well-deserved assassination in 1942 was followed by widespread reprisals when hundreds of Czechs were murdered. The massacre at Lidice near Prague included 172 people: the men were shot; the women shot or sent to concentration camps; and the children sent to concentration camps or foster homes. Heydrich's name was abominated in Czechslovakia. Once more World War Two had obtruded upon my journey; the museum did not intend that Heydrich or his doings should be forgotten.

My wayside café turned out to be a popular meeting place and was crowded when I went to have a drink there in the early evening. I found a single seat at a small table otherwise occupied by a solitary black man. The man had the distinctive Hamitic features of the Horn of Africa: thin face and high cheekbones. I did not speak English but gestured towards the unoccupied seat and he gravely inclined his head. When the waiter came I ordered my wine in German. Then we eyed each other. He knew me to be foreign but had not placed me as English. Each of us waited for the other to make an opening. Finally, sure it would be so, I asked whether he spoke English. He smiled: 'Of course.' He reminded me of the Germans who always said, 'Naturally I speak English.' He came from the People's Democratic Republic of Yemen (the former Aden colony) and not Africa at all. So we talked about British imperialism. He was on a three-year study course in Czechoslovakia. He had wondered about me as I approached his table, he said. How often it is that in such circumstances people hesitate, although they would like to talk, each waiting for the other and neither knowing quite how to begin.

When he went to meet some friends I was free to study the gypsies who occupied an adjoining table. I had been conscious of them for some time but only now was I able to give them my full attention. They merited it. There were several women, a number of children but no men. Their table was covered with empty glasses which represented an afternoon's hard work. Two small children were becoming increasingly irritable, attracting alternately slaps and commands to behave or petting and fresh ice creams and Pepsis. The leader of the group had a wide Mongolian-shaped face, slant almond eyes, a long broad forehead, flat heavy cheeks, large thick lips and long, straight, shiny jet-black hair. Hers was a striking rather than a handsome face yet when she smiled she radiated compulsive pleasure. A second woman of identical build and similar, if coarser, features had startling henna-coloured hair. They were entrenched and drank brandies and coffees with a steady concentration whose end was clearly not yet in sight. It was the first woman who attracted my attention. Her hair hung loose across her broad shoulders, her long black lashes slanted upwards with the corners of her eyes, her gold-plated teeth flashed every time she laughed and her skin glinted olive-brown. She carried half her wealth on her hands: every finger bore a ring. These were gold with large stones on them and each time she gestured with her hands they flashed and glinted and when she spoke or smiled her broad face lit up in animation. Two other women could only have been mother and daughter: the girl, pudding plain of face, was about 17 while the mother resembled the other two women. I think the three must have been sisters. All four of them, including the daughter, had achieved bodily heaviness. Their talk became increasingly raucous as they toasted one another with growing abandon, tossing off their brandies, calling for replenishments—two glasses each at a time—which they lined up like enemies waiting to be demolished. A great deal of brandy was consumed at that table by three strong women in their late thirties surrounded by their offspring, all of whom were girls. Clearly they did not favour male children.

An extremely pretty girl, thin of body and delicate of feature, came from another table to talk with them. Under the pressure of laughter and insistence she took a glass of brandy, held it for a long time at her lips without attempting to drink before finally taking a reluctant mouthful. She kept this in her mouth for a while, her cheeks bulging and her face contorting before spitting a jet of brown fluid onto the ground with an expression of supreme disgust. Then, volubly denouncing the brandy to the delight of the older women, she returned to her table and the pale young man she had left there.

From time to time these gypsy women wandered between the tables greeting people; everyone seemed to know them. They never paused in their steady consumption of brandy and trouble loomed ahead. They were a busy group: they shouted to friends at other tables; they hailed the waiter in expectation of instant service which they always got; and occasionally they fell silent although animation was the rule. At another table nearby a young soldier was equally fascinated by them. He eyed them, eyed me eyeing them, then eyed them again. A youth approached the soldier and offered him a small coin for a cigarette but the soldier refused the coin and gave the youth a cigarette, at which he went off with a smirk of triumph on his face.

The best capitalist fifth column in the eastern countries consists of the American hotel chains–Hiltons and Intercontinentals–a subject to which I shall return. There was a Hilton in Bratislava, the only place where I could get a decent beer. No doubt the hotel provided other luxuries not easily obtainable elsewhere in the city, though it was a Hilton of only the second class. Such hotels attract tourist dollars much needed by Czechoslovakia as by every other east European country, but to view them simply as a source of hard currency would be naive. That drab hotel was also a centre of attraction, an advertisement for the different life of non-austerity, the thin end of a Western wedge.

A young barman who spoke tolerable English served me with best Pils lager. 'The strongest beer in the world,' he beamed with pride. However, most of it went for export, he told me, and was rarely available in Czechoslovakia where they had to make do with weaker beers. Beer, I discovered, was only served in certain bars while many pavement cafés would only serve wine and spirits or the ubiquitous Pepsi which has penetrated to every corner of the world–capitalist, Communist, Moslem, Hindu. Pepsi's spread may represent a triumph of Western salesmanship, matter over mind, but hardly an advertisement for good taste.

I dined in the Hilton where nine Czech businessmen or *aparatchniks* enjoyed themselves at the next table. The dining room did a brisk trade that evening and caused me to reflect upon the differences between the capitalist and Communist worlds. Greed for money, whether by individuals, governments or systems, invariably spells an end to the purity of any would-be ascetic regime, although whether Czechoslovakia ever aspired to Communist purity is altogether another question.

I walked back from the Hilton to my hotel increasingly aware of mounting dissension and shrieks of laughter ahead of me. It was approaching ten o'clock, the more or less universal closing time in eastern Europe, and sure enough on the corner near my wayside café I witnessed the inevitable end of the gypsy brandy-drinking party. The henna-haired woman, now very drunk, was down on her knees, her hands raised aloft as though in supplication to some primeval god.

No sign was forthcoming. I think she was calling upon her companions, perhaps not quite as drunk as herself, for an understanding of her case. But when she went to her knees they paid her no heed. So she heaved herself to her feet again to round upon them in more vigorous terms. Then, still disregarded, back she plonked onto her ample knees to repeat the supplications. She had a fine sense of the dramatic. The large mother of the seventeen-year-old, who now looked close to collapse, had her face slapped by an even larger man, presumably her husband though he had not been in attendance earlier in the day. She accepted the slap as her due; no one else paid any attention. A crowd gathered, half-amused, half-embarrassed and not dissimilar to a voyeuristic English crowd in such circumstances.

Then a policeman and an army officer came to make peace. They remonstrated quietly and to apparent effect. The black-haired woman of the flashing gold teeth and Mongoloid features stood quietly to the side, a spectator of all these happenings although she had almost certainly consumed as much alcohol as anyone else. My last view of them as I reached the corner near my hotel was of the redhead once more down on her knees supplicating heaven.

Only a short stretch of the Danube acts as the border of Czechoslovakia: first, briefly, with Austria and then for a somewhat longer distance with Hungary. Like Austria, Czechoslovakia is involved in an ecological controversy: it is planning to construct as a joint venture with Hungary, a major dam on the spectacular Danube Bend. Thereafter the river crosses the Hungarian Plain, neatly cutting that country into two halves.

On the day I left Bratislava, true to form, it poured with rain. I wanted to find the bus station and asked directions of a big fat, jolly-looking man who, on discovering I was English, said: 'For you, English, anything.' He misdirected me.

The bus station was large, drab, an uninviting place like bus stations the world over. I went to cross between bus bays to be waved back by an angry armed guard who ostentatiously put his hand on his leather pistol holster. I retreated into a great overhead waiting room from which separate staircases led down onto each bus bay.

I had a three-hour bus journey to Komárno whose Hungarian twin across the Danube is Komárom. The countryside was flat and uninteresting, the bus radio endlessly played the song *Rosetta, are you betta* as we weaved our way through villages, picking up and setting down passengers.

Chapter Fifteen

Budapest

Ar Komárom the Danube has become an industrial river: docks and warehouses line the banks and cranes like vulturine birds of prey droop over the barges moored at the quays as these load and unload. It is very much a working river, dirty and businesslike; when I crossed the bridge into Hungary the water was oily, grey and smooth. The border posts between Czechoslovakia and Hungary are in the middle of this bridge across the Danube. I was quickly passed through the Czech formalities, then I continued to the Hungarian post. No one else was on foot though a few cars with Czech registrations and some lorries were in line awaiting clearance. The officer. showed surprise and interest at my British passport. 'Have a seat,' he invited, then took my passport and left me in the bleak control hall. Through the window I watched other customs officials examine cars until my official came back accompanied by another man. I had already noticed this character prowling up and down the line of cars without apparent purpose. He was small, wore a loud check cap, thick horn-rimmed glasses but otherwise nondescript clothes and looked like a bookmaker's clerk. I had not thought he was anything to do with officialdom. Together they went to unlock a door off the hall, then disappeared inside with my passport. At this manifestation of his importance I revised my opinion: the check cap was a disguise; I suspected he belonged to the secret police.

The uniformed officer now returned. 'What was your mother's maiden name?' My visa form was in my passport; it contained a box for the name of the applicant's mother which I had filled in. 'Shaw,' I told him. He nodded and went back to the little room and several minutes passed while I continued to watch the cars being processed outside. At last he came back with my passport. 'Your mother was called *Margaret* Shaw,' he said, holding my passport out to me. 'That's right,' I said. He watched me with just the suspicion of a smile. My passport had been stamped and I realised that I had just been treated to a display of considerable efficiency. I had not filled in 'Margaret' in London, nor had I been asked to do so. But the London Embassy must have investigated as a matter of routine through Somerset House and passed the information back to Hungary. I wondered about that little room which the man in the cloth cap was now relocking: a computer tuned into headquarters in Budapest? Or merely a telephone? They had been remarkably quick; it was impressive.

Beyond Kómarom–Esztergom in Hungary–the River Danube, now a huge volume of water, is once more enclosed by hills as the Borzsony range from the north which rises to 700 metres (2,296 ft) and Mount Visegrád on the south bank forces it into a narrow canyon. Then it follows a semi-circular bend and after completing 90 degrees heads due south to divide the great plain of Hungary in two. But where the mountains come down to the river (the Danube Bend) great forests approach the water's edge, cliffs add drama and old ruins testify once more to the attractions which this great river has exercised since earliest times for Church and State alike: always the monuments are the castles of power and the monasteries of faith.

I had a beer in a lively but dirty little station buffet while waiting for the train. I shared a table with two old men in railway uniform who were immersed in a conversation about the railway. The train was crowded but I managed to find a seat; we reached Budapest at seven in the evening.

Normally on arrival in a new town I would wander in search of a place to stay, but since a prominent tourist bureau occupied the middle of the station concourse I sought guidance. After some misunderstanding they found a woman who could speak English.

'Can you tell me the address of a reasonably priced hotel, please?'

'There are no cheap hotels in Budapest.'

'What price are they, what is the range?'

'There is no range.'

'What price are they?'

'They are all very expensive, Budapest has no cheap hotels.'

'What price?'

'Three thousand forints a night.' That was fifty pounds.

'There must be something less expensive than that; what about middle-price hotels?'

'There are none; they are all expensive, three thousand a night.'

'Surely everybody does not stay in such places. You must have something less expensive. I am not an American,' I added.

'Of course we have: we can arrange for you to stay with a Hungarian family.'

'That would suit me very well; then I can get to know some ordinary Hungarians while I am here.'

'Of course,' she said.

'How much?'

I did not appear to have any choice of place: or, rather, it was Hobson's choice. I told her how many nights I wished to stay, she consulted a register and wrote out a chit for me. I paid in advance; it came to an absurd figure of four pounds a night.

'Present this to your landlady,' she told me.

I suppose that in due course my landlady would receive this very modest payment from the state tourist agency. I asked about food but was told she did not supply food but that I might 'make an arrangement' with her.

'How do I get there?' I looked at the incomprehensible address.

'Very simple: take the underground to the end of the line, then take a trolleybus,' she told me the number, 'and go for five stops. It is right there.'

It sounded easy enough but such instructions usually only work when you know the place. I took a taxi and was rewarded by a superb view of Budapest as first we sped alongside the Danube in Buda and then crossed into Pest and along another broad street to the suburbs. The taxi-driver had considerable difficulty finding the address; I should have become hopelessly lost had I taken the underground and trolleybus. Later the journey by trolleybus and underground became my daily 'commuter' route into the city. My road, when finally the taxi-driver did discover it, was unpaved and dug up for drains but the detached suburban houses, each with their own garden, were pleasant enough. The taxi-driver deposited me outside a high iron gate and promptly drove off. The gate was locked, the house appeared deserted and I could not find a bell, but after a short while an elderly, dried-up little woman appeared. She spoke only Hungarian but at once opened the gate and bade me enter. I gave her my chit which she examined perfunctorily while treating me to a voluble welcome. I tried my German but to no avail. There did not appear to be anyone else in the house.

My room was separated from the rest of the house in a semi-apartment which included a bathroom. It was sparsely furnished but clean. The landlady, whose name I never worked out, took my passport to note its details while I unpacked. She gave me a set of keys—one for the front door and one for the outside gate—showed me the lavatory, gave me a towel and said goodnight. I tried to ask about food but drew a blank. She withdrew smiling and nodding into the front room where the television was on and shut the door, presumably to rejoin her so far invisible family. All the way in the taxi I had been relishing an evening with an ordinary Hungarian family, so that I could learn something of Hungarian life. This, clearly, was not to be despite the assurances of the lady at the station. My window gave onto a sunporch which contained an old, rusted man's bicycle: perhaps there was a husband and I should meet him later. Closer examination of the bicycle, however, prompted a quite different speculation: it was ancient, rusted and flat-tyred and would, I felt, work only under protest. I think the husband had died long ago and his widow left it in the sunporch, conspicuous in its masculinity, as a message to her boarders that there was a man, somewhere about the house. I was not to see my landlady again, let alone anyone else in that house, for the duration of my stay in Budapest until the morning of my departure. There was to be no living with a Hungarian family for me.

By then it was eight o'clock and I was hungry, so I set out to find a café. I was in outer city suburbia and though frequent buses and trolleybuses passed along the nearby main street there was no sign of a café or shops except for a tiny tobacco kiosk. I asked directions of a young woman who, it so happened, spoke excellent English. The nearest café was back in the city, she told me, and then she instructed me in the bus system. My informant was delighted to have the chance to use her English, so we stood talking for 20 minutes and she would have been quite happy to go on indefinitely but I wanted food. I congratulated her on her English which she said was mainly self-taught. 'There is a building at the bus terminal,' she searched for a word, 'like a mushroom. There you can buy tickets for the bus.' She could not tell me how to travel on the bus if I did not have a ticket to begin with.

I took the next trolleybus and began a battle to understand the ticket system for Budapest public transport. There was a small boxlike receptable by the entrance and I watched other passengers to see what they would do but everyone ignored it. I had no ticket and the driver was sealed off in the front. Everyone who got onto the bus simply sat down and I assumed they all had passes.

The underground was the same. Masses of people walked through the barriers and onto the trains without tickets or check. I had purchased a dozen blue bus tickets at the 'mushroom' building but these I later discovered were no use on the underground. I chose a familiar name, Astoria, where I left the underground. The stop was close to the centre of the city. It was dark by then and I found a lively café-bar near the opera.

The bar was dimly lit by green-blue lights, taped music played continuously and most of the clientele appeared to be young, casually dressed and relaxed. I found a small table and was served by an elegant waiter in black who spoke good English. I wanted soup, but those on the menu looked uninteresting so I asked for something

97

better. He apologised–there was nothing. Resigned, I simply ordered a main dish yet five minutes later he returned with a bowl of goulash which he placed before me with a flourish, compliments of the house. It was a friendly gesture and that goulash was the best I have ever tasted. The meal, including wine, cost a mere three pounds. On my return journey I was once more baffled by the ticket system, for again I did not see a single person insert a ticket in any machine. My house, when I found it, was dark and silent.

I established a Budapest routine. Since breakfast was not available at my lodgings, I left at about eight and travelled to the centre of the city. Near the Astoria station I found a self-service municipal restaurant which, as far as I could judge, was patronised only by workers. A curious selection of food was on offer and this differed each day: a bowl of tinned apple chunks, two dry rolls and a tiny cup of coffee was a typical breakfast–odd yet quite satisfying.

Budapest is an elegant city in a spectacular setting. Buda and Pest, its twin cities on opposite banks of the Danube (west and east respectively), have equally dramatic fronts on the river. The Danube sparkles its way through, crossed by eight bridges of which the old Chain Bridge, restored after the War, is the most dramatic. Below Budapest the river divides into two channels but between Buda and Pest it runs wide and majestic, an elegant sweeping curve of water which the breezes whip up into flashing ripples of waves. Strings of low-lying black barges can almost always be seen passing along the river and once, standing in the centre of the historic Chain Bridge, I looked down on a string of familiar barges as they passed directly beneath me. I took a photograph and a member of the crew waved back at me from the bridge, putting on a grin for the tourist. Little did he suspect that I had travelled in such a barge. The thought of my experience, unknown to him, gave me a simple unlooked-for pleasure.

Few cities so obviously use a river to enhance their glory as does Budapest. Both Buda and Pest line its banks with boulevards, gracious or majestic buildings and from many vantage points in old Buda the great sweep of the Danube below provides a breathtaking panorama. Each side of the city begins on the river and then grows outwards from it. Only when the Chain Bridge, a superb example of early nineteenth-century suspension architecture, was opened in 1849 were Buda and Pest permanently linked to one another. Eight bridges of widely differing yet dramatic design now span the Danube to connect the two parts.

Budapest was devasted by six weeks' fighting in 1944 when the Germans fiercely resisted the advancing Russians and blew all the bridges. Yet today, so well has the restoration been done, there is almost nothing to remind even a searching visitor of the War. The old medieval buildings look medieval again, though perhaps too well preserved (Col. pl. 13). The dome of the Roman Catholic Cathedral was being recovered with copper when I was in the city; it is a gloomy pile and inside I found it to be a dark, forbidding place and unlike all the other Roman Catholic churches which I had inspected, not a single candle was burning at any side altar.

I remarked upon this feat of restoration to a friendly Hungarian I met. We were walking near the Parliament in search of somewhere to have a coffee. 'Not so,' he said. 'Look, I will show you' and after a few minutes' further walk he pointed to the facade of a large office block. The unmistakable pockmarks of machine-gun bullets were visible on the stonework. 'You see,' he said, 'there is evidence of the war–we have not restored everything as you thought. The war of 1956,' he added.

I found that most of the goods in a leading department store were the equivalent in quality perhaps to Littlewoods in London, although certainly there were also some more elegant shops with goods to satisfy Budapest's increasing number of tourists. There did not appear to be any shortage of things to buy.

The city's grandiose parliament buildings were partly modelled upon Westminster. I approached a solitary policeman on guard outside. 'What building is this you guard?' I asked. 'Parliament,' he growled with a certain grim satisfaction.

Budapest is enjoyable, a lively city. It bustles and apart from large red stars on top of prominent buidings (including churches) and a good sprinkling of uniformed soldiery, I was otherwise unaware of being in a Communist capital. None the less soldiers with automatic weapons seemed to be stationed at the oddest places. They occupied incongruous corners: on the watch for spies, insurgents, traitors or maybe saboteurs? As a rule they looked so bored that a dozen dissidents could have passed them undetected. I often wondered why Communist regimes consider it essential to have so many soldiers in evidence in public places. In the end I decided it was for reasons of propaganda: to demonstrate perpetual vigilance.

I walked the length of Népköztársaság Street. It is, or rather was, the Park Lane of Budapest with its large blocks of once elegant, balconied apartments and decaying mansions standing in their own grounds. Some of these mansions now serve as embassies. Eventually I reached the spectacular entrance to a park: Heroes Square was constructed in 1896 to commemorate 1,000 years of Hungarian conquest of the Carpathian Basin (Col. pl. 14). The great open space is dominated by a tall column; the base surrounded by statues of the chiefs who originally led the tribes into Hungary. Beyond this stands the park gateway: heroic allegorical figures in chariots ride on top

99

of either side of a half circle of columns, between which stand the most famous Hungarian kings. Museums set off two sides of this square and a wide boulevard, which is used for military parades, runs past the park. Rows of tourist buses were parked to one side while their occupants were lectured by guides about Hungarian history. A group of army officers, elegant and superior in dress uniforms, stood by the foot of the central column and a pretty, vibrant girl walked diagonally across the huge open arena, her breasts bouncing with the joy of being alive.

I was determined to hear some good music while in Budapest but came across my first concert by accident. In Buda I visited the former royal palace which is now a museum and gallery. I paid five forints, a tiny sum, which I assumed was the entrance fee but the elderly woman who had taken my money now gave me a programme. Then, from above, came a burst of music, Rossini, played by a full orchestra. Under the central dome people were crowded, some with seats, others standing, some sitting across the wide stone steps that led to the galleries above to enjoy a lunchtime concert of Rossini, Chopin, Bizet and Ravel. It was popular but performed with panache and much enjoyed by the audience.

I went to another concert that evening: I had been told that tickets would be available at the concert hall. A man behind a counter appeared to be dispensing tickets to anyone who approached him and he gave me one as soon as I asked. I tried to pay but he waved me away. An elderly woman usher showed me to a seat near the back of the large Liszt Ferenc Hall but promised she would look after me. What this actually meant was that just before the performance began she moved me to a splendid seat near the front.

The first violin was a tall, austere young woman in a simple long black dress with straight black hair to match. She spent the ten minutes after the orchestra had come onto the platform organising the players. She wandered up the ranks of the first and then the second violins, between the brass and woodwind, periodically playing an A on her violin, then standing by in case someone required a repeat. Hers was an oddly officious performance; the concert, however, was superb.

On another occasion, this time in Buda, I discovered the Musical Courtyard where an elegant quartet performed Vivaldi and Bach. For this I paid the princely sum of 40 forints. The quality of the music in the city was excellent: for one concert I paid a derisory five forints, for the second nothing, for the third 40 forints and yet there were empty seats. In Western capitals, seats for comparable music would have cost a fortune and in most cases it would have been impossible to obtain any seat on the day.

There were several expensive hotels along the river front, among them the Hyatt, the Duna Intercontinental and the Forum Intercontinental. These were presumably the hotels alluded to by the lady at the station tourist centre when she insisted that all the city's accommodation was the same price. A few years earlier, Hungary had raised a substantial loan from Austria to invest in her tourist industry and the country now attracts millions of visitors a year. A growing proportion of these tourists come from the West and prices have been increased accordingly to ensure a maximum take in foreign currency. Orange juice and coffee in the Hyatt cost me four times the price of breakfast in my municipal café, but this was still cheap at the price.

The interior of the Budapest Hyatt consists of a huge central lobby which pierces the entire height of the building. From each floor balconies overlook this open space which features a suspended model of an ancient aircraft. Plants trail over the balconies and the general effect of this extravaganza is similar to the Ford Foundation building in New York. The Hyatt was engaged in that most American custom of hosting a convention and the banners draped from one of the balconies advertised 'McDonald's Managers' Convention'. Presumably the big American hotel chains would soon be followed behind the Iron Curtain by McDonald's hamburger joints and Colonel Saunders with his 'finger lickin' chicken'. The hotels were already spearheading an onslaught on the Communist way of life.

What happens on the tourist front has become of considerable economic importance to Hungary, and Budapest too is set to capture and then increase a substantial tourist business. As a city it deserves to succeed: its setting is spectacular and beautiful, its music excellent, its food as good as that to be found anywhere outside eastern Europe and still at half the price. But the high prices of the big hotels, and perhaps more important the absence of medium-priced hotels, reflect the greed which tourism always contrives to encourage: in the case of Hungary this greed appeared to be shared equally by the government and trade. The presence of these hotels in Budapest epitomises the most open aspect of life under the Kádár regime.

János Kádár is one of the most astute political survivors of the Communist world. Since 1968 he has combined economic reforms that have allowed Hungarians a greater choice than anywhere else behind the Iron Curtain with a hard-line foreign policy which has persuaded Moscow that the country remains a dependable ally (*Glasnost* may change this). Shops displayed a considerable range of goods, while the amenities–hotels, restaurants and entertainments–are many and attractive. In 30 years of power Kádár has persuaded Hungary to accept the structures of a rigid Communist straightjacket as the price to pay for some freedom. His performance has been no mean political feat. Many Hungarians, I discovered, do two jobs and the second of these (on the black economy) enables them to keep their heads above water in the most advanced economy of the eastern bloc.

As in Austria, an ecological argument was raging about the Danube. Despite well-organised protests, Hungary has decided as part of an agreement with Czechoslovakia to build a dam at Nagymaros, upstream from Budapest. The effect of this development will be to ruin one of the most picturesque stretches of the Danube Bend. Unlike their Czech neighbours who are already constructing a dam north of Györ, the Hungarians have hung back, although pressure from both Czechoslovakia and the USSR now seems to have forced them reluctantly to go ahead with the project. The dam is scheduled to be completed by 1995. Yet another beautiful stretch of the Danube will be flooded and, according to the scientists, rare species of fish will be destroyed. It is not a popular decision.

One morning I took a three-hour bus tour of the city: the guide spoke English and German. We began by visiting old Buda, inspected the cathedral and then had various landmarks of Pest pointed out to us across the river. The trip included a twenty-minute break in a hotel for soft drinks and cakes and then we were efficiently shepherded out to the bus (processed is a better word) as other tourists arrived for their break. We were shown the railway stations which, we were told, represented fine examples of nineteenth-century English design. Near parliament our guide indicated the working office of Comrade Kádár. I could not quite place her tone of voice and spent the remainder of the drive speculating as to whether she had sincerely referred to Comrade Kádár with pride as her head of state or because to do so was *de rigueur*. She told us an anecdote set suitably far back in Hungarian history in which a Hungarian had acted treacherously. 'I am ashamed to have to relate this,' she remarked primly of this piece of historical nastiness. She also told us that Hungarian is related to that other impossible European language, Finnish. 'The sounds are very similar,' she said, 'but of course we cannot understand one another,' she added with satisfied pride.

We finished where we had begun, at Roosevelt Square, appropriately near the big hotels. I set off to find a place for lunch only to be seized upon by the moneychangers who regard Roosevelt Square as their best hunting-ground. Normally, when I asked a stranger for directions he would most likely look blank, shrug and inquire '*Ungarisch?*', perhaps smiling in the certain knowledge that no visitor would speak his language. But around Roosevelt Square I was approached as though to be asked for a light: 'Deutsch? English?

American?' 'English,' I would reply. 'You want to change pounds? Very good rate.' And walking beside me, the cigarette forgotten or returned to his pocket, the changer would make a quote, perhaps three times the official rate of exchange.

I discovered an especially attractive restaurant in old Buda which was made memorable for me by the spectacle of a Hungarian 'intellectual' (at least he so appeared) gorging himself upon caviar. Hungary may be a Communist state but Budapest has the appearance of a wealthy capital city in a thriving capitalist society.

To the end I failed to master the ticket technique on the trollybuses until, on my last ride in the city, I finally saw a passenger push a ticket into the little boxlike contraption by the door until this clicked and dated the ticket. With a sheaf of pristine tickets in my pocket I was not prepared to demonstrate my low level of mechanical aptitude by going up to the machine to punch one of my own. Instead I brought home with me all the tickets I had purchased at the 'mushroom'.

Throughout my stay I had not set eyes upon my landlady or anyone else in that silent house after my initial encounter. Living with a Hungarian family had turned out to be a myth. But on the morning of my departure the door from her sitting room into the hall was open; she was moving about to remind me of her presence and came the moment I called. I returned my keys and thanked her for her hospitality and she gave me voluble goodbyes.

Chapter Sixteen

A Bus to Baja

I travelled by bus across the Great Plain of Hungary along the east bank of the Danube to Baja, near the Yugoslav border. The bus was not full and its passengers were treated to the comedy of a daughter and her father. She was a middle-aged woman, perhaps 45, while he was about 70, a man of exceptional selfishness, a petty exacting tyrant who expected his every whim to be met at once. They sat together in the middle of the bus. He plonked himself in the window seat with a sigh as though bus travel was only to be endured as a last resort while leaving his daughter to arrange their luggage on the rack. The tapering bullet shape of his head betokened obstinacy and reminded me of the little man searching the *Ratskeller* in Munich for the roll of his choice. His daughter was plump and naturally friendly; she was also long-suffering, a quality which in her case was also a necessity.

As soon as they had settled and the bus had started he wanted to change seats: he did not like the middle of the bus. They moved back two rows to another empty seat and resettled themselves. By then we were passing through the outskirts of Budapest. The man removed his hat which his daughter placed up on the rack. Then he shut their window and promptly complained to the woman in front of him that her window was open and causing a draught. Obligingly she closed it. By this time most of the passengers had become aware of his cantankerousness and were ready to side with the daughter. Now he opened his window, just a little–he held his finger and thumb apart to indicate how much–for some air. His daughter shrugged. But he then felt a draught on his head and demanded his hat. Exasperated, his daughter got up to retrieve it for him; he took his time setting the hat straight on his narrow head. Finally he appeared satisfied and sat back as though ready to endure his journey and collectively we sighed in sympathy with the daughter.

But after a mile, certainly no more, he complained to his daughter.

I did not understand the subject of his complaint although everyone else clearly did for the general head-shaking, eyebrow-raising and clucking which followed showed he was up to no good. His daughter was obliged to stand in the gangway so as to allow her father to stand in his place, turn and survey the bus behind him. He pointed. He wanted to sit at the rear of the bus where there was an entire row of empty seats. Again they moved. When they had settled out of everyone's sight at the back he did not allow us to forget his presence for he insisted that his daughter should fetch their luggage from the rack above their original seats. This took her three trips up the swaying bus; at the back he directed her as to where each item should be stowed. The daughter showed extraordinary self-control but she had forgotten something which remained on the rack in front and after a while the old man demanded to know where it was and sent her forward to retrieve it. The sympathetic cluckings from the other women passengers were now more pronounced and some of the ladies made them loud enough to ensure that the old man understood where their sympathies lay. It made no difference: such people are not concerned with opinion. Later, when I looked back, he had gone to sleep.

Although for most of the journey we travelled parallel to the Danube, tantalisingly we never glimpsed the river from the bus. Yet it was there and provided constant evidence of its presence across the flat plain by a line of trees marking its banks or a small town rising unmistakably on its invisible far bank. Our direction southwards was determined by the Danube.

The Great Plain stretches eastwards from the Danube to Hungary's borders with Rumania and south into Yugoslavia. Flat and uninteresting, it appears endless. It was settled 1,000 years ago by nomads, the Cumanians or Jazygians, who moved westwards to escape the Mongols. We meandered through small villages, stopping everywhere to pick up or set down passengers. Most knew one another and the bus acted as an exchange mart for gossip.

Watching the different types who travelled on my bus caused me to reflect upon the Hungarian character. Intensely nationalist, with a reputation for adaptability–a necessity their geographic position has forced upon them–they also have a reputation for loose morals, a swashbuckling disposition, in short a people to be watched. The sterotype of Hungarians I had learned in my youth was 'not quite dependable'. Reflecting, no doubt unfairly, upon a people through whose country I was passing I recalled a comment upon Hungarians made decades before. Then I had been questioned by an elderly lady, a family friend of immensely snobbish inclinations, about the guests at a party I had attended the night before. When, rather proudly, I produced in my list a Hungarian count she raised an eyebrow. 'My dear,' she said, 'counts are two a penny over there.'

Now the bus was to be enlivened by the antics of a Hungarian Lothario whose behaviour reinforced the idea of the macho, sexually swashbuckling Hungarian male: an image they certainly like to encourage. Halfway on our journey we had a ten-minute stop. By then most of the original passengers had got off. Three attractive teenage girls came to sit in front of me, one in the double seat immediately ahead of me and her two friends beyond that. These two half-turned to talk with the girl behind them. Meanwhile, idly, I watched a scene outside the bus.

A man was taking farewell of his wife. He was about 40 and extremely handsome, his greatest assets being his liquid blue eyes which at 20 must have had all the girls chasing him. Now he looked at his wife as though she were the only woman in the world. She was younger than he, no more than 35, yet work and a hard life had aged her in a way which had not touched him. She was dumpy of figure, poorly dressed, her wispy untidy hair already turning grey. Once her face must have been very pretty and despite its now careworn appearance it still retained something of its youthful attraction. The man waited until the last before entering the bus, allowing the other passengers to board ahead of him. He had eyes only for his wife. He held her, he looked full into her careworn face, a long passionate stare as he protested his love, so that she took on a new sparkle, her face reflecting pleasure at attentions which were obviously rare. He behaved with passion like a young man with his first love. She responded with growing, deepening pleasure. She could not help it, she became more like the girl who once had attracted him. She looked almost as though she would rediscover long-forgotten passions. He kissed her, turned her to the light, hugged her so that her face looked over his shoulder at me in the bus window. But she did not see me. She was happy in that embrace. Once more he held her at arm's length, searching her eyes with his own. Then, at last, he boarded the bus. She moved with him to the door at the front but he did not look back. Instead, and at once, his eyes came to rest upon the three teenage girls as though it would have been absurd to expect him to notice anyone else. He took the seat next to the single girl in front of me. He turned to give her a minute appraisal, looking directly and closely at her face to compel attention. 'Hello,' he said while he examined her features with critical approval. The girl blushed. He laughed and redoubled his attentions, never taking his eyes from her.

Outside the bus meanwhile his wife peered up at the windows to see where he had taken his seat, but when she could not find him her face gradually changed, its brief glow of happiness fading as a mask of weary ordinariness once more took control. Yet people insist on hoping when, in their hearts, they know it to be pointless; and so still she hoped, searching the windows urgently for a further exchange, one more of those adoring glances which for her meant everything and for him were routine. But she was too close to the bus and could see only the people at the window seats. She realised this and moved back. Then she saw him.

Lothario meanwhile had forgotten his wife and was engrossed, all his magnetic charms at work, upon the girl beside him. He could not take his eyes from her and teased her into blushing so that to save herself she looked firmly out the window, a useless exercise which merely served to make him laugh. He settled himself more comfortably in the seat, closer to her. The other two girls now became conscious of his attentions to their friend but were far from sure how to act. The driver started the engine and casually, as an afterthought or an obligatory interruption of more serious business, the man remembered to look out the window where he discovered his wife's eyes upon him. Earlier pleasure, whose companion had been suspended belief, had been replaced by resignation, a hopeless acceptance of what she had always known. After one dismissive glance he turned back to the girl beside him. He did not relax in his attentions to the three girls and so became the scandal of the other passengers but, though the women muttered, none dared to remonstrate with him for his behaviour.

For the remainder of the journey I divided my attention between this passionate yet meaningless little saga of the 'macho' Hungarian male being played out before my eyes and searching from my window for evidence of the Danube. Hungarian passion—and they are a passionate people—is perhaps both a reaction and compensation for the flat dreary plain which forms the centre of their country.

Now Lothario, who was a big man, tried to make conversation with the girl beside him but she was too shy and nervous—not afraid but certainly nervous. He took off his watch to show her: it was nothing special as watches go but he made a story out of it, turning it in his hand and pointing out its very ordinary features as if they were jewels, so that over his shoulder even I became fascinated, wondering which of its points he would romanticise next. Then he touched her lightly on the arm and examined a strand of her hair while laughing softly into her face with his lovely blue eyes.

He turned his attention to the girl in front of him. She had long fair hair which reached down to her shoulders and shone from much brushing. He stroked it and at once she tossed her head, freeing the golden hair from his clutches. This delighted him and he laughed, then stroked it again. She turned to the third girl and they both laughed disdainfully. He attempted to take a strand of her hair in his hand but she wriggled it free of his grasp and the game continued for some time. The girl was shy, resigned, irritated and a little afraid but she also enjoyed his attentions. At last he did secure a strand of her hair which he placed with exaggerated care in his pocket book, nudging the girl beside him while he did so to make sure she recognised his prize. She could not quite prevent herself laughing but then looked angrily out of the bus window. He liked that and brought his head close to hers demanding attention with his ever-moving, liquid eyes; meanwhile, the two girls in front of him ostentatiously engaged in serious conversation.

At this point he became aware of my obvious interest in the proceedings. He turned, gave me a hard look and said something to which I responded in German. He shrugged, not understanding, then turned back to the girl beside him; but he was irritated at my presence behind him and after further attempts to secure hair from the girl he again tried to make conversation with me, only to give up at my lack of Hungarian.

All this took place while we were running more or less parallel to the invisible Danube and intimations of its nearness constantly aroused futile hopes of an actual sighting. At the same time my attention was repeatedly drawn back to the little saga unwinding in front of me. By then the three girls had become embarrassed, annoyed and also a little afraid–for the man was persistent as well as being large, powerful and slightly drunk. Yet such is human perversity that they enjoyed his attentions too, the more so because they were the innocent parties and could do nothing to stop him anyway which allowed them the exquisite double enjoyment of taking pleasure and being outraged simultaneously. Once, at mutterings in the bus, he looked round with slow deliberation to survey the other passengers, all of whom promptly stared primly ahead. Two teenage boys sat across the aisle from the girls. They would have liked to become acquainted themselves but had missed their opportunity to do so and were now obliged to be spectators only. They were out of it and lacked the man's maturity and panache so there they sat, jealous at the fun he was having and regretful that they had not contrived an immediate contact with the girls before his arrival. The remaining good citizens registered growing outrage. Having sized up everyone else, the man turned back to me and we engaged in a sort of shrugging match at the uncooperative, incomprehensible nature of girls. Then we reached Baja and the passengers got off, still manifesting disapproval, while the man bowed to the girls and at once left them. They were astonished at his abrupt departure; I think they had been wondering how to shake him off but he had other prey in mind and his byplay had been no more than an automatic reaction to pretty girls–any pretty girls.

I found Baja an interesting town. It was raining once more but at that stage in my journey I had become indifferent to rain. A wide square formed the town centre: there were buildings on three sides of this and an arm of the Danube on the fourth; in a corner by the river was the Hotel Duna. This had a dilapidated air about it but the rooms were spacious, comfortable and cheap.

Baja is a market town but it was crowded with young people for a sports festival. Over lunch I became aware of a party in a side room: they were all giant young men, Americans, who turned out to be the Harvard basketball team which was taking part in the sports festival. 'They are very good for amateurs,' the Hungarian who shared my table informed me, but he avoided elaboration as to whether they had won or lost their games. In the main square I watched chanting crowds of youths returning to the town centre from the day's sporting activities. They surged over the bridge, spread across the square and then disappeared into the surrounding side streets, leaving behind a sudden silence. As dusk descended I watched a pair of highly skilled sportsmen scull swiftly over the still, glassy waters of the river below.

The dining room of my hotel had been turned into a dance hall for the night. It was crowded, the crush of people dancing with growing exuberance to a crescendo of sound. The scene had an old-fashioned quality reminiscent of a Saturday night hop in pre- 'rock-and-roll' Britain. Somehow this seemed apt, an accurate representation of Hungary which is a curious blend of authoritarian one-party Communism and almost universal moonlighting. There is a longing for the contacts and the goods which come from the West and this longing is coupled with a forlorn realisation that for most people such goods must remain an unfilfilled dream.

It is curious how often helpfulness hinders. On paying my bill next morning I asked directions to the bus for Sombor in Yugoslavia. The receptionist tried to explain, got confused, then suggested that I should ask the taxi-driver outside. He gave me totally conflicting advice. I assumed he ought to know so followed his directions but after a while became certain I was heading in the wrong direction. I sought help of a man with a limp. 'That is the wrong way,' he insisted. He wanted to show me and we turned back the way I had come. I protested but he insisted. 'Follow me please. Not so fast,' said my guide, 'I have a limp.' Contrite, I apologised but time was passing and I did not want to miss the bus. He brought me back to the corner of my square to point triumphantly to the hotel. Language! I thanked him, waited until he had limped from sight and then headed back the way we had just come. I found the bus station in the end, at a different place from the stop where I had been deposited on my arrival.

I still had half an hour to wait before the departure of the Sombor bus. The other travellers in the bus station were peasants and local people, some with live chickens which squawked resignedly. Everywhere there were small containers, tied parcels and packages with which the poor always manage to surround themselves when travelling. I found a seat in the crowded hall next to an old woman who was chewing her way with toothless gums into black bread and raw onion slices. She cut the onion with a blunt penknife which she wielded in stubby, gnarled fingers. While watching her I realised that I myself was under observation. Across the other side of the hall a young man of round, florid face, short mouse-coloured hair and bloodshot eyes scrutinised me with a kind of fixed determination. Whenever I looked directly at him he turned away. I watched the animated scene but also kept searching out the young man and each time I looked his eyes were full on me, though when they met mine he would at once redirect his gaze elsewhere. Then I looked again; he was gone.

I went to locate the Sombor bus and wandered along the bus bays checking destinations. At the end of the bays I came face to face with the florid-faced young man. He spoke to me in Hungarian and for a moment I thought he must be a border moneychanger, less slick than those who frequented Roosevelt Square in Budapest, on the lookout for foreigners about to leave the country. I replied in German. Then he produced identification: 'Police–your passport.'

I think he was some kind of secret policeman. He had difficulty deciphering my passport for he was not a very bright young man but when he realised that I was British became quite friendly. 'Ah, Engleesh,' he managed and nodded several times. We shook hands, I said 'Yugoslavia' and he led me to a different part of the bus station altogether, where people were already boarding the bus for Sombor. Being a secret policeman in a small border town must be a boring occupation. I doubt if a great deal of action came his way, so that the sight of an obvious foreigner had stimulated him to challenge me if only to find out who or what I was. At least I had broken the monotony of his day. As I sat in the bus for Yugoslavia I saw the policeman again, this time in the company of an older, fatter and altogether more sinister-looking character. They were deep in conversation and when he thought I was not watching the policeman pointed me out to his companion.

Chapter Seventeen

Into Yugoslavia

The man who sold the tickets on the bus from Baja had a cleft palate and apart from me knew every passenger on board, for apparently everyone regularly crossed back and forth on 'family' business. At the border posts only my passport excited any interest for Western tourists did not enter Yugoslavia by means of this peasant bus. Sombor is an attractive little town, heavily tree-lined, somewhat off the Danube. A modern hotel, the only one I could find, provided a double room for 17 American dollars. Out of my hotel window I looked down on trees, for Sombor boasts more trees than any town in Europe. It had been the practice, now unfortunately abandoned, for fathers of new-born sons to celebrate the birth by planting a tree for the town.

Sombor possessed a tiny state theatre, all red plush and gilt, with boxes at the sides and back of the stalls, a small balcony and an elegant painted ceiling. The theatre could seat a maximum of about 250 people. There was a cabaret that night and I went in good time to get a seat, only to be told I could go in free; by eight o'clock the house was full. The cabaret would not have been out of place in a film of the 1940s. Three men in baggy black trousers, red shirts, huge white spotted ties and grey braces came onto the side of the stage to play a piano, a mandolin, a saxophone and percussion. The players' costumes were set in a time warp, everything was 1940s and Humphrey Bogart raincoats and fedoras for the men and two-piece square-shouldered costumes for the women. Frequent jokes about Communism caused half the audience to chuckle with pleasure while the rest kept quiet, though whether from disapproval I could not tell.

Afterwards in the bar of my hotel I got into conversation with another solitary drinker. Lack of common language does not prevent conversation. He gave me his address, insisting I should write to him from England, and a cognac which later I repaid. Thereupon he returned the favour and the ritual escalated. He lived 30 kilometres (19 miles) from Sombor and was a chauffeur. I am not sure about Yugoslavia's drink-and-drive laws and in any case it took me a while to work out his occupation. In Sombor, he said producing his one German word, everybody *schlafen*. Then he started; he had had far too much to drink and now in the big bar mirror he spotted his boss, a high-ranking army officer. We shook hands and he departed, not without an effort to look at ease. Later, when I left the bar, the poor man was standing stiff, being dressed down by his colonel.

I took a bus to Novi Sad back on the Danube. At first sight the town is ugly, a jungle of huge high-rise apartment blocks, but the old city centre is more appealing. In the centre is a long open square, part pedestrian precinct, faced by the townhall and the cathedral, and dominated by the large statue of a past hero. I found a friendly B class hotel which boasted a certain fading elegance; the receptionist promised me a room in an hour's time when they had been cleaned, so I found a pavement table where I watched the midday bustle over a beer.

From Novi Sad I still had another 1,255 kilometres (780 miles) to travel before the Danube reached the Black Sea but I had covered more than half my journey. I certainly felt that I had travelled a great distance: the days of walking between small medieval towns and cities in Germany were long past; I had finished with the barges and already two of the Danube's great capitals, Vienna and Budapest, were behind me.

Novi Sad has a population of a quarter of a million and is a modern industrial town, the capital of the autonomous province of Vojvodina in the Republic of Serbia. Originally a Roman settlement, in the Middle Ages it was a centre for Cistercian monks and then in the eighteenth century became known as the Serbian Athens since Serbians from many parts came to make it their cultural centre. Today it remains a city of ethnic groups including considerable numbers of Germans and Hungarians.

At Novi Sad the Danube is wide and steady flowing, its waters deep and strong. Whenever I watched the river here I invariably glimpsed long strings of barges, black and low in the water under the weight of their loads, or riding high and light, empty on a return trip. Across the river from Novi Sad, rising on a massive rock, stands the huge, grim fortress of Petrovaradin. The great fortifications are an ideal place for a holiday afternoon stroll and from the ramparts high above the Danube the whole of Novi Sad and long stretches of the river are spread out below. Grass overgrows the ramparts, two museums and a hotel are hardly noticed in the sprawling grounds of the fortress, while tucked away in part of the massive walls is a little art gallery. Petrovaradin was once a great outpost of Europe designed to face south against the common enemy. The Turks stormed it in 1526. Later it was refortified and then, after Prince Eugène had taken Belgrade in 1717, the Austrians turned Petrovaradin into one of the greatest fortified strongholds of the eighteenth century. It has ten miles of passages within its massive walls and an estimated 18,000 loopholes for use by its defenders. Across the river in its shadow the town of Neusatz grew to prosperity to be renamed Novi Sad and was created a royal free city by Maria Theresa.

It took well over an hour to stroll round the overgrown bastions and walls. Dilapidated and unkempt, these still impress by their sheer vastness. The fortress exercised a greater appeal for me than many an English castle whose beautifully mown lawns with 'keep off' signs emasculate them. Here was nothing to prevent you throwing yourself off the battlements if you so chose and the overgrown, deserted aspect of the ancient parade grounds and courtyards seemed nearer to historical reality. I suspect, however, that such considerations of historical aesthetics were less the reasons for its unkempt appearance than a lack of municipal funds for its upkeep.

In Yugoslavia, as in Hungary, I was aware of the military; there were always soldiers about in uniform. In Britain these disappeared off the streets with the ending of national service. More than once I saw Yugoslavian military policemen stop young soldiers to check their papers. Down the hill from the fortress of Petrovaradin I went into a bar for a beer–it was an unusually hot day–to find half the occupants of the small establishment were uniformed soldiers. In West Germany, on the other hand, although many NATO troops are stationed there I saw little evidence of their presence.

Novi Sad boasts a fine modern theatre and I booked for a performance of *Swan Lake*. As in all the Communist countries, theatre is heavily subsidised and very cheap. The performance given by a visiting Russian company was no more than fair. During the interval I got into conversation with a young student in the next seat who spoke good English which he claimed was self-taught and though he spoke slowly he managed remarkably well. He was, he told me, a first-year philosophy student at the University of Novi Sad but his chief interest was athletics and, in the American tradition, he had an athletics scholarship.

Our conversation proceeded in an oddly jerky fashion. He would proffer an isolated piece of information about himself or Yugoslavia in answer to a question from me: he was off to an athletics meeting the next month to run for Yugoslavia in Italy; education in Yugoslavia is free; he had a girlfriend but she was unwell so he had come to the ballet alone; he had pulled a muscle the previous season which

113

had prevented him running in an important race, but he was young and other opportunities would come his way. He wanted to improve his English but lack of books was a problem, so he asked if I would send him a book from England on my return. Although he insisted that he had come to the ballet to relax, at the first interval he said: 'It is over!' Surprised, I raised an inquiring eyebrow. 'Yes, it is over,' he repeated; so I suggested some refreshment. I am not sure whether he really believed that the ballet had finished or that he had merely become bored: I suspect the latter. We found an open-air café where I had a beer but since he was in training the ubiquitous Pepsi appeared on the table. He described himself as middle class but 'there are millionaires' he added, an intriguing statement about the Yugoslav socialist economy which I should have liked to pursue but we got sidetracked into something else. My friend had an appointment at half past nine to meet other students at a disco; perhaps the real reason why he had insisted that the ballet was over after the first act. We shook hands and parted, he to his disco and I to the theatre in time for the last act.

Observing people is always instructive and sometimes amusing. In eastern Europe, on the whole, men dressed astonishingly badly in ill-fitting suits a size or so too large for them, cut from drab material in styles that went out of fashion 40 years ago in the West. Likewise, many women wore dresses which added years to their ages. Greetings between friends or casual street encounters, however, turned into events attended by an elaborate ritual of handshaking, hugs and kisses. I smelt honeysuckle wherever I went in Novi Sad yet, curiously, I never actually saw any.

I visited a small war museum whose guardians, a man and a woman, seemed surprised that I wished to see it at all, although it was open to the public. The man accompanied me round the exhibits which consisted almost entirely of photographs and documents. The earliest of these illustrated Serbia before World War One and showed something of that turbulent little state's history of uprisings and revolutions. There were endless fading enlargements of groups: fierce, moustached partisans, arms crossed, staring proudly into the camera. Many photographs covered World War Two: the Nazi occupation, traitors being hanged, Tito and the partisans. Once more I had encountered the German factor as so often throughout my journey, yet on this occasion I could not help reflecting that it had been 'little Serbia' which actually sparked off World War One.

A waiter at my hotel adopted me and, whenever possible, made a point of serving me. He spoke good English and was pleased with an opportunity to use it, for Novi Sad is not on the main tourist route. When I left I gave him a generous tip which he had certainly earned from my point of view but he was hesitant to take it and, when pressed, explained he did not want me to think he had spoken English and taken time to answer my questions solely in order to obtain a tip. Such an attitude is all too rare; in his case it was genuine.

The river ran a murky brown, bearing silt from Germany, the Alps, the Carpathians; a wide swift-flowing waterway whose surface had a deceptive appearance of sluggish smoothness. I took a long walk on the path beside it and once I was clear of any possible shelter, the clouds which had been banking steadily above unleashed their heavy rain to drench me. The rain changed the character of the Danube, made it fiercer, swifter, more turbulent. The rough aspect of the river beneath the sheets of driving rain provided a dramatic backdrop for some heavy barge traffic which was passing. One tug pushed six barges slowly upriver at a painful three or four kilometres an hour; the barges were coupled in pairs, heavily laden and well down in the water. The throb of the tug's engines came fitfully across the swirling rain-spattered water. At the same time another six barges, equally heavily laden but travelling much faster, came downstream. The two strings of barges passed one another exactly opposite my vantage-point on the riverside path. The general gloom, the sudden wailing hoots from the tugs, the great mass of the old fortress of Petrovaradin across half a mile of water combined to show off the grim forbidding side of the mighty Danube.

I spent the evening investigating Novi Sad's high life. I began in the huge cellar bar of my hotel. Seats were partitioned off in sections. It was very full and many of the customers were young soldiers in uniform. I was forcibly struck by the general quietness: it was like being in the common room of a strict boarding school where a special holiday relaxation has been allowed. The people were enjoying themselves but authority—the prefects—were just around the corner. This subdued effect was astonishing, although everyone appeared totally relaxed. I imagined a bar that size, that full, at that time of night in London—the noise would have been deafening.

I set off to find a place to eat. I had seen many notices in town advertising a music group described as Novi Sad's best and after a while I discovered the hotel where the group was due to perform. I had no difficulty getting a table and took my time ordering a meal. Meanwhile four young men, smooth-faced and inclining to stoutness, took over a corner of the dining room where they set up their apparatus. They fiddled for the best part of an hour, laying down wires and placing microphones to which they connected their instruments until, eventually, they were ready to swamp the room with electronic vibrations.

Bing Crosby pioneered one of our modern revolutions when he began a career maundering into a microphone instead of singing with his voice. There was a time when four artists with four instruments would simply mount the platform and perform–but not anymore. Almost no one was wearing a tie or formal clothes of any kind except for a sprinkling of military in their uniforms. Small children, however, were taken everywhere: they had been at the ballet the night before; they were present now. Most of the people in the dining room had only come for the music and there was a table division: certain tables were reserved for eating while at others it was sufficient to order a drink, the most common drink being the abominable Pepsi. Once tuned into the electronic vibrations the music was melodious, pleasant, nondescript–a bromide.

At the next table to me a young-old man with a huge nose and drooping moustaches–a picture-book Serb–had come with his family to enjoy the music. His wife wore a headscarf and had a pale white face more like an Iranian or high-caste Arab than a Yugoslav: she might have been an Armenian. One child was a pretty girl of three who wandered all over the restaurant; the other child in a pram was no more than six months old. The couple held hands and stared into each other's eyes. The three-year-old went from table to table irritating people and the baby choked. I looked on fascinated. Only when the baby produced a desperate strangled gurgle and started to retch violently did the mother notice its plight.

Observing is what makes travel so enjoyable. Across the road from the hotel dining room, through a gap in the curtains, I saw a senior police officer come down the steps of his police station, his face glistening under the street lamp from a good meal just demolished. He carefully patted his uniform and adjusted his cap before setting off on the evening's hunt.

There could not have been much money about for people nursed their drinks for half the evening and this was one of Novi Sad's best hotels. The band would play for 30 minutes and then take as much time resting before returning to provide further entertainment. These long intervals were a strain on the Pepsi-drinkers.

At another table near me an important burgher forced lettuce leaves into his mouth. The band improved and was now joined by two singers: two fattish young men with round, boyish, smiling faces. Sometimes they performed together, sometimes singly. I think everyone else in that room was a Yugoslav; visibly they relaxed more and more as the music decibels increased. The burgher near me called the waiter to complain: something had been wrong with his salad, although he had taken care to eat it all, and now he demanded another one. The waiter, his face expressionless, brought a second salad. I wanted to make notes about that burgher but found I had left my notebook in my other jacket which had been soaked by the afternoon rain, so had to content myself making mental notes. Had I taken out a book and made the most obvious jottings about him, I doubt the burgher would have noticed. After despatching the second salad he commenced a concentrated and furious gorge, demolishing at speed his main course: a plate piled with rice and stew. Then he ordered a third salad. Every time I looked at him, for his performance was mesmeric, he was busy forcing yet another mangled lettuce leaf into his capacious mouth.

The music and brandy improved together. The burgher, like a certain type of Frenchman, needed to dispose of the serious business of eating before he could turn his attention to anything else, and in his case relaxing was out of the question. Two young men who wanted only to listen to the music approached his table to ask whether they could sit at the spare seats. He looked up grudgingly from his task and half agreed, but the waiter came to tell them it was an 'eating only' table so they drifted off through the crowded restaurant. The burgher looked relieved. He promptly had a further row with his waiter, this time over the bill whose every item he questioned with pernickety care. Finally he placed a 1,000 dinar note on the the table. The waiter brought a 100 dinar note in change. The burgher thought for a moment, for he had undoubtedly given the waiter a bad time, and then, with a grand gesture, he pushed the 100 dinar note across the table as a tip. It was not that he wanted the waiter to have the money but he did want to make the correct gesture. The waiter, however, showed a splendid sense of socialist dignity, refused to take up the note, said something and walked away. The burgher wanted to pick up the note and almost did so but instead, ostentatiously, he placed it in the middle of the now cleared table before getting up to leave. He was the only man in the entire restaurant wearing a dark suit and tie. He rose, placed an old-fashioned trilby hat on his head, donned a heavy mackintosh and stumped out.

Chapter Eighteen

Belgrade

It is a pleasant bus ride from Novi Sad to Belgrade: up and down hills with the Danube often in sight, a big river meandering through the plain. Belgrade sprawls along the south bank of the Danube at its junction with the River Sava. The weather was a mixture of rain and sun from behind fast-moving clouds.

People are always quick to spot the helpless stranger; then they are happy to demonstrate their superiority by coming to his assistance. It is a characteristic upon which I prey ruthlessly. I found a small pizzeria for lunch and sat at a table waiting for service but none came, although a waitress busily wiped tables round me. Eventually an elderly man at the next table asked whether I spoke English and then explained the system: I must go to the cash desk, order what I want and pay for it, present my chit at the food counter and wait to be called. I did all this to find that, in the meantime, three girls had occupied my table. I tried speaking English with them but they only knew a few phrases. When I collected my pizza the three girls, in turn, gravely wished me *bon appetit*. They were working girls and left before me. Then, the elderly man who had instructed me also left. On his way out he inquired, courteously, where I came from and helped me again, this time with the language. He pointed to my wine. '*vino*,' he said. 'Thank you,' I replied and we shook hands. I finished my *vino* and went to explore the city.

Unlike Vienna, which is frozen in the past and relies upon tourists to bring it into the present, or even beautiful elegant Budapest, Belgrade is very much a working city. Although it has attractive sights it is a much used modern city rather than one preserved for history. The River Sava joins the Danube at Belgrade and I walked along its bank leaving the bustle of the downtown city behind me until, quite suddenly, I found myself walking alone with the old citadel rising to one side of me, the river on the other. Only heavy vehicles came thundering past on their way to the docks; otherwise it was a curiously deserted road to find in the middle of a great capital. I investigated a dilapidated sixteenth-century Turkish defence tower and then came to tramlines and people again.

The old fortress area dates from Roman times and Belgrade, like Rome and a growing number of other cities which make the same claim, was originally built on seven hills. Today most of the city is modern, extensively rebuilt after the damage sustained during World War Two. But part of the ancient fortress remains: the area of the Kalemegdan has been developed as a beautiful park overlooking the junction of the Sava and Danube, the latter now a huge, majestic waterway.

Belgrade's covered fruit and vegetable markets are colourful, lively places where peasant stallkeepers bring their cherries and tomatoes from the country to sell in the capital. I once nearly caused a riot in a West Indian island by taking a photograph without first asking permission of the subject. That taught me a lesson: a stranger has no automatic right to take photographs of people, particularly close-ups of interesting faces. I was contemplating this market when a determined young American woman arrived on the scene. She produced a complicated camera with which she wanted to take faces, stalls, piles of cherries, indeed anything from every conceivable angle. She proceeded in a businesslike fashion, oblivious to the stall-keepers' feelings on the matter. Most blanked their faces and stared into eternity which was rather nice of them.

The Belgrade authorities had a mania for watering the streets though whether to clean them, to keep them fresh and cool or to catch unwary passers-by was debatable. Men from water trucks wielded powerful hoses to send great jets of water onto the pavements, catching the unwary. Pedestrians leapt to safety or, if trapped, shouted at the men to desist until they could get clear. The water men complied with cheerful grins, deflecting the streams of water long enough to allow the agitated citizens to pass out of range before giving play to their jets again. I walked along March 27 Avenue, back along Revolution Boulevard and visited the massive Cathedral of St Mark in Tasmajdan Park. Inside, the cathedral is not unlike a small Istanbul San Sofia. The buses, trolleybuses and trams were always full.

The area of the old citadel had a wonderful array of attractions for the visitor: an outdoor war museum of mid-century howitzers and field guns, an avenue of heroes whose stern busts looked down on an indifferent generation, the remains of the medieval fortress and a futuristic monument to the conqueror of Kalemegdan who stands naked on a great pillar looking across the city. There was also a charming, decaying little zoo of grottoes. You can tell a good deal about people from their zoos. I saw no keepers though I did stumble upon a man sweeping leaves.

In a corner of the park I came upon a group of elderly men standing hunched in concentration. I peered over their shoulders to see the object of their attention: they were watching two chess players who occupied one of the park benches. I came across other chess players and card players as well–it was certainly a place of relaxation. Basketball teams practised under the walls in the remains of moats and half Belgrade seemed to have turned out to enjoy the sudden fine weather. A famous café occupies a corner of the battlements and from its veranda there is a breathtaking view of the junction of the Sava and Danube. Another of the park's attractions was a tiny hunting museum of elegantly arranged stuffed animals: bears, wolves, boar, civet cats, foxes, deer and many birds. The woman at the door was not ready for visitors, she was enjoying her morning coffee, so she waved me in without charge.

Pavement cafés along a pedestrian precinct served wine, coffee, ice creams, beer and cakes. At my favourite establishment I watched four old men meeting by appointment. They shook hands ceremoniously and dusted the seats with their handkerchiefs. They ordered their refreshments deferring to each other in order of seniority. Then they got down to the serious business of gossip. It is a canard invented by men that women are the only gossips; get a few old men together and they will outperform women in the line of gossip nine times out of ten.

Near this café an old woman had established her pitch under a large coloured umbrella shade. She was positioned behind a little desk and immediately in front of her was an old-fashioned set of scales for weighing people. Her customers would stand patiently on the scales while she adjusted the weights until the arm tipped. Then she told them their weight in return for a trifling sum of money. She had a great sheet of paper mounted on a clipboard; this was divided into tiny squares covered with figures and she entered each customer's weight in one of these squares. Was she working towards a total of 1,000,000 tons of weighed people or did she have her machine oiled and serviced after every 5,000 tons? Was it for her income tax returns or was she merely concerned that at the end of her life she would have a written record of all the Belgrade citizens for whom she had provided this service?

Watching passers-by I decided that the Slavs are a handsome people. Men's faces are thin and raffish with fine bone structures; comparatively few show the effects of overeating that is all too common in Western countries. Girls are lovely in both feature and figure. In Belgrade many of the passing faces were seamed, ancient, wrinkled with outdoor toughness and belonged to peasants from the

The interior of the baroque chapel attached to the Benedictine monastery at Beuron. (*See previous page*)

The Benedictine monastery at Beuron which has long been a centre of learning and music. Here the Danube is still a small stream. (*Opposite*)

A castle on a crag dominating the downstream end of the first dramatic gorge through which the Danube passes. (*Below, right*)

The spring or source of the Danube in the grounds of the castle at Donaueschingen which is 2,840 kilometres (1,765 miles) from the Black Sea and 678 metres (2,224 feet) above sea level. (*Below*)

The thirteenth-century castle at Ingolstadt which was long regarded as the strategic centre of the Bavarian Danube.

The castle of the Hohenzollerns at Sigmaringen with a holiday fair in the foreground. (*Opposite, above*)

The Danube passing over a weir at the attractive medieval town of Riedlingen. (*Opposite, below*)

Kelheim in the rain from the Michelsberg hill that dominates the town which was the old ducal seat of the Wittelsbach family. From here the Altmühl Canal (upper left in picture) will connect the Danube with the Rhine, so that from 1990, it will be possible to travel by river from the North Sea to the Black Sea. (*Above*)

The docks at Linz (Austria) where there are huge iron and steel works. (*Opposite*)

The docks at Regensburg (the city of rain) which is the northernmost point of the Danube where the barge traffic to the Black Sea begins and ends. (*Below*)

The Hofburg Palace, Vienna, a city of past imperial grandeur. (*Above*)

Bratislava (the former Pressburg) from the citadel; it was the capital of Hungary from 1541 to 1784. It is now a major industrial city of Czechoslovakia and Danube port. (*Below*)

View of Pest across the Danube from Buda with the Roman Catholic Cathedral in the centre of the picture.

Donji Milanovic (Yugoslavia): a new town
built after the great dam at the Iron Gates
further down river had created this lake-like
bend to the river, and flooded the old town
which lies beneath the waters in the
foreground. (*Above*)

Heroes Square (Budapest) which was designed
in 1896 to commemorate 1,000 years of the
Hungarian conquest of the Carpathian Basin.
The seven conquering tribal chiefs are on
horseback and the most famous Hungarian
rulers stand between the columns.
(*Opposite, left*)

Turnu Severin (Rumania): a former Roman
town where Trajan bridged the Danube, now
nearly a mile wide. (*Opposite, right*)

On the road to Calafat: typical cart used by peasants in Rumania. (*Opposite*)

Vasili Rosu who had played soccer for Rumania in Munich, Mongola, Wembley and Mexico, where he broke his shoulder and ended his football career. (*Below*)

The Danube Delta. (*Above*)

Rumanian holiday-makers in the Danube
Delta. (*Below*)

countryside rather than city-dwellers. But to speculate along such lines as I did is to provoke Providence. A succession of quite extraordinarily ugly individuals now paraded past my wayside table as if sent to prove me wrong in my idle thoughts and to round off this special procession a grim, battle-axe of a woman, a cigarette clamped between her lips, strode past. At sight of her I began to despair of the Slavs but then a group of laughing, pretty girls came by to restore my faith in my judgement.

One evening I booked for a much advertised folk dance company—Kolo. I wanted something traditional. With an hour to kill before the performance I strolled into a little park. It was a charming, grubby place, much used, and I sat watching children, dogs, oldies enjoying an evening stroll and two boys fighting, cheered on by a small excited crowd. Standing in the centre of a bed of poorly tended flowers was the statue of a nineteenth-century dignitary, a handful of dried grass carefully inserted in his extended statue hand. Then in a small square I came upon a group of musicians playing folk tunes to raise money for the South West Africa People's Organisation (SWAPO).

The group I was to see at the theatre, a professional folk dance company, called themselves Kolo. They performed dances from different regions, each dance in the appropriate national costume, for Yugoslavia is a country of several nationalities. Originally these dances would have been performed in the open for a wedding or some other such festival. The theatre was large and almost empty when I arrived. My seat was in the fourth row of the rear section of stalls and I was one of no more than two dozen people thinly scattered over the auditorium. Had Kolo such a bad reputation? But then, with five minutes to curtain time, the organised tourist groups arrived. They came wiping the dessert from their lips, the evening's entertainment neatly slotted into their tight schedules. They were tended by their efficient minders like flocks of sheep. Their guides even purchased bundles of programmes and handed these out, a take-home souvenir for each person, part of the all-in price. One large group filled the front four rows and a second group took up the three rows immediately in front of me. Without these last-minute arrivals and two smaller groups which also arrived late and slightly breathless, the dancers would have had to perform to an almost empty house. The dancing was colourful and the music gay and noisy. Half the tourists were armed with cameras and flash guns and, as though by arrangement, they kept standing up to take photographs from different parts of the house so that the first half of the show was punctuated by a constant popping and flashing of bulbs. Two Japanese in front of me were persistent offenders in this respect:

they took at least one shot of each dance and there were about 20 on the programme. At the end the tour guides shepherded their flocks out into the street and counted them carefully back into their waiting buses. 'That was good,' said one large American gentleman smacking his lips as he left, for all the world as though he had just devoured a large steak. The dancing had been good: it was also routine and without inspiration, designed for the package tourist, a taste of old Yugoslavia to take back home.

I went to the Moskwa, one of Belgrade's leading hotels, for a late supper. At the next table a weary Yugoslav ate cheese and drank white wine. He was studying the locale. A party of four dull Americans occupied one table; a young man with his girl, whom he had clearly brought to impress, sat at another. They were uninteresting. Then a new party arrived: a Yugoslav and his wife with two English guests, businessmen. They conversed in English and the woman described a number of food recipes. Then they talked business for a while until one of the Englishmen told a silly story. The solitary Yugoslav and I each found them boring too. But then they broached the subject of soccer: Brussels again and I pricked up my ears. The Yugoslav host, on to a winner, became aggressive. He delivered a lecture on British soccer hooliganism and the general brutality of British fans and put his English guests suitably on the defensive. The Yugoslav pressed home his attack: 'Why,' he asked, 'is your television so full of foul anti-foreign jokes? Why are you always going on about the Germans, wogs or foreigners in general?' He had a point and his guests offered no adequate defence, though one of them did make half-hearted gestures, less of explanation than of personal dissociation. It was not the first time I had heard the Brussels affair raised to spark off a tirade about British behaviour.

What interested me was not the reaction to Brussels, which seemed to be routine across Europe, but the fact that such an event was seized upon as a convenient introduction to something deeper. British aloofness, arrogance, insularity—what you will—is not appreciated on the Continent. Much earlier on my journey I had become increasingly aware of a deep divide between myself (cosmopolitan as I like to believe I am) and Europeans, whose many divisions do not prevent them from regarding themselves as Europeans, something the British have still to learn to do.

I had become absorbed in this scene and had not noticed that my neighbour had finished his cheese and wine. Now he got up to leave and his weary face suddenly creased in a smile of complicity: he too had been listening and enjoying himself, though whether he spoke English I do not know. He had also been watching my absorption in their conversation.

I was awakened at two in the morning to the sounds of a terrific storm and out of my hotel window saw the streets of Belgrade awash with water. Yugoslav plumbing, even in the better hotels, leaves a good deal to be desired. The basic principle of plumbing–that water flows downwards–seems to be defied by hotel bathrooms. The same pattern of flooding occurred in hotels of classes A, B and C. Generally bathroom floors were of stone or tiles with a drain in the middle of the floor covered by a small metal grill. At first I assumed this was to meet an emergency in case the water was left running in the shower or bath but on numerous occasions I discovered otherwise. Repeatedly, after a shower, I found my floor awash with water and only after several near disasters did I realise that the drains were simply unable to cope with the normal outflow of water, so spewed up half of it onto the bathroom floor. I learnt to regulate the outflow with my foot, so as to keep the floor moderately dry.

On first reaching Belgrave I mistook the River Save for the Danube for here the Save is a large river, twice the width of the Thames in London: it is Yugoslavia's main Danube tributary. Rising just south of Villach in Austria among the Karawanken Alps it flows for a total of 724 kilometres (450 miles) south-east across Slovenia and Croatia until it joins the Danube at Belgrade. It is navigable for 563 kilometres (350 miles).

I wandered along the bank of the Save opposite Belgrade. The river sparkled blue under a bright sun and rising beyond it the citadel of the old city presented an uneven skyline dominated by the nineteenth-century tower and spire of the Orthodox Cathedral, whose gilding flashed in the brilliant sunlight. Below, along the water's edge, drawn up smartly and gleaming white, were the passenger hydrofoils that do a brisk business up and down the river from Belgrade.

The walk beside the Save ended in a promontory, a fisherman's paradise among willow-like trees that grew half in the water. Here an arm of the Danube which skirts a large island at the junction of the two rivers joins the Save, as its waters finally merge with those of its grander cousin.

I came upon a number of old men sunbathing. They appeared to be regulars and to know one another at least as nodding acquaintances. They each affected outmoded, old-fashioned bathing shorts. These were, without exception, too large for their shrunk shanks, floppy, as though designed to emphasise their advanced physical decrepitude. They were bronzed by the sun, some indeed were nut-brown in colour, but their muscles were drooping and flabby, their skin wrinkled and ugly. They had reached the stage in life when bodily deterioration had set in and when it would have been more seemly not to indulge in public displays of the flesh. But they were enjoying the sun and had probably long ago relinquished concern as to the effects of their appearance upon others.

On my last night in Belgrade I went to the opera and enjoyed a superb performance of Verdi's *Il Trovatore*. I had purchased a seat in the third row of the stalls for the princely sum of 200 dinars (about 70 pence). The part of Leonora was sung by Yugoslavia's leading soprano, Ljiljana Molhar-Talajic. She was a lady of Wagnerian proportions with a plain pudding face yet when she sang the love arias she became radiant. At the intervals and the final curtain red roses were thrown down to her from the balcony, and the audience gave her a rapturous ovation.

I was to depart from Belgrade by hydrofoil at three in the afternoon so found a restaurant near the hydrofoil port for lunch; it was an interesting, lively place, the food was good and the prices reasonable. The toilets were below the dining room, approached down a small spiral staircase at the bottom of which, between the doors marked 'ladies' and 'gentlemen', sat a little old lady: the guardian of the lower regions. As far as I could determine, her sole function was to collect tips in her prominently displayed saucer. I had left my wallet in the jacket over the back of my chair and that held even my ten-dinar notes. When I emerged from the lavatory she had her beady eyes upon me in expectation. Guiltily I fished in my trouser pocket and found one or two worthless coins. These I deposited with a rattle in her dish; then with swift though nonchalant strides I made for the little staircase but though I spiralled quickly out of sight I was pursued by irate and shocked protests.

Chapter Nineteen

The Iron Gates

From Belgrade the Danube flows eastward to the Kazan defile where the river used to narrow to a dramatic width of only 146 metres (160 yd) with a depth of 45 metres (150 ft). Now the flooding which followed the building of the great dam below the Iron Gates means the waters are no longer so swift or so dramatic although the gorge remains spectacular. East of Belgrade the Danube is Europe's greatest river. It runs for 105 kilometres (65 miles) through fertile plains and then for 210 kilometres (130 miles) it forms the boundary between Yugoslavia and Rumania.

At Smederevo stand the impressive remains of one of the greatest fortresses of the Middle Ages with five-metre (17 ft) thick walls. This was built in 1430 by Prince Djuradj Branković as a defence against the Turkish advance into Europe. The peasants had to scour the countryside for every available stone to use in its construction. Legend has it that these same peasants had to supply thousands of eggs to mix with the mortar in order to cement the stones more securely. The fortress has changed hands many times in its history. The Germans made it an ammunition dump during World War Two and it suffered from a massive explosion in 1941. Downstream from Smederevo the Danube widens considerably and there are a number of large islands such as Ostrvo, which is 19 kilometres (12 miles) long.

Further downriver, set against dramatic rocks, stands Golubac Castle, which was built to guard the entrance to the gorge. It stands on the site of the Roman Castrum Calumbarum and it has been of strategic importance for 2,000 years. Near the modern town of Donji Milanovac at Lepenksi Vir archaeologists in 1965 discovered one of the oldest neolithic sites dating from 6000 BC. At the great bend in the river at Donji Milanovac the Danube looks more like a lake so wide has it become as a result of flooding, even though the Iron Gates dam is still another 50 kilometres (31 miles) downstream (Col.

pl. 15). Before the flooding the gorge was known as the 'Great Cauldron' because of the rapid currents and whirlpools, but now the water is deep and calm.

The Djerdap Dam is the largest hydroelectric work in Europe. Its waters have covered the Roman road which Trajan cut along the rockface on the Yugoslav side of the river. The plaque commemorating Trajan's ancient feat of engineering which made possible the conquest of Dacia (Rumania) has been moved higher up the rockface. Now it can only be seen from the river. Between Kladovo on the Yugoslav side of the Danube and Turnu Severin in Rumania, Trajan's great bridge once spanned the river and traces of its massive supports may still be seen. These two towns lie 10 kilometres (6 miles) downstream from the dam.

I travelled this dramatic part of the Danube by passenger hydrofoil from Belgrade, stopping in Donji Milanovac on the way. The journey from Belgrade to Milanovac took three hours. At first we passed through flat plains: there were islands in the river and sometimes swamp-like vegetation at the water's edge, while forest-covered hills crowded to the river banks.

A friendly Yugoslav with passable English sat next to me. He wanted to know where I came from; then he provided a commentary upon the places we passed. He described the great explosion at Smederevo in 1941 as though he had been there in person, a member of the Yugoslav partisan forces, to supervise the event. In fact he was probably not then born.

We turned to politics in a cautious, casual way: I not to embarrass, he uncertain how far to venture with a stranger. After a while he relaxed and we discussed Yugoslavia's relations with her eastern neighbours. Those with Czechoslovakia, Hungary and Rumania were good, he said. 'No real problems.' But relations with Bulgaria and Albania were 'problematic'. He produced the word with emphasis after a mental search. Bulgaria was more Communist, more hardline than the Soviet Union. I was to be told this more than once. 'As for Albania,' he shrugged his shoulders eloquently–there was really nothing to say. Otherwise he did not mention the Soviet Union. Indeed, a failure to talk about the Soviet Union was a feature of the political discussions I had in the east European countries. 'Big Brother' was a taboo subject and the determined way the topic was sidestepped spoke volumes of Russia's standing in those countries. When the Soviet Union entered the conversation it met with elaborate courtesy or ironical jibes.

We passed dredgers at work in the river which prompted my friend to tell me his business. He worked for a company which ran barges on the Danube and was responsible for dredging a section of it. He, however, was going on a personal trip to Rumania, a business deal, nothing to do with the company. He did not elaborate. We went to the small bar for a beer, although he only accepted one from me after much persuasion. They were expensive beers, almost twice the usual price. Then, suddenly, on a wide loop of the river we found ourselves bumping up and down quite fiercely as the hydrofoil hit a patch of choppy water with white horses flying all round us.

It was a gloomy day and when we passed the castle of Golubac it stood grim on its crag, wreathed in trails of mist. The town below is a centre for sports. By then the northern bank of the Danube was in Rumania.

The hotel at Milanovac was an astonishing feat of modern design built in layers on the hillside. The hotel pick-up was at the quayside waiting for me. I had booked a room from Belgrade: it was the only hotel in Milanovac and this the only occasion on the entire trip that I booked ahead. Everything was in dark brown wood, the effect not unlike a North American 'lodge'. I signed in and the receptionist said in American-English: 'Have a pleasant stay.'

From the balcony of my room I could look down on the modern town of Milanovac; the old town, all save the church, had been totally submerged by the rising waters after completion of the dam. Beyond the town the Danube curved like a wide lake. Far out, heading downstream, was a long string of barges, the chug of the tug's engines coming faint yet powerful across the water. The hotel was packed with holidaymakers. I went to a balcony bar which also faced the river and the distant Rumanian hills. Two young men at the next table listened to me ordering drinks; one of them asked me the time in English. He had a smattering of English and wanted to practise it on me. Like almost everyone else in the hotel, they belonged to a group.

The rooms were well appointed and the general layout of the hotel was attractive with wide, open-plan features. There was a pristine newness about the place which was really a superior 'people's hotel': it deployed the pretensions but could not quite match the middle-class standards of a Hilton, even though the decor suggested a stan-dardised American chain hotel. The dining room gave the show away. The tables–there were no individual ones–were laid out in rows as in a school, the people sat in their groups and the menu was a fixed one. The effect was that of a superior barracks, though the food was good. When the waitress discovered I was not part of a group, she brought me an à la carte menu which was still cheap. Across the middle of this huge dining room hung a kind of Chinese screen to divide it into equal sections. As a foreign visitor, I paid four times as much as the Yugoslavs on holiday but that seemed appropriate in a country desperate for foreign exchange.

A quartet of musicians plugged in their electronic instruments and got to work on the assembled diners while everyone remained in place to enjoy the music. There was a dance area in front of the band but as yet no one ventured onto it. I retreated to the bar which overlooked the dining room and so I now had the band directly beneath me. By this time all the diners had finished eating but continued to sit in their rows to listen to the music. I was the sole occupant of the bar and I do not think the barmaid approved; I ought to have been below enjoying myself.

Eventually, four people made their way on to the dance floor. They did not dance as couples but held hands in a row, as if to do the Lambeth Walk. This brave example was soon followed and they were joined by others. The newcomers did not dance in couples either but attached themselves to one or other end of the original foursome and the line steadily grew until it was obliged to curve into a circle. The lively music continued, more people came onto the floor and the circle curled in on itself to become a Catherine wheel with one man in the centre and the circle twisting out in peels from him, so that additional newcomers could only attach themselves to the outer end. Eventually the first circle became so tight that a second was formed and later a third: these also developed into Catherine wheels. A hearty organising man of constant jokes and jolliness had created the first Catherine wheel and was now at its centre, and his exhortations kept it pulsing like a distant star. The dance went on for a long time: three steadily weaving, breathing Catherine wheels, a huge one in the centre, the two smaller ones on the flanks.

When the dance came to an end the revellers remained on the floor ready for another group effort. This time they squared off–or tried to do so, for there were now about 150 people on the small dance floor. They clapped and swayed and moved in and out to the identical rhythms which had worked for the Catherine wheels.

I was leaning on the balcony surveying this scene, engrossed in sociological calculations upon the nature of organised group entertainment, when I became aware of the severe barmaid standing beside me.

'We are shut now, you must go,' she said and pointed to the exit.

'But I want another drink.'

'Of course. You can have one upstairs, there is another bar there.'

It was then ten o'clock. Below, the diners had finished their square dance and returned to their seats. I found my way to the other bar which was crowded with those anti-social elements who did not wish to dance or sit in ordered rows in the huge dining room. I ordered a *slivovica* (plum brandy).

Nearby a drunk and a talkative army major held forth to a couple who wanted to escape: after a while they managed to do so and the major headed for the bar to collar a small, inoffensive man as a substitute audience. He ordered a drink for him, then led him back to his table. However, after a while he, too, tired of the soldier's harangue, made his excuses and departed. Back went the major to the bar in search of a successor. He repeated this exercise twice more. Once, bereft of his latest audience, he looked in my direction but I evaded his glance and stared stonily into space. Although the dining room made me think of a British Butlin's holiday camp, yet there was something ordered and different about it, a certain quietness despite the lively and un-English response to the dancing.

At breakfast the next morning new friends from the night before greeted one another with the cheery heartiness that becomes second nature on group holidays. The coffee was execrable: almost cold, strong with chicory, otherwise watery; on the other hand it was produced so quickly and served with such a friendly 'I hope you are enjoying your holiday' smile that I did not have the heart to complain.

A busload of us went to visit Lepenski Vir, the ancient mesolithic site, which was an hour's drive back upriver from Donji Milanovac. The road runs high above the river through steep hills. The bespectacled man who had led the dancing the night before was on the bus, jollying and organising once more. He turned out to be a professional tour-guide. This stretch of river, with dramatic hills on either side, is one of the most exciting of the Danube; it must have been still more awe-inspiring before the dam was constructed at the Iron Gates.

Lepenski Vir is one of the most complete mesolithic sites in Europe, a place where migrants settled on their ages-long journey up the Danube into central Europe. The site may predate migrations from the Middle East; it is dated between 6800 and 5300 BC. The excavations have been covered over for protection and to a layman's eyes the site reveals little. We were a group of 40, a full busload. We walked a quarter of a mile from the bus to enter a covered area where we crowded onto a viewing platform. There was hardly room for so large a group and to see anything one had to peer over shoulders. We were treated to a twenty-minute lecture by a student attached to the museum. A man who was clearly not archaeologically inclined stood behind me and muttered angrily throughout the lecture. Finally we were permitted to leave and then spent a more interesting time in the little museum where the ancient village had been reconstructed in miniature. There were some marvellous stones fashioned into faces, in the style of early Picasso.

Enforced culture is a funny thing. Everyone looked suitably impressed, lingering beside the more interesting objects and talking in hushed tones. But most of the group were not really interested; they were making the visit so as to say 'I have seen the oldest mesolithic site in Europe' and also because within the group situation they wished to appear superior. Group holidaymakers are expected to set aside one morning for higher things, in this case history. When we left the museum and returned along the path to the bus, voices rose happily again: we were out of school and back to the normality of the holiday.

I did not want to take lunch in the big dining room so wandered down into the little town where I found a small café with garden tables under an awning. I had a beer and asked for the menu: all fish, fresh from the Danube. A girl brought two fish on a plate for me to inspect. They looked very ordinary uninteresting fish but in view of the nature of my journey I felt I ought to sample them. I began with fish soup and salad. Then came the two fish dry-fried in breadcrumbs. They tasted very ordinary indeed.

It was a popular lunchtime place. The proprietor came out to talk with me. He was small, plump and bald with a huge beaked nose. He knew a little German and a little English. He presented me with a coloured postcard of the old town before it had disappeared under the dam waters and explained at length how beautiful it had then been. He was very friendly and kept coming to see that everything was to my satisfaction. Four boys at a table behind me were enjoying Pepsis and bread with some form of dip and their English-speaking member gravely inquired my name. His was Branca.

It is amazing how easily one can be impressed by one's own importance. As I drank my coffee I mused that they were flattered by my patronage, hence the repeated visits to my table by the host. Yet though the service was good the meal was indifferent. When I was ready to go I asked my friendly host for the bill. 'Of course,' he said and disappeared. Shortly afterwards a total stranger came out from the back, a large man I had not seen before. He presented me with my bill and I understood why: it came to almost twice the cost of my dinner in the hotel the night before. The little host remained conspicuously absent while I settled and left. They *had* been thrilled to have me but not for the reasons I had believed. I never argue in such circumstances. I left the coloured postcard which the host had presented to me squarely in my place, since I did not believe I had paid enough to deserve it. That lunch upset my stomach: the Danube fish must have been contaminated with Danube pollution.

I went to the quay to book a place on the evening's hydrofoil to Kladovo. Then I sat outside an otherwise deserted waterside bar drinking *slivovica* to settle my stomach. Upstream from my wayside vantage-point was a vast stretch of water: wide, misty, with hills rising steeply on either side, in appearance more like a Scottish loch than a river. The far end of this stretch of water must have been eight kilometres (five miles) distant before the river became lost in the grey-purples of the hills. Here the Danube had taken on another of its many cloaks, a different mood entirely from those I had seen hitherto. Now it was a gentle, placid lake, the man-made result of the great dam farther downstream–a lake though which could easily be whipped up into rough and dangerous waters in a storm.

Back at the hotel I settled my account and then sat on the bar balcony until it was time to leave. The holidaymakers must have been on an excursion or have departed for new destinations for the place was all but deserted. Then, just before I left, a bus disgorged a new crowd of holidaymakers. These were quite different from the previous groups and must have come from another part of the country altogether. They were older, peasants, with lined, weathered, shrewd faces. They crowded into the reception area and got in each other's way while waiting to be shown their rooms.

At the river again I watched the tiny smudge of the distant hydrofoil eight kilometres (five miles) up the 'loch' as it came towards us, until I could distinguish the wake of white spray from the darker white of the vessel. Unfortunately something had gone wrong: two hydrofoils arrived but one had to be taken out of service and everybody was crowded into the second vessel. Consequently I had to stand as we raced down one of the most spectacular, historic stretches of the Danube. Kladovo lies below the dam. The hydrofoil drops its passengers above the dam and a bus takes them 20 kilometres (12 miles) to the town. The rawness of the new hotel at Kladovo showed it had only just come into use.

This hotel was also full of group holidaymakers but it had none of the pretensions of the one at Milanovac. It provided down-to-earth workers' fare without frills. The men in the large dining room drank hard, the noise was deafening as the band and singer brashly performed, assisted by overpowering electronic aids. At the desk I asked about the morning bus to Rumania. A man overheard me and got into conversation. He spoke some English and a little German. He warned me to be careful once I reached Rumania. 'All Rumanians are cheats,' he said, 'watch them, they are very corrupt, they will do you down. We never trust a Rumanian.'

Chapter Twenty

Into Rumania –
Turnu Severin

A bus left Kladovo for Turnu Severin in Rumania at seven in the morning. I had been warned that I would not be allowed to walk across the dam. Everyone on that bus, except for me, was making a day trip to Turnu Severin and would return on the same bus that evening. They were supposedly going shopping, but I think had other purposes in mind. The bus made the trip every day of the week and it was a popular excursion.

We returned 10 kilometres (6 miles) upstream from Kladovo to the great Djerdap Dam. This huge construction, a joint Yugoslav-Rumanian enterprise, is the largest hydroelectric dam in Europe. Here, finally, the vast waters of the Danube are harnessed at their last defile of the 'Iron Gates', where the great westward-reaching spur of the Transylvanian Alps turns southwards to crowd in on the river and the Danube passes over the Prigrada Rock. From my hotel balcony ten storeys up in the early light of dawn I had looked upriver to the distant dam as the sun broke through the mist to catch the stonework and make it glint. The river was about one kilometre (half a mile) wide and Trajan's bridge is reputed to have measured 915 metres (3,000 ft) in length.

They were a friendly crowd on the bus but I could not discover the attraction of a visit to Rumania; by common consent Rumania was poorer than Yugoslavia and had few goods worth purchasing. There was a distinct holiday atmosphere and one passenger paraded up and down the bus imbibing steadily from a litre bottle of red wine: he was already happily drunk. We were cleared through the Yugoslav checkpoint in five minutes, though my British passport on that bus provided a mild sensation.

I asked the man sitting next to me why they were visiting Rumania. He spoke some German.

'You are going to visit relatives?'

He laughed, 'No, no; we are going on a day trip.'

'Who–all of you?'

'All of us,' he nodded and gestured at the bus, 'we often go.'

'Is Turnu Severin so interesting?'

'We go shopping.'

'But Rumania is poorer than Yugoslavia.'

'Oh yes, poor. But we shop and return tonight.'

'What do you buy?'

He shrugged, 'Many things, we go for the day.'

He was not very enlightening.

There were four lanes of cars waiting for clearance; the bus was waved into an empty fifth lane. An official collected the passports from the bus and the passengers remained seated. I saw my passport separated from the rest to be handed to a more senior officer. Then we were told to leave the bus and the women went off to a special room to be searched. Personal searches were not being made of those travelling by car; our bus, clearly, had a special reputation. I was separated from the rest to have my luggage inspected, though not with any great thoroughness. I was then told to join the other men from the bus and we crowded into a small room to be searched. I found myself at the head of the queue. A huge Rumanian official told me to take off my jacket. At that all the men laughed uproariously. 'He is English-British.' They chorused this. 'British?' and the guard stood back, surveyed me and said, 'I love the British.' Then he gave me a great bear hug. He waved me from the room. The men all grinned, not in the least put out that I was allowed to go while they remained to be searched.

I doubt the search revealed much. Whatever the smuggling purpose of that trip they had reduced it to a fine art and the border search was a matter of form–for both sides. I had noticed earlier the drunk passing cigarettes to the guards. Meanwhile I had to change the equivalent of ten dollars hard currency for each day I intended to be in the country. Then the customs officials, three of them, asked whether it was my first visit to Rumania. It was and they wished me a happy visit.

When they had been cleared the men trooped to the other side of the barrier where the bus had already been allowed through; there was no sign of the women. They, no doubt, represented the real problem for the authorities. We watched a game of 'throw penny' between the bus-driver and his ticket collector. A line was drawn on the ground, the two men stood three metres (10 ft) from it and, in turn, pitched a coin at the line; the coin falling nearest the line taking its rival. Both men were extremely accurate, casting their coins within a few inches of the line but the ticket collector won every time. A young man stood by the line to act as judge, calling out what we could all see. They shouted, they laughed, they got angry–or rather, the driver got angry for no matter how well he cast, his ticket collector cast better. Yet the driver went on playing, cast after cast, losing his money. He changed a note for more coins. He threw nearer the line; the ticket collector just beat him. He touched the line, so did the ticket collector who won every single cast with practised ease. It was a ritual: they always played and the driver always lost. Everyone looked on with pleasure and the drunk passed round a newly opened bottle of wine.

The young man who had spoken German with me was one of many that day to advise me on how to change money on the black market. 'Watch out,' they said, 'the Rumanians are *all* crooks. Corrupt.' They nodded seriously. They instructed me in the various ways in which I could double or even treble my money. 'But beware,' the chorused, 'we all know what the Rumanians are like. You cannot trust a Rumanian.'

I enjoyed that bus ride. I had become an object of interest to the Yugoslavs on the bus and the Rumanians at the border post. Nearly half the men, though none of the women, approached to wish me a good journey or a successful money change. As soon as they discovered I was English they spoke German.

The ride into Turnu Severin was short. We parked at a large shopping complex and once off the bus everyone disappeared at speed. Whatever they had come across the border to do required despatch and was unconnected with Turnu Severin's historic attractions.

The present town of Turnu Severin was founded between 1835 and 1841 but its history dates from Roman times (Col. pl. 16). It also played a substantial role in medieval days. The town featured in both world wars: it was captured by the Austrians in 1916 and by the Russians in 1944. It was a busy, bustling place with a dramatic water tower in the centre.

After a short walk I found a hotel where I had breakfast: it was still only nine in the morning. My waitress spoke good English of which she was inordinately proud. I congratulated her and she promptly brought me more coffee. That was a class A hotel and expensive so I set off to find the tourist office. There was only one other hotel, the Parc, and that was equally expensive. There were no cheaper places in which to stay; Turnu Severin expected to trap incoming tourists and make them pay but I decided otherwise. The main sights of the town consisted of a huge festival hall, where a culture feast was in progress, the dramatic water tower and an interesting market selling only tomatoes.

I returned to the tourist office. The staff were charming and did their best to help. We struggled–the man, a woman and I–with a little English and German. Carefully they explained that Turnu Severin only offered the big hotels at high prices but that in small towns, perhaps 20 or 30 kilometres (12–19 miles) away, I would be able to find a cheap hotel. This suggested interesting possibilities and we settled upon Vinju Mare. The woman telephoned the bus station; there was a bus at half past three that afternoon.

I set off to explore the town. Down by the river I came upon some huge overgrown ruins which could have been almost anything: there was no one to ask but I think they were the remains of Trajan's bridge. Then I went to the Hotel Parc for a drink. I ordered coffee, brandy and a mineral water and sat on a low stool by a small occasional table. Once settled my attention was drawn to a wispy man in his early forties. He had a three-day growth of stubble, a pointed ravaged face, sharp dark brown eyes and a small black moustache. He was so thin that a good breeze would have blown him across the bar. When I first caught sight of him he was talking with a couple who seemed unwilling listeners but then he caught sight of me, smiled as though we were old friends, winked, nodded, excused himself (much to the couple's relief) and came across to me.

'Deutsch? Französisch? English?'

'English.'

'Ah, English. Good.' We shook hands. 'Have a drink with me. I insist. What is that? A brandy, good. You stay.' And he went to the bar. Intrigued I watched him get into conversation with a man already at the bar and it was this second man who ordered a brandy which he gave to my wispy friend who brought it straight back to me.

'Your brandy.' He had nothing for himself and shook his head at me as though he did not drink. This was interesting. We talked, slowly, his language was limited to a little English, more German, a few phrases in French.

'I can show you a far more interesting place for a drink, down by the Danube, the blue Danube,' he laughed.

We came to a large, open beer garden. He saw someone he knew. 'A footballer,' he said and introduced us. We found a table and ordered drinks and this time he did have one. I paid. What did he do, I asked. 'I am vagabond,' he replied. 'Vagabond,' he repeated with pride. Earlier he had flourished his keyring so I could see attached to it plastic discs with pictures of nude women on them. He was a fixer and I was, or so he hoped, a customer. Coffee and brandy were brought. The footballer went off to meet some friends, promising to return. What would I like him to arrange, to fix for me: girls? Something else?

'What you want? I vagabond, I can fix.' He asked me for a souvenir. I had nothing, no Western cigarettes which is what he really wanted, as did everybody else. So at his continuing insistence and because another thought had struck me I gave him one of the spare passport photographs I always carry with me and he kissed me on both cheeks and ordered two more brandies. I paid.

Periodically during this disjointed conversation he repeated the phrase 'I vagabond.' I was fairly certain he had another occupation. He kept greeting people as they passed; it was a busy place, and he was clearly known to half the customers. Some, I noticed, were less than pleased at his recognition, yet none actually brushed him aside. He managed to convey the impression that he knew both the people and their business. He behaved with a calculated air of discretion. We sat over cognacs until I discovered that the clocks changed an hour at the border and I would only just have time to get to the bus station for my bus to Vinju Mare. I had, in any case, exhausted all the conversational possibilities. I made my excuses. He insisted upon coming with me but only just outside the beer garden; there, away from prying eyes, he asked for 20 lei for his lunch which I willingly gave him. He had been good value. I think he was some kind of border policeman or, rather, informer, in return for which he was left to his dubious devices.

The bus station was like Heathrow in the morning when the overnight jumbo jets arrive together. After lengthy queuing I got a ticket for Vinju Mare but, despite a struggle, found it impossible to get near the three-thirty bus, which was besieged by a fighting crowd. That bus departed bursting at the seams. The next bus went at five so I wandered off to find food but discovered only a sleazy bar serving warm beer. Rumanian beer was almost always warm and weak. At the bus station the second time round I succeeded in fighting my way to the door of one bus only to discover it did not go to Vinju Mare at all. So I fought my way to the door of another bus which was already packed with people standing solid down the centre. However, by dint of pushing–the pack on my back was a useful weapon in such circumstances–and then flourishing my ticket at the driver who stood guarding the door and speaking at him in foreign tongues, I persuaded him that I should somehow be allowed to force my way on board. Other people he was busily turning away. The bus was meant to seat 60 but at least 90 were crammed upon the seats and a further 50 were standing. Somehow I moved about a third of the way down the aisle and lodged my pack at my feet. Still more people forced their way onto the bus until finally the driver shut the door and took his seat. He just had room to manipulate the steering wheel. On the stroke of five we departed. Two girls in the seat by me, one perched on her friend's knees, kept asking me questions in Rumanian. Every time I replied in German they relapsed into delighted laughter.

It was only an hour's journey. A man two people away asked me something; he sounded slightly aggressive and I think he meant me to move down the bus which was a sheer impossibility. I replied in German, 'I do not understand.' At once he became friendly and we conducted a conversation of sorts for the rest of the journey over the heads of the people standing between us. He would reach across, touch my shoulder and draw attention to the scenery. We were passing through wine-growing country, the area which produces Rumanian champagne. From the top of the hill we saw the Danube, a large silver slug winding through the green countryside to disappear again behind trees.

The bus stopped at the Vinju Mare turn-off and I was cheered through the crowd to the door, the only person to descend. I walked about a mile along a pleasant, tree-lined avenue to the centre of the little town. There stood the hotel. A girl and a sleepy youth looked surprised at my appearance. I asked in English, German and finally French for a room. They did not understand so I made the sign for sleep at which they both laughed. The girl led me round to the back and through a huge open bar under a high corrugated roof. There were dozens of tables, half of them occupied. She took me to a hatch from which two more girls served the drinks. There was much laughter when they discovered I wanted a room. They asked for cigarettes. I had been warned to carry Western cigarettes since they are not available in Rumania, except for hard currency in shops reserved for tourists, but since I do not smoke I had forgotten to bring any.

I was watched by an interested audience while I filled in the hotel form. The girl then laboriously copied details from my passport into the register. She asked for a souvenir so I gave her one of my biros since I was without the more desirable cigarettes. My room cost me seven pounds: it had a shower, lavatory and washbasin as well as a balcony overlooking the rooftops of Vinju Mare. I returned to the bar for food. There was only beer to drink but after a while they brought me a cabbage salad, bread, three sausages and three very tasty meatballs. Anyone who came near my table made a smoking sign or said 'cigarettes?' A trio of musicians arrived to play lively music and the bar filled with the Vinju Mare elite.

The bandleader played the accordion and as soon as they took a break he came to my table. He wanted to know where I came from, why I had come to Vinju Mare and where I was going, but all this was leading up to something else: had I cigarettes? As it happened the 'vagabond' at our parting had pressed a packet of Rumanian cigarettes into my hand in return for his lunch money. I had tried one: they tasted like weak imitations of Gauloises and lasted for three puffs. I produced the crumpled pack and offered these to the accordion player. He looked at them in dismay and then laughed, half in disgust and half in admiration at my guile. I kept that pack for a week and produced it on similar occasions until it crumbled apart in my pocket.

A family came to occupy a neighbouring table: a peasant, his wife and a son of about twenty, handsome but slightly simple. The woman, her head in a traditional scarf, peered between her husband and son to get a better look at me. By some deft trick with his hands and without the aid of an opener the son now removed the tops from three beer bottles all together. This feat greatly delighted the mother: her eyes sought mine. Had I seen and approved? I nodded and smiled which redoubled her pleasure.

Much handshaking took place whenever a newcomer joined a table. He might just approach to greet a friend but always he would be introduced all round and shake hands with everyone, the warmth or perfunctoriness of his handshake indicating the degree of friendship or acceptance.

At dusk I went for a walk through the town. Vinju Mare was a crumbling little place; several shop windows were cracked or broken with virtually nothing on display. In the window of the main store were plastic bags of noodles and what looked like dog biscuits. A photographic studio displayed peeling prints of young men and women dressed in fashions at least 20 years out of date. The doors to the cinema were broken. Rising behind trees were grey dilapidated blocks of flats. Nothing looked new, nothing had been painted in a long time, yet there were many trees and sweet-scented roses.

In the outskirts of every village or town I entered in Rumania would be an array of posters: for peace; against war; for socialism; for other things I could not decipher; and, above all, extolling the leader, the fearless Ceauşescu. Vinju Mare had its share of such posters and not all on the outskirts.

Two boys, one about 14, the other 11, followed me round. They approached: Polish, Yugo? Czecho? Deutsch? 'English,' I said. English? They were nonplussed. 'British,' I tried. *British*. Their eyes lit up. 'Cigarettes?' demanded the elder. 'Gummi,' demanded the younger. I shook my head, I had neither. I was not believed. They drifted away.

Along a quiet, pretty, tree-lined avenue with high fences round small gardens I came upon a man supervising another man and a woman as they swept the pavement and street in front of a house. I assumed the house belonged to the man who was so obviously in charge but who were the sweepers–his family, servants, paid workers? Bent over her task the woman worked nonstop. Pigs grunted in back yards and hens squawked. It was very much a peasant town and Rumania was more obviously a peasant country than anywhere else on my trip. The dirt, the poverty, the old-fashioned dresses and the sometimes awesome interest in a stranger were signs of a peasant mentality I had not encountered earlier along the Danube. Invariably I was asked for things and not just cigarettes; the stranger was seen as a source of otherwise unobtainable luxuries.

Near the hotel stood a charming little church with icon-style paint-ings round the top of the walls. The boy who had asked for 'gummi' appeared. 'British,' he said tentatively, then he felt the stuff of my shirt which was of green towelling. 'Car?' he asked. I shook my head, 'bus.' *Bus!* He did not believe me. He called to his friend who was some distance away but the older boy did not have even the few English words the younger had mustered and seemed shy to approach. I tried the door of the church: it was locked. The boy shook his head emphatically as though I ought to have known it would be locked. I said goodbye and headed back to the hotel followed by 'bye bye' and then a second 'bye bye' from the other boy.

The beer garden was crowded and rowdy. I did not want anything else to drink but was keen to observe the local scene and doubted Vinju Mare had much else to offer. A large man, whom I took to be the manager, was controlling a drunk. A man in a beret at a neighbouring table constantly rose to greet newcomers as they walked past: he seemed to know everyone who came in. The band had now dispersed but the accordion player sat at a table with friends and played whatever they requested. An old man sat gloomily contemplating the empty bottles in front of him, he had done well but had now run out of money. Reluctantly he got up to leave when the man in the beret insisted upon giving him another beer and, nothing loath, the old man resumed his seat and his drinking.

Late that night a band went joyfully and noisily through the sleepy town, the trumpets blaring, the big drum banging out a steady beat as the revellers from a wedding finally made their way to the bride-groom's house, oblivious to the lateness of the hour.

Chapter Twenty One

Journey to Calafat

Cocks crowing from one backyard to another set the dogs barking and Vinju Mare woke to a bright, cloudless day. From my hotel balcony I looked down on red roofs and backyards alive with rooting pigs and furiously quacking ducks. The little town was like a great farmyard upon which a village had been mysteriously superimposed. I went to wash but my shower, the basin taps and the lavatory, in collusion with one another, merely hissed back at me like female cats defending their young. I went below in search of water but there was little sign of life except for an old woman carrying a great bucket of water to the men's lavatories. I followed her into the street where she filled her bucket from a hand pump. I came back with her. 'Coffee?' I asked. 'No, no!' came the stern reply. I made signs for shaving water, so she motioned me to wait and from the kitchen brought me a large, long-handled, copper coffee jug full of water. I took this receptacle of precious liquid to my room and performed my toilet.

I sensed a difficult day ahead for it was Sunday and I had no idea how to get to Calafat, my next stop. Once packed I descended again to the large yard at the back which acted as the centre of hotel activity and found the two serving girls of the night before sweeping the floor and taking the chairs down from the tops of the tables. 'Coffee? Breakfast?' I asked. But they just laughed. There would be nothing in that line, I gathered, before midday.

Then I said 'Calafat'. The second girl nodded vigorously. She pointed to my watch, it was then ten past eight, and indicated that there would be a bus at half past eight. 'Down the valley,' and she pointed, 'on the main road.' In fact where I had alighted the day before. Quick, quick, she signalled. So I shot up to my room, grabbed my bags and came down again. Amazingly, another woman in a white coat like a doctor's was standing in the corridor waiting for me: she wanted the key. The two girls, laughing, waved me on my way.

I went at speed up the road–almost a twelve-minute mile–and already the day felt very hot. For the last quarter of a mile I could see the main road ahead, but no bus passed. I got to the road junction with two minutes to spare before the eight thirty deadline. A handful of people were sitting along the wall by the bus stop. They had bundles of luggage, small cases at their feet and the general appearance of those about to travel. 'Calafat?' I asked. 'Oh yes,' they nodded. So I was in time. I removed my pack and relaxed, wandering up and down to cool off after my fast sprint from the hotel.

The little group sitting on the wall looked me over with interest. I asked again to make sure there was a bus to Calafat. They passed a bottle of red wine between them and insisted that I had a drink: relax was the message. So I took a good swig of the wine which was harsh but not unpleasant. Other people drifted up to the bus stop. One important man arrived with two cases but he stood carefully apart from the peasants sitting on the wall.

People tell you what they think you want to hear and I was by no means certain about that bus. So crabwise, coming at it from several angles, I asked different people when the bus for Calafat would appear.

'Of course there are buses for Calafat.'

'Sometimes there are buses.'

'I expect there will be a bus, why not?'

'Perhaps the bus won't come *today*.'

'Who knows?'

I continued my gentle inquiring for 30 minutes. I was offered another swig of the red wine. I was becoming suspicious. I approached the important man with two cases who had stood apart from the crowd all this time. He had a little English although he gave me a look of great suspicion before he replied.

'Yes, of course there will be a bus to Calafat; I myself am going to Calafat.' That did seem to clinch it.

By a quarter past nine I had been told, mainly by signs and with much good-humoured banter: of course there will be a bus; maybe; soon; sometimes; it depends; we are going to Calafat; something usually comes; tomorrow there will be a bus; there is plenty of time; maybe; be patient.

In the light of this range of advice I decided there would be no bus to Calafat. Already the sun burned down harshly and the day threatened to be scorching hot. Meanwhile, a newcomer had come to the bus stop: a youngish man with a small pack. He stood a little apart, downstream as it were of the bus stop, and every time a vehicle passed he tried to hitch a lift. I wandered over and asked him. 'No', he insisted, there would be no bus to Calafat. He was trying to hitch a lift. So I went back to my pack which I put on and the peasants sitting along the wall, their bottle of wine empty, nodded in unison as though they had known all along that this was what I would do. I set off walking. The sign at the edge of the village told me that Calafat was 70 kilometres (43 miles) away.

Micawber-like I decided that something would turn up. I walked, contemplating a perfectly flat plain which stretched for miles on either side of the road. Tall poplar trees zigagging into the distance marked the course of the road across the plain. A few people were coming into Vinju Mare on foot but many more clip-clopped along in open carts drawn by small ponies or donkeys. I greeted people. Some replied with ready warmth, others looked startled, though whether at my greeting or my alien appearance I could not tell. By the time I was well clear of the town the vista of the plain before me looked endless and I began to think grimly of 70 hot kilometres. Then I heard the sound of a heavy vehicle coming up behind me, hooting. I stood to the side of the road and turned as a great lorry jerked to a halt beside me.

The door opened and looking down, gesturing me aboard, was the young man from the bus stop who had been trying to hitch a ride. I climbed up. The driver, a man of about 28, had a tough, humorous, flattened ugly face as though he had tried boxing before his bones had set. He grinned a cheerful welcome and we shook hands. I tried English and German on him only to meet uncomprehending shrugs and laughs. Then we were off. His small daughter sat beside him on top of a box cover over the engine while my friend of the bus stop and I occupied the big leather-covered bench seat of the large comfortable driving cabin. The girl, who was no more than four, had curly black locks and was prettily dressed in blue. Her tiny green glasses and purple-painted finger nails turned her into a demure, miniature woman. She was dressed in her Sunday best. The driver was visiting rather than delivering a cargo. He played his radio loudly; popular Rumanian-style country music.

We had an animated discussion in Rumanian and English, neither side understanding the other. He drove fast, a lord of the road high up in his great truck, swearing aside the peasants in their little horse-drawn carts. The girl became drowsy and the hitcher placed her on top of the engine cover where she promptly fell asleep. The little horse-drawn carts which formed the bulk of the traffic presented a constant hazard for the big lorry, though the driver never diminished his speed. We covered about 30 kilometres (19 miles) before the driver stopped at a village which was his journey's end, so we shook hands and descended. I set off walking once more, this time with the other man beside me. A sign told us that Calafat was 39 kilometres (24 miles) distant.

After no more than half a kilometre my companion halted and pointed to a house across the road; we shook hands and he headed for the house wishing me luck over his shoulder. I got back into my walking stride, contriving wherever possible to walk in the shade of the roadside poplars. In a field a group of peasants, eating bread and raw onions, waved to me and a youth called 'cigarettes?'. They never had any problem with that word. Then I came to a tourist café–signs along the road had proclaimed its excellence for several kilometres–but it was closed and shuttered against the world. Quite a few cars with holiday gear piled on the roofs passed me; these were the wealthier Rumanians, making for the Black Sea Delta. At the bottom of a long steep hill the roadside trees came to an abrupt end and I really felt the full effects of the sun as I walked up to the village at the top. By the time I reached it I was hot, thirsty and hungry.

In a tiny corner shop I bought a bottle of lukewarm beer which I drank straight off. It was a busy little shop visited by a constant stream of people; adults bought bottles of beer to take away with them while children purchased sickly, sticky green sweets. The village straggled along a ridge and about 3 kilometres (2 miles) distant, far below, I glimpsed the Danube. It glinted silver under the hot sun, its wide waters winding lazily across the rich grass of the plain until once more it disappeared into the darker greens of a thick wood. The village street was lined with small trees whose symmetry was broken at strategic intervals by large posters detailing the ceaseless Rumanian struggle for socialism and peace and the dominant role played by comrade Ceauşescu in the pursuit of these goals. Just as I reached the outskirts of the village a great truck thundered along and, encouraged by my earlier lift, I turned to thumb a ride. The big lorry, with an equally large trailer behind, crashed noisily to a halt. The driver motioned me aboard with a grin and asked in Rumanian where I came from before we settled for good-humoured silence.

After a few kilometres we came upon a soldier operating a road check. He had just stopped a truck from the other direction and was busy questioning its driver so we went straight through: 'one at a time' seemed to be the motto. My driver, clearly relieved that he had not been obliged to stop, muttered angrily and twice I caught an unmistakable 'Hitler, Hitler' spoken with venom. We came to a T-junction where he went to the left while the road to Calafat, now 13 kilometres (8 miles) distant, was to the right. I shook an oil-stained hand and once more found myself walking.

After three kilometres (2 miles) I entered another village. By then it was two in the afternoon and I felt really hungry. A sign beckoned me: *bufet!*. I took this to mean food but it was only a pub, flyblown and dirty. Talk came to a stop as I threaded my way through the tables to the bar to ask for a beer. It was mid-Sunday drinking time for the men of the village, as in villages the world over. My pack interested them as did the small bag in which I carried my camera. The host produced an ice-cold beer from the refrigerator in my honour; he opened this and handed it to me (there were no glasses), and I found my way to an empty table.

Someone approached. 'Deutsch?' he asked tentatively.

'English.'

'Car?'

'No, foot.'

'Good heavens.'

They reflected on this fascinating information. One, inevitably, asked for cigarettes. I had none. Another asked what I carried in my small bag; he had picked this up and was judiciously weighing it in his hand.

'Camera.'

Could he see?

'Of course.' I took it out and they passed it round. I have an old Leica. Someone pronounced it German. I confirmed this.

Would I sell it they asked, and how much did I want for it?

'Not for sale!' They laughed.

'We would give a good price,' they said. Then everyone laughed again. One who had acted as spokesman and to whom the others deferred now came to sit at my table. He had tiny scraps of English and German, unconnected phrases which he had picked up somewhere. He went to the bar to bring me back another beer which I did not want; this one was lukewarm but out of politeness I drank some. Then he asked if I was hungry.

'*Mangare?*' he said and made a sign of eating.

'Yes indeed.' I was ravenous by then. But where?

'Come, I show you,' he signed.

He went up to the bar and bought four bottles of beer and then we left together. Outside he placed the beers in the pannier of an ancient bicycle which he pushed along the roadside path while he made smiling comments to me in Rumanian. I realised that he was taking me to his home for lunch; there was unlikely to be anywhere else. We met a woman pushing a cart and stopped for a talk. Then he went to answer the call of nature behind a tree. He led me up a side street away from the main road until we came to the last house. The backyard was dirty, a puddle occupied the middle of it, but a tree offered shelter to a bench and table. I took my pack off and he insisted I should leave my things inside the house, in the best bedroom. The room was very cool and I felt tempted to sleep. I could hear my host telling his wife to prepare a meal. Back in the yard three shy little girls came and in turn, gravely, shook hands with me.

We sat on the bench talking, while noises from the kitchen signalled that food was being prepared. A duck followed by a string of tiny ducklings waddled across the dirt to the puddle and the children disappeared about their business. The wife now appeared with two dishes which she set before us. My host was a small spry man with close-cropped, iron-grey hair; his wife was younger, larger, tending to fat and untidiness, her black hair falling in wisps across her big cheeks. She had brought us two dishes of rice with a chicken leg on each: this, clearly, was their Sunday lunch and she would now go without. 'Soup?' he asked. 'No, this is fine,' I assured him. His wife looked relieved at the shake of my head rather than my words. She herself had begun to shake her head when her husband said 'soup', however he insisted. She turned angrily away and came back reluctantly with a single bowl of soup, the broth in which she had cooked the chicken legs, with some noodles added. She placed this in front of me. I looked at my host: 'But you?' he shook his head. 'It is for you.' His wife went grumpily away. Poor woman, she had hoped to have at least the soup while I was eating her chicken leg but now she would get nothing. I ate every last drop of that soup but felt awful doing so. Only when my bowl was empty did we tackle our rice and chicken. It was a simple enough meal, the best of their week.

When our food was finished my host opened two of the bottles of beer he had brought back from the *bufet* and we settled down to talk. The children came back and he was about to order them away when I said I would take a photograph. He was delighted at this and arranged the three girls in a row–they were aged about eleven, eight and six–but he refused to join the picture himself. I took a photograph and then insisted he joined his daughters for a second shot. I promised to send copies from England. The children left us and painfully, in large script, he wrote his name and address in my notebook. Gradually in the course of a disjointed and difficult conversation I learnt that he had played football for Rumania: at Wembley, where he had met Bobby Moore; in Munich; Mongolia; Bulgaria; and finally Mexico, where he had broken his shoulder, bringing his football career to an end (Col. pl. 14b).

When the beer was finished I went to take my leave. He suggested a rest but I knew that would be fatal. I collected my pack from the house yet when I came out found he had opened the other two beers for a farewell drink. Eventually, reluctant to let me go, he accompanied me back to the main road to see me on my way. Halfway along his own short, dusty street he greeted a pretty young woman who stood in a gateway, holding a baby. I took her picture too. Then we reached the main road. We shook hands and he kissed me on both cheeks and I set off on the final stretch to Calafat. I looked back to wave. He stood to watch me go, his face sad with nostalgia for a wider world, one he had once travelled during his triumphant football career. That was why the others had deferred to him in the *bufet*. Vasili Rosu was his name and back in London I had prints made and sent these to him, so I hope his wife forgave me for eating her Sunday lunch.

My parting from Vasili had been witnessed by two old men, who were sitting on a long bench beneath the thick foliage of trees lining the village street. They eyed me with interest as I passed. Vasili remained standing where we had parted, clearly expecting to answer questions about me. The two old men duly obliged: they called him over to their bench. The last I saw was Vasili holding forth in front of the old men, though what he made of me I do not know.

I had just cleared the village when I heard a horse and cart clip-clopping up smartly behind me (Col. pl. 18). I badly wanted a photograph of one of these peasant vehicles and now had time to get my camera ready. The driver saw what I intended to do and stopped his cart. I took the photograph and he then motioned me to come for a ride. Nothing loath, I dumped my pack in the empty cart and climbed up beside him. We shook hands. He established that I was English, laughed happily at the thought, cracked his whip and we set off along the road to Calafat.

That horse was a splendid creature, full of character. The carter made noises to encourage greater speed; the horse pricked up its ears in a gesture of interest, made more speed for about nine metres (30 ft) then lapsed into the precise rhythm it had previously maintained. The carter cracked his whip though never touched the horse which rolled its head from side to side at the sound, otherwise ignoring the suggestion that it should move faster.

By sign language and finger count he indicated his age: fifty-one. I returned the information, indicating that he had the advantage of me by two years. He laughed happily: we were two of a kind and he pointed first at me and then at himself to make this clear. We had covered about two kilometres when we met a crowd of people spread right across the road. We could hear the fiddling, the singing and laughter as they approached. It was a wedding. The bride, veiled, all in white, walked demurely in the middle, the groom self-conscious rather than happy beside her. We drew to the side to allow them to pass. Bottles of wine were being passed round. I took out my camera for a picture and at sight of it two men came over to ask who I was. My driver explained and we shook hands. One of them went back into the crowd to return with a two-litre bottle of red wine. We each took a long draught and then shook hands again. When I went to hand the bottle of wine back the men insisted we keep it. The wedding procession, meanwhile, had gone on and the two men hurried away to catch up. To the dwindling sound of fiddles scraping thinly in the hot afternoon air, my companion flicked his reins and cracked his whip and we were off. I placed the bottle of wine–it had no cork–on the floor between my feet to hold it steady. I never got a photograph.

In my naivety I thought that at least my kindly carter would be left with a large bottle of best wedding wine as a reward for his courtesy to me. I was, of course, hopelessly wrong. It is amazing what you can drink, without hurrying, over eight kilometres (5 miles). He offered me a cigarette. 'No thanks'. He slowed down to light his and gestured to the wine. I offered it to him but he insisted I drink first. Then he followed suit and we clip-clopped up to speed again. A little further on he slowed again, gestured at the bottle and once more we had a drink. This pleasant process, interspersed by attempts at Rumanian-English conversation aided by signs, continued to Calafat.

On the outskirts of Calafat we passed a mile-long queue of cars waiting at a garage for their monthly allowance of petrol (a full tank). The spectacle delighted my companion who waved his whip, stood up to laugh and gestured at his horse smartly eating up the road into town. He only slowed down as we came along a broad attractive street which brought us into the centre of the town. We had another drink of wine. Was I going across into Bulgaria, and could he take me to the ferry. But no. I wanted a hotel. Fine! He cracked his whip once more and shortly thereafter drove me into the large open space beside the Hotel Calafat. It was the town's best, an A-class hotel. I invited him to have a beer with me but he had to go about his business, so we finished the wedding wine between us, shook hands, then he waved his whip and clip-clopped away.

The Calafat Hotel charged 350 lei (£20.50) a room so I walked along to the Hotel Dunarea which charged only 129 lei (£7.50) a night. There was a young woman in the reception and between us we spoke a little German, a little French, even a few words of English. Yes, she could let me have a room: a moment. She opened a vast ledger and slowly, painstakingly, examined long lines of entries, page after page. She flipped the huge pages back and forth, a puzzled frown on her face, to find nothing. She took down a second, equally formidable ledger from the shelf above her head and began a similar examination of that. Still nothing. She thought I was getting impatient and looked up: 'Do not worry, I shall find something.' Full of excellent wedding wine I was not in the least impatient, but happy to wait and watch her search. She returned to the first ledger, checking slowly and carefully across double pages of entries, eight columns to a page. Just what all the columns stood for baffled me. If the size of the ledgers was any guide that hotel was an exceedingly busy place. At last she ran a room to earth. Then followed the slow process of entering my details, also across a double page. My passport and currency form were scrutinised, their information noted. When finally she had entered everything to her satisfaction she gave me a key. I was about to go when she held me back with a gesture: 'money', she said, as though I intended to cheat them and she turned to laugh at the placid young man who all this time had sat motionless and expressionless at her side. In Rumania payment was always in advance but I had forgotten. I paid for a night's lodging and went to my room. I needed a rest.

Chapter Twenty Two

Rumanian Trains

Calafat was a pleasant town of many trees and some interesting architecture. The dining room was the most elegant feature of my hotel. The chairs were large and comfortable, covered in light green material. Every table was elegantly laid with a fresh damask cloth and decorated by a single rose in a glass. The woman in charge was quick, friendly, efficient.

'Soup?' I asked. There was no soup.

'What is there to eat?'

'Cutlets,' came the reply; so I had the inevitable cutlets. The term 'cutlets' was invariably used in Rumania; it covered whatever meat was on offer. On this occasion I was given a small tender steak, potatoes, beans and peas. I had a bottle of red wine which was automatically accompanied by a bottle of mineral water.

At the beginning of my meal I sat in a solitary state. Loud music came from the hotel's inner courtyard where people sat drinking. Three young boys entered the dining room from the door onto the street. They did not see me and one placed a tricorn folded napkin on his head; then, giggling, they were about to go when from my corner I shouted, foreignly: the boy hastily put down the napkin and the three departed.

I was constantly being asked for souvenirs and my waitress now followed convention. She wanted cigarettes but I had none. Then a man who spoke some German came over to talk with me; I think he was the local secret policeman checking on me–Rumania employs more secret policemen than any other east European country–so I asked about buses to Corabia the next day. He was certain one went at eight in the morning and gave me instructions how to find the bus station. In the event he was proved wrong; there was no bus to Corabia.

The food was cheap in the hotel; people came to buy bottles of wine or beer to take away. The door between the dining room and the main part of the hotel became stuck and could not be opened from either side, so that guests wanting a meal had to go out into the street and then enter the dining room through the street door and diners who had finished their meal had to go back to their rooms the same way. Much of Rumania, it seemed to me, was suitable country in which to play out a Graham Greene novel; the readiness of things not to work coupled with a fading decor of genteel decay was emphasised by the constant suspicion of secret policemen or informers casually going about their doubtful professions.

After dinner I walked down to the Danube where big lorries were manoeuvring into line for the early morning ferry across to Bulgaria. The night was pitch dark, though across the wide expanse of the river an occasional light from the town was reflected, glistening and shimmering back from the rippling Danube. Almost everything in Rumania closes at ten in the evening and most lights dimmed at the same time. But the dark cloudless sky now carried the hint of a moon to come and, sitting on a bank high above the millpond-smooth waters, I realised that I had passed all the dramatic gorges: now huge, stately and steady the Danube flowed out to the distant Black Sea which was still 1,000 kilometres (620 miles) away. For some time I had been conscious of the approaching throb of an engine and then, blacker than the river, a long irregular shape loomed in mid-stream: six barges were travelling steadily through the night. As they came level with the ferry the tug sounded its single eerie hoot, like a great river owl. Long after the barges had passed, ripples from their mid-stream wash began to lap the bank below me until gradually the river lapsed back into its mood of silent peace.

Trajan founded the ancient province which became Rumania. He was the last Roman Emperor to have a 'forward policy' and after constructing the great road along the Danube, carved into the rocks approaching the Iron Gates, he crossed the river in force to conquer the Daci and their King Decebalus in 106 AD, adding the final major province of Dacia to Rome's huge empire. The Emperor Aurelian withdrew the Roman garrison from Dacia in 275 but Roman influence was to remain strong for centuries afterwards and today frequent references to Trajan and Dacia are to be found in the names of streets and squares.

I experienced a night of insomnia and became aware of the silence of Calafat. There were almost no night noises in this town: no traffic, no late revellers, no doors banging, nothing. I lay for half the night listening. Once I heard a far-off lorry and once, softly tapping, someone entering the next room in my corridor. He or she was obliged to knock three times before gaining entry. Once, much later, a cat screeched but its screech was a subdued affair as though it, too, realised that noise was forbidden. There followed an answering yowl, equally subdued. Then, in the early hours, my next-door neighbour's visitor–he or she–went softly away. Only with the light of day was there a return of sounds: cocks crowing and then birds heralding the coming day.

Lavatories and hygiene are not a subject upon which I wish to dwell but I cannot pretend that Rumania excelled itself in this regard. Some hotel lavatories were unspeakable and I found myself retching in their vicinity. More than once I constipated myself rather than use the lavatory. Many Rumanians using hotels do not appear to have been house-trained.

Early the next morning I watched the great lorries drive onto the ferry and took pictures of the Danube, here wide and grand. I found there was no bus to Corabia; instead I would have to take a train to Craiova and then begin again. I returned to the hotel for breakfast then, after exploring the town, I collected my pack from the hotel and went to catch the midday train. The waitresses from the restaurant waved me on my way.

I grew fond of Rumanian trains in which I frequently travelled. They had character, a hint of a more distinguished past, even if they now looked scruffy and unkempt. They did keep time. On this occasion the train was already standing in the station at Calafat to begin its journey. The seats were a mixture of leather and wood, the carriages had once seen better days and had also, once, been cleaner. I found a place in a compartment with a drunk smelling of garlic but he slept on peacefully. A tiny peasant woman came into the compartment. She was so small that she was obliged to heave herself up into her corner seat and then her feet no longer reached the floor but swayed uncontrollably with the rhythm of the train for the whole journey to Craiova. This took two and a half hours since the train stopped at every wayside station to take on passengers until its corridors were packed solid with people.

Craiova is a large busy city. Outside the railway station I asked directions of a friendly, helpful man who did not understand a word I said. So, peremptorily, he called over a youth who spoke a little English and they jointly directed me to a hotel. The Hotel Jiul was the biggest, the best, the most expensive and as far as I could gather, the only hotel in town. I was not prepared to search further: I wanted a shower and my own lavatory.

On my evening stroll I discovered a huge church behind high railings hidden by a dense jungle of bushes; the entrances were locked and barred. Then from a nearby ivy-covered building I heard the plaintive notes of a solitary flute. This building was a museum, the flautist the doorman. He interrupted his playing to tell me the museum was closed but I lingered in the porch to listen when he resumed his haunting refrain.

I took my evening meal on a veranda overlooking the crowded courtyard of the Jiul Hotel. That courtyard was a popular place where people jostled, joked and ordered endless replenishments of beer. Groups at adjacent tables argued with each other as to whose turn it was to be served next by the overworked staff. A woman came round selling lottery tickets. These were threatened like keys on a great ring which she swished round endlessly to attract attention as she weaved her way among the tables. I had the usual discussion about cutlets. There was no menu: a paper shortage. No soup. I asked for wine. 'Red or black?' my waitress inquired. 'What is black wine?' I asked. 'It is very good,' she told me. 'Rumania's best.' So I ordered a bottle which turned out to be champagne. It had a black label.

Even in Rumania, which is far from being a wealthy country, the car has become a problem. Often when I asked directions people assumed I was travelling by car. When I inquired about buses or trains they looked in amazement and asked, 'But your car?' They were astonished that I should be travelling on foot. Such revelations were fun for me.

In most hotel rooms little complimentary pincushions, complete with needle and thread, act as a reminder that time seems to have stopped 30 or 40 years earlier. The custom is an elegant, old-fashioned one reminiscent of an age in keeping with the generally decayed decor of Rumanian hostelries. I spent a day visiting Craiova's museums and galleries and discovered that the museum of the flute player specialised in local history. Its displays began with Trajan and the story of Dacia and came through to the Communist revolution and the achievements of Comrade Ceauşescu.

Fighter jets flashed low over the city sky: ever alert, I thought, to safeguard the revolution from the West, a mirror image of NATO jets I had seen on earlier stretches of my journey.

At the railway station I purchased a ticket for Corabia and then repaired to the busy station buffet for a beer. I had to queue. Women collected the large dirty glasses from all over the buffet and crowded these upon the counter in front of another woman whose only function was to serve beer. She would seize one of these dirty glasses mechanically, swill it round once in a bowl of greasy water, draw beer into it and plonk it down on the counter in front of the next customer. It was not hygienic but the draught beer tasted better than the awful weak brew from bottles which was my normal fare. I have long adopted the rule that when in Rome do as the Rumanians do and apart from the Danube fish I had the misfortune to consume in Yugoslavia, I had no stomach troubles the length of my trip.

Rumanian trains look as though they like being dirty. Not even token gestures towards cleaning have been made: the sills are thick coated in dust, the windows filthy with grime so that it is almost impossible to see out. The plastic walls of the compartments ought to be easy to wash down but feature dirt stains which have been there so long that they have taken on the character of decorations and lay claim to permanence, so that a regular traveller would be able to recognise a particular compartment by its designs. The railways were much used. There were double-decker trains made in East Germany which were employed on short-haul commuter journeys. At stations ancient railway staff came along the tracks tapping the wheels of the stationary trains with long-handled hammers. The journey to Caracal, my first stop, was over flat dusty plains.

I had two hours between trains at Caracal so walked into the centre of town, passing on my way a charming little church with outside frescoes, all peeling, but as usual its doors were firmly locked. Half the town seemed to be under the hammer with massive demolition in progress. At least the trains kept to their timetables, although my next one also specialised in dirt. Nearly all the travellers were peasant farmers. Covertly I inspected two men in my compartment: two peasants with thick-fingered hands, their forearms massive from a lifetime heaving hay. One had a bovine face totally devoid of intelligence, but in the features of the other could be detected a little hope. As before we stopped at every wayside station and weaved our way over the same flat, dry, endless countryside.

When anybody left the compartment, which was always full, the space would at once be taken by someone from the crowded corridor. One such replacement was a huge doddering man with a great stomach hanging over his belt in front and a huge bottom sticking out behind. His face was covered with two days' stubble of dark beard, his close-cropped hair stood up in surprise. He carried a massive walking stick and had huge flabby arms which quivered with a sort of Parkinson's disease. He was afflicted with a permanent rasping wheeze.

He was followed into the compartment by a matriarch; no other word describes that woman. She wore a bright blue dress, a silver filigree headscarf, a thin gold chain and medallion and a fine gold watch. Her hair under the scarf was pure white. Her hands were large and strong with thick, powerful fingers, her wrists were thicker than those of many men, her forearms massive, her biceps rounded and firm, her calves bulges of powerful muscle. In her youth she must have been a match for most men and plenty would not have been able to stand up to her even now. She must have been about 65 and possessed a serene, confident, handsome face. She would have ruled any roost where she came to rest.

At Corabia North I asked the assembled peasants whether I should get out but was assured that another Corabia station was just down the line. My query startled them into renewed interest in my presence. When we arrived I headed for the centre of town but saw no sign of a hotel, so I asked a man directions in English, German and French, although the only word which registered was 'hotel'. There was only one, he signalled, and insisted on leading me to it. We returned towards the station; I had missed the correct turn. I invited him for a drink but he declined. The hotel was dilapidated though with pretensions to a grander past, which was the normal and predictable state of affairs.

I had a long discussion about rooms (in sign language) with the receptionist. She told me I must share with two others which I did not want to do but I took the room anyway and had it to myself for no one else appeared. It was quite clean and included a washbasin and cold water; the lavatories were unusable.

When I went to the restaurant for supper I was not permitted to eat there. Word of my status both as a guest and foreigner had been passed on, and the waitress who spoke some French led me to a deserted private room where I was obliged to eat alone. It was a small, dark, wood-panelled room and the entire space was filled with an oval-shaped table surrounded by ten tall-backed dining chairs. The table was covered with a great white damask cloth and was elegantly set for ten, each place laid with two knives, two forks, three glasses and a white napkin.

My meal consisted of brandy and mineral water, bread and salad, veal cutlets (very good), potatoes, cheese and olives. There was no wine so I was reduced to bottled beer which, for a change, was cold. Although she knew a few French phrases my waitress and I relied upon sign language and got on famously doing so. The room was intentionally exclusive–but for whom? A large card on the centre of the table announced in red and blue: RESERVE–*autotourist*. But the autotourist party had not materialised, there was only me. There was no coffee. 'It is *good*?' asked my waitress carefully, having slipped off to look up the phrase. I felt like a nineteenth-century English lord touring the Continent and being kept safely away from peasant riffraff. Food in Rumania was often in short supply but the Rumanians made up for this by the panache with which they served the shortfall.

In the rapidly gathering dusk I walked along a high embankment that overlooked a broad meadow beside the Danube. Everywhere I came upon gaggles of geese being driven home for the night, sitting in huddles at the corners of streets, waddling and hissing when taken by surprise. Down by the water's edge I found the river was much faster flowing than it had appeared from above: a swift, steady current bearing silt endlessly eastwards.

Nowhere else have I seen so many men with long straight noses. Back at the hotel I went into the main bar where originally I had tried to eat and there I had a final beer. The bar was full and I watched Corabia's nightlife: or rather, until ten o'clock life, for then everything closes down as though in observance of a wartime curfew. At the next table two young men, the proud owners of motorcycles, were the envy of their friends.

Chapter Twenty Three

State Farms

From Corabia to Turnu Măgurele was 30 kilometres (18.5 miles) and I set off at seven in the morning knowing it would be useless to wait in expectation of any breakfast. For some distance out of the town the road looked down from a height upon a lush green flood-plain beside the Danube; this was dotted with ponds and alive with geese whose gaggles and formations criss-crossed it, wandering in clusters which managed to maintain a sort of disordered orderliness. At one point I looked down upon the diminutive figure of a shawled peasant woman, back bowed, scurrying along with fixed determination as she drove a gaggle before her: to better pastures or to market?

This stretch of road passed through rich farmland. I came level with a huge pig farm just as a truck disgorged its complement of about 20 men who headed towards it for the day's work. The neat rows of sties lay 200 metres (656 ft) back from the road and the slightest breeze wafted the stench across my path. There were no hedges on that road though trees marked its course for miles across the plain.

Peasants in their donkey carts headed for Corabia and most returned my greetings while some greeted me first. With my pack on my back I must have seemed an unfamiliar sight. After nine kilometres (five and a half miles) I came to a village but saw no sign of a place offering food or refreshment. The day was strangely dull and though there were no clouds there was no sun either. It was stifling, preparing for a storm.

Huge combine harvesters were at work in the fields and distant lines of workers bent over hoes or carried out other back-breaking tasks. There were more women than men in that meadow while lookout soldiers occupied high wooden watchtowers which rose gaunt and menacing out of the flat fields: on the lookout but for what? Agricultural saboteurs? Or were they just guards in a state

156

that takes nothing for granted? Once at the roadside I passed a woman of about 30 giving a group of older women their working orders for the day. These older peasant women, in thick and heavy clothes despite the heat, looked as though they had been born working in the fields. They stood listlessly round their mentor, resting on their hoes, the dull expressions of their faces blank to her pep talk and instructions: she, it was clear, was not going to break her back doing such work. Their lives would be hard by any standards and all the farm workers I saw had a tough, weathered appearance and were old before their time.

The little carts passed me all day long as I tramped towards Turnu Măgurele and I saw many cast-off horseshoes. This stretch of plain beside the Danube is one of the most productive areas of the country. I came to a checkpoint where a lorry was drawn up, its driver talking with the soldier on duty. Both men had watched me approach along the open road and as I drew level we exchanged greetings before soldier and driver in unison asked: 'Cigarettes?' 'Alas no,' I said, and shrugged. 'English?' They showed their surprise.

It is curious how you can walk near a river, not necessarily in view of it yet always aware of its presence. I suppose on this particular walk the nature of the landscape helped. The Danube was to my right, though usually the huge fields of the state farms lay between me and its course. At times I could see trees or lines of bushes marking its bank but at others nothing–just a fading away of the landscape, for by then the river was well over one kilometre wide. Later, as I approached Turnu Măgurele under a sky that was shimmering with thunderous intent, the hills of Bulgaria loomed purple-grey eight kilometres (five miles) away, where they descended precipitately to the river's shore. The Rumanian plain ends abruptly, cut off by the Danube, and on the southern bank a more rugged terrain at once rises steeply from the river.

Turnu Măgurele was an interesting town. I located what I think was the only hotel and had a couple of watery beers to quench my thirst followed by a lunch of sausages. When I paid the waiter I also tipped him, at which the two men sharing my table protested that he had cheated me. I do not think he had but they assumed I did not understand the money and since the thought appeared to give them considerable pleasure I did not undeceive them.

I found Rumanians relaxed about strangers. When first I presented myself at the reception I was told a room would cost me 350 lei (£21); I reacted with horror and protested it was too much. As usual I had to pay in advance but had only traveller's cheques which the hotel did not change, so I left my pack and went to the bank, to find it had just closed. This frustration paid off, however, for on my return the receptionist said I could pay in the morning and that my room would now only cost me 240 lei (£14), a reduction of a third. I think the pack had persuaded her that I was not a Western capitalist with money to spare and the price had come down accordingly. Just as I completed the lengthy registration formalities a furious thunderstorm crashed upon us and the curious dull day of my walk exploded in thunder and lightning followed by torrential rain.

The bar of that hotel was patronised exclusively by men and that evening I noticed the receptionist pointing me out to the waiter who had served me at lunchtime. As a result I got more attentive service though I had not complained. I shared my table with an army major. We tried conversation but achieved only good-humoured nonsuccess. He had a long wait for service so I offered him a glass of wine from my bottle but he excused himself by indicating that he was driving; when eventually service did come he had a Pepsi. A lottery man came round jangling his ring and the major had several tries, each ticket giving him another chance. I watched this process bemused and when a second lottery man appeared decided to have a go myself. I held my small change on my palm and he selected a five-lei piece. I took a ticket and asked the major to read it for me. He burst out laughing: not only had I won nothing, I had to give the lottery man a further ten lei. Both were vastly amused at this result, the only time I ever ventured my luck with a lottery.

When I sought breakfast in the morning the restaurant was closed but the receptionist took me to the kitchen and spoke with the cook. 'All is taken care of,' she said and a big fat man led me up a back flight of stairs to a locked door. This he opened to admit me to a splendid dining room. All the tables were laid with shining white cloths, elegantly shaped napkins and gleaming glasses. The dining chairs, armed and capacious, were of green upholstery. 'Five minutes,' he said and left me in solitary splendour. I was getting used to such treatment: deserted but ready-laid dining rooms appeared to be a Rumanian speciality.

He reappeared in exactly five minutes to place before me a huge omelette, a large baked tomato, two big sausages, six toasted bread rolls and a bottle of sparkling green mineral water. He came back a little later with a pot of tea. I ate this splendid meal in silence and since more often than not I failed to get any breakfast at all, I determined to do justice to this large yet tasty offering. When finally I left I met the big cook shepherding a portly, well-dressed woman up the stairs, presumably to partake of an equally solitary repast.

I went to change traveller's cheques at the bank. This was an old-fashioned building surrounded by railings and trees. At the entrance an elderly uniformed guard, armed with revolver, respectfully inquired my business before escorting me inside. There was a high hall down either side of which opaque-glass wicket windows gave visual access to rooms where business was transacted. Customers remained in the hall where leather seats ran back to back down the centre until summoned to one of the wickets. The porter escorted me to the first glass wicket and tapped. A woman opened this, heard my request and directed me to a second wicket. My guard continued to accompany me. Here an elderly clerk thumbed slowly, carefully through the traveller's cheques which I had presented to him and then retired to his desk. He took out a thick ledger which he consulted laboriously. Exchange rates, I wondered? He took his ledger to the window at the far side of the office and peered at my cheques, one at a time. He looked up to see me at the open wicket, came over and gently closed this in my face so I sat down. The first 15 minutes passed.

Two well-dressed men, not accompanied by the guard, now came to tap at my wicket which the elderly clerk opened. He listened to their request, pointed to me over their shoulders and then left them. Courteously they turned to me and we chatted in snatches of tongues. They realised there was a problem and sat talking together with resignation. This time the clerk had left the glass wicket half open and unobtrusively I pushed it wider. My clerk was back at the window under a fading poster of the young Ceauşescu and now he was thumbing through a different-sized ledger, periodically referring to my traveller's cheques. I had given him £100—three twenties and four tens. He was joined by another elderly clerk and they had a consultation. The second clerk disappeared to return clutching a large magnifying glass: perhaps they were checking watermarks for forgery? By now 30 minutes had passed.

Meanwhile somewhat more brisk banking business was being transacted at the other wickets in the old hall and the two men who earlier had come to my window had moved elsewhere. The clerk returned to his desk, again closing the glass window on me. I sat back to wait but someone else came to the window for service; he, however, was dealt with by a woman who until then had been out of sight. She left the wicket open. By this time my clerk was back at the window with his elderly companion, the ledger, the magnifying glass and my cheques. Finally he came to the wicket and showed me my three £20 traveller's cheques: the serial numbers were not in sequence, had I the one which belonged in the middle? I referred to my wallet and luckily did have it, although for some reason they had got out of order. Much relieved the clerk took the cheque I offered and returned the out-of-sequence one to me. Forty minutes had now passed.

At last the clerk inserted papers in triplicate in an ancient typewriter; one by one the details of my traveller's cheques were noted–by then I thought he might have known them off by heart. This done he came into the hall and courteously invited me to follow him to a grille on the other side, through which he handed the typed orders to a large smiling woman. 'Will you please sign?' and he handed me my cheques for counter-signature. Then through her grille the woman handed me marvellous crisp, brand-new lei notes, the first such I had handled. The clerk extracted my copy from his triplicated record of the exchange and handed it to me. The entire transaction had taken exactly one hour and six minutes. I felt the clerk deserved a reward so, gravely, I took his hand in mine and shook it solemnly.

The centre of Turnu Măgurele lies five kilometres (three miles) from the ferry across the Danube to Bulgaria. Near the point of the ferry a huge factory belches and splutters its fumes over the countryside, its stark outlines a dramatic, polluting presence on the banks of the river. A breeze was stirring the water into tiny horses right across to Bulgaria more than three-quarters of a mile distant. At this point the Danube is both a major highway and a formidable military obstacle, one of the great natural divides of Europe.

My next destination was the large river port of Giurgiu. After consultation with the receptionist I discovered I could only get there by train. The station did not sell tickets for Giurgiu and I was referred to an office in town. My friendly receptionist offered to come with me to the ticket bureau situated in the post office near the hotel. I was glad she came, for Giurgiu turned out to be complicated. It was not far in a direct line but the only way by train was to travel three sides of a quadrilateral whose base was the Danube. A stern-faced, grey-haired woman in railway uniform sold tickets at the special railway counter and I noticed my receptionist became stern too, referring to me as the *Tovarich Breetish tourist*. She wrote out for me the names of the two towns where I had to change trains, and the times. Together we returned to the hotel. Proudly my guide asked whether I liked their town; I assured her I did.

The train was crowded but eventually I found an almost empty compartment though people were standing in the corridor. I took a seat opposite an old man who asked me something to which I replied in English. A well-dressed man of about 35 who was standing in the corridor turned to ask in good English, 'Is there anything wrong?' He sounded aggressive but I realised that he was merely shy at using his English. The ticket collector appeared and only then did I realise that I had taken a seat in a first-class carriage. He indicated this forcibly. 'Can I pay the difference?' I asked and took out my wallet, but at this he looked outraged and went away. First class was comfortable but as dirty as the rest. I had to change trains at Rosiori de Vede where I went to check the information board; the English-speaking man followed me from the train. At my elbow he indicated that I should take the six thirty train to Bucharest and, since he was also waiting for that, I suggested we should pass the time over a drink. 'If we can find anything,' he replied dubiously; however, there was a flourishing beer garden just outside the station. My companion insisted that he would get the drinks and I sat at a little table in the hot sun until he returned with four large glasses of draught beer, two each.

I had an interesting talk with Dudu. After he had satisfied himself that I was a passing stranger and posed no danger he relaxed to become expansive, happy with the opportunity to talk in English about things which must normally have been taboo. We spoke principally of economics. He was the agent of a major British company and despite his excellent English he had never been to Britain. Even if the company offered to pay his expenses he doubted whether he would be allowed to go: this led him on to describe the obstacles facing a Rumanian who wishes to emigrate. We tried to compare British and Rumanian salaries but this proved difficult. The average monthly salary in Rumania was about 2,500 lei (£150) and the range varied between 2,000 (£120) and 3,000 (£175). Dudu suggested that the real value of a professional salary for a year was no more than $800 (American) while tourist exchange rates were greatly inflated.

Dudu had taken his family on a two-week holiday to the Black Sea Delta which had cost him 7.000 lei (£410): this was nearly three times the average monthly salary (Col. pl. 20). He said that wages and salaries generally allowed people to just get by without luxuries. In his case, he said, he needed to speak English for his job but no English books or papers were available. I asked him about the rich farming area through which I had walked. He became quite heated and scathing about the way workers on state farms were treated. He agreed the area was rich agricultural land but said the peasants who worked it were not allowed to earn more in a good year while all the best crops went for export.

I asked him about Rumanian national dishes–food on this part of the trip had become something of a preoccupation with me–and he described a speciality which he promised to make for me if I contacted him in Bucharest. I asked about hotels in the capital and he said he would not dare to offer me a room himself, for someone would inform on him. The authorities insisted that visitors should stay in hotels in order to make them spend their hard currency–also, no doubt, so that they did not have the opportunity to influence their hosts. We went over my map together and he told me of the

161

beauty of the Delta where he liked to take his family whenever he could afford to do so. We returned to the station for the Bucharest train. This conversation saddened me: not so much because Dudu did not have Western things but because he so obviously longed for them.

The Bucharest train was a crowded express; I stood with Dudu in a first-class corridor. The run to Videle where I had to change again took a mere 30 minutes. From the window I glimpsed yet more geese. I asked Dudu what happened to the geese: were they to be found on sale in Rumanian shops or did they all go for export? Evading my question he answered, 'Geese are very good for Christmas.' The door to the first-class compartment immediately behind us was open and from the corner of my eye I noticed that one of its occupants had picked up my English and was curious. He was a fat-faced young man and had earplugs and a cassette machine–an unusual sight in Rumania–attached to his belt: it was a good one too. He came out into the corridor where, arrogantly, he moved a more humble man aside so that he could stand next to Dudu and myself. He lit a cigarette. He had come out to join our conversation but had made the mistake of not removing his earplugs first and to do so now would be too obvious. He smoked his cigarette with an air of concentration while he thought out his next move. He was a fixer of a type to be met all over the world. In a society where most people were lean he was fat; he was well dressed where most were dowdy; he flaunted his electronic gadget where few had anything to flaunt. Smooth-faced with smug complacency, he represented the sort who will survive anywhere in any situation because they always know how to ingratiate themselves with those in power and become useful to them. He returned to his seat to remove his earplugs, then came back into the corridor. I had deliberately engaged Dudu in a further conversation about geese. The fat man was not going to find out anything from me. Then the train began to slow down and I asked my companion whether we were approaching Videle and this he confirmed. The fixer, misinterpreting my interest and assuming I was going on to Bucharest, said, 'Yes, only Videle, we don't get to Bucharest for another half-hour.' I raised a polite eyebrow, then shook hands with Dudu and picked up my pack ready to leave the train. The fixer's face betrayed his chagrin: he had been all set to force his way into our conversation, though what he imagined was in it for him I do not know. I suppose he acted upon principle.

With half an hour to wait in Videle I found an astonishingly clean, smart *bufet* where a few people were queuing for a drink. I had brandy and mineral water and watched the antics of a tiny black kitten until my train came. This turned out to be the cleanest in which I had yet travelled: open-plan carriages with brown leather seats. The train was not full and I had a section to myself. I sat watching the flat plain as we headed back to the Danube. As we approached stations men or women in the blue and orange uniform of the railway would stand stiff outside signal boxes holding up yellow flags for the train to proceed. They looked awkward, posed, like extras in a film about railways in Tsarist Russia.

We did not reach Giurgiu until nine thirty and from experience I knew I had no chance of an evening meal. In the rapidly fading light I walked to the centre of the town along a street of curious old-style architecture until I came to a large square. There I inquired the whereabouts of two hotels; one of the first and the other of the second class. By then it was dark and street lighting was minimal. I found the second-class hotel; it appeared more sleazy than I liked and could only offer shared accommodation in a room with two others. I declined this offer and set off in search of the first-class hotel. This was fully booked but the receptionist told me of a motel three kilometres (two miles) distant, near the ferry to Bulgaria. Back in the square a drunk gave me exact directions to the motel in slow, perfect German. I decided to take a taxi. I had seen several pass and stood waiting with my pack on my back. presenting an obvious target. Sure enough a voice came from the darkness behind me: 'Taxi?' A man materialised. 'Yes.' I named the motel. He nodded and beckoned me to follow him into a dark unlit street where stood a battered old car. He gestured towards it. He was certainly not a licensed taxi-driver. I got in and after some difficulty he managed to start the engine and off we careered at speed. I lost my sense of direction in the dark; street lighting everywhere was minimal (evidence of national economy) but before long we drove through a line of parked vehicles. A soldier shouted at us but my driver took no notice and drew up before the motel. 'How much?' I asked. He wanted 100 lei which I felt to be exorbitant. I fished in my pocket and gave him 30 lei and he laughed good-humouredly at his defeat, we shook hands and I went into the motel.

A young man with good English was at reception. The motel was full but I had no intention of leaving and nowhere to go anyway. 'Food?' I inquired. He pointed me towards the dining room but without conviction. He was quite right: no food, they were closed. 'Drink?' No drink. But after a good deal of badgering I managed to purchase two bottles of green mineral water which the man in the kitchen agreed to open for me. At least these would quench my thirst during the night which I now foresaw as a long and difficult one.

I returned to the receptionist but there were no rooms: the motel was full of school children, three or four to a room, on a holiday

163

trip to Bulgaria. They would cross by ferry the next morning. If I came the next day, he said, there would be plenty of room. 'There is nowhere else and I want a room tonight,' I told him. He shrugged. In a corner of the reception area were some large, comfortable-looking armchairs while on the other side of the reception a happy group chatted together on a big couch. I asked if I could sit out the night on one of the big armchairs. Why not! So I settled as best I could in an armchair with my two bottles of green water on a table beside me, my pack at my feet. I was comfortable and thought I might not pass too bad a night. A crowd of school children, early teenagers, now came in and for the next half-hour the reception was in chaos until they had been escorted to their rooms.

Then the mosquitoes came. I loathe mosquitoes. They search me out anywhere in the world. One of my nightmares consists of that zizzling drone as they home in on their target. These were large, the battle became constant. I sat up and tried to make conversation with the group across the lobby. Then the receptionist 'discovered' that they did after all have a room at 300 lei (£17.60). I think he had done a deal with the teachers to double up some children. By then I was so mosquito-bitten I would have paid anything. Another 20 minutes passed while I signed the register and the receptionist recorded my passport and currency details. I asked about a boat down the Danube to discover that one of the big tourist steamers from Vienna had arrived that evening. If I got to the docks by seven the next morning I should get a passage to Cernavodâ. Greatly cheered by this information I retired to an indifferent room after arranging to be called at six. When I left in the morning the receptionist, covered in a blanket, occupied the chair in the mosquito corner where I had briefly made my bed the night before. It was his usual nightly spot and perhaps that had also spurred him to find me a room.

Chapter Twenty Four

Bucharest

Shortly after six the next morning I was heading for the centre of Giurgiu and the docks. The trucks outside the motel were in line, revving up to cross the ferry into Bulgaria; the checkpoint was nearby. From the centre of town I became part of a growing number of workers heading for the docks. The docks are extensive with bustling quays, cranes and wharves crowding the waterfront; for after Constanţa, Giurgiu is Rumania's largest port trading in petroleum from the nearby oilfields, salt and grain. Giurgiu is the principal centre for commerce with Bulgaria and lies a mere 64 kilometres (40 miles) southwest of Bucharest. Somewhere in this region, probably upstream of Giurgiu towards the river Yantra which flows into the Danube from Bulgaria, Alexander the Great crossed the river in 335 BC on his campaign against the Getae before he set off to conquer Asia. The port is believed to have been founded by the Genoese. It was destroyed by the Russians in their war against Turkey in 1829 then recaptured by the Turks in 1854. The Giurgiu oilfields were bombed by the Allies in 1944 before the advancing Russians captured the town in August of that year.

I had no idea where the tourist steamer would be. I picked upon a group of three well-dressed men coming along behind me in the hope that one of them would speak some German. They turned out to be Russian technicians working on a Soviet project and all three roared with laughter when they realised that I was English. They stood round me repeating the few phrases they knew 'very good' and 'thank you', but they pointed the way–or so I thought.

What I came to, however, was a Rumanian naval vessel. Petty officers were marshalling sailors for some task and one of them directed me back the way I had come. I looked in dismay at the endless docks spreading the other way. Time was passing and if the tourist steamer was at the other end of the docks I needed transport.

At that moment a man drove by in a car and I flagged him down. To my surprise he stopped but when I turned and he saw the pack on my back he became nervous. I think he believed I had jumped ship and was smuggling, an impression reinforced by my foreign speech. He did not want me in the car. Carefully I explained about the tourist boat from Vienna and suddenly his face cleared with relief, he did not need to give me a lift, the dock I wanted was just beyond the naval yard. He got out of his car the better to point where I should go.

I found the DDGS vessel *Carpathia*. A solitary soldier with a rifle slung across his shoulders was on guard at the gangway. He was talking with an elderly, nondescript-looking man. I wanted to go on board and see the captain; I went to do so but the soldier stopped me. 'Captain?' I asked. 'I–Captain,' said the nondescript man. I tried speaking German but he only knew a word or two. Then the purser came ashore to see what I wanted. He was an Austrian and spoke fluent English. I asked if I could get passage to Cernavodă where the tour ended. He said it was not possible. I asked why not, and stressed that I would pay. He asked the captain who shrugged. They did not take on single passengers. I persisted. Then I told him I had come down the Danube all the way from Donaueschingen which certainly intrigued him and he softened. 'Perhaps,' he said; they would talk about it. The two of them left me with the soldier and wandered back across the gangplank deep in conversation. The young soldier assumed I was up to some kind of dishonest enterprise and smiled with friendly complicity.

The purser now returned alone. He was sorry but no. The ship had been chartered by a group to take them from Vienna to Cernavodă and back. He wouldn't mind, it was a nice idea, but the captain would get into trouble. The Rumanians, he added, checked the manifest and the passenger list three times a day and there would be a great commotion if they suddenly found me aboard. The captain did not dare, it was more than his job was worth. This did not quite fit with the relaxed attitude of the captain but I could tell that bureaucracy and fear of officialdom had won. As a matter of form I made a last effort then we shook hands and I headed back to town.

Back at Rumanian Railways I discovered I could only get to Cernavodă via Bucharest which I intended to visit anyway. I repeated the journey of the night before to Videle where I caught one of the double-decker commuter trains to Bucharest. The train was crammed, mainly with peasant farmers, and stopped everywhere. I was surrounded by peasants on their way to the Bucharest markets: they carried buckets of produce and live chickens tied by their legs. They were gnarled, seam-faced, dirty, garlic-smelling and they smoked and talked nonstop. People crowded on at each stop while hardly anyone got off. At last we reached Bucharest; by then it had turned into another wet grey day. I asked a man directions. He spoke some Italian and insisted on walking a distance with me to ensure I went the right way. I always met extraordinary courtesy when I sought directions.

I saw a number of food queues and thought of taking a photograph then decided against doing so, an instinct which turned out to be correct.

In the centre of the city I found the main tourist agency. I wanted quite a bit of information: about trains to Cernavodă, about the Delta and about trains home when my trip came to an end. On the whole they were not helpful. They spoke English but they hassled me and seemed concerned only to sell tours or flights and preferably those which would extract the maximum foreign exchange from my rapidly diminishing stock.

I lunched at the huge Intercontinental Hotel which rises a dominant skyscraper in the centre of the city. The more such hotels I saw behind the Iron Curtain the more convinced I became that they represent a contradiction in terms, but the Rumanians are desperate for hard currency. The first, special item on the lunch menu was Russian caviar which had to be paid for in American dollars. I had decided to have an expensive lunch as compensation for my cramped railway journey of the morning although, despite the general crowding and dirt, I had developed an affection for the CFR (Rumanian Railways). Huge American portions of food were served, yet there was no fresh fruit on offer in a fruit-growing country. I ordered one of the few Rumanian dishes on the menu–a mincemeat wrapped in cabbage leaves and served with spicy sauce–and when I told the waitress that it was one of the most tasty dishes I had eaten since coming to Rumania she was astonished and then, suddenly, pleased.

At the next table sat nine smartly dressed men, seven Rumanians entertaining two Americans. It was a business lunch. The maître d'hôtel, a portly woman dressed in black, hovered about their table, fussing and laughing at their comments so I surmised they were important comrades.

At the central railway booking office I managed, after a good deal of effort, to obtain a ticket and a reserved seat on the late afternoon train to Cernavodă. The two women who dealt with my request pressed relentlessly for cigarettes which I did not possess. Then, with the afternoon free, I set off to explore Bucharest.

I came upon an interesting square whose far side was occupied by an ornate building which I took to be a museum. I decided to take a photograph, especially as I had taken none of the capital. At the

167

corner where I had entered the square was a substantial building with half a dozen steps leading up to large, double glass doors. These were locked and inside was a bare rotunda-shaped hall without any sign of occupation. I put my pack on the top of the steps and took out my camera. When I had taken a photograph of the 'museum' I noticed a small, interesting-looking church wedged between two much larger buildings on the second side of the square. For this I needed my telephoto lens and, still on my vantage-point at the top of the steps, I proceeded to change lenses. Twice while taking these pictures I noticed people looking at me oddly as they passed but the fact only half registered.

I had just completed the second shot when I became aware of a large military gentleman who had materialised at my side. He had various insignia, crossed weapons and pips, on his epaulettes and also seemed to be in a high temper. 'Come, come,' he said. At least that is what he appeared to mean. He delivered the words with the peremptory knowledge that the military are obeyed. I then saw that the double doors of the building on whose steps I had been standing were now open. He had come from inside and other soldiers were moving across the hall between its various doors; the place had come to life and it seemed I had taken up my position on the steps of a military establishment.

There was a low table to one side of the hall with a chair behind it. My officer led the way to this and sat abruptly in the seat facing me across the table.

'Passeport, passeport,' he demanded, pronouncing an 'ee' in the middle of the word.

'Do you speak English?' I asked.

'Passeport, passeport,' he reiterated.

'*Sprechen Sie Deutsch?*'

'Passeport.'

'*Parlez-vous francais?*'

'Passeport.'

So I produced my passport. He took out a small pocket book into which he began laboriously to transcribe my passport details. Since there was no other chair I perched on the side of the table. Another senior officer came up. He inquired of the first who was busily writing in his notebook and the word 'photo' was the only one I understood. The large hall had suddenly become busy with a variety of military personnel scurrying back and forth. I got the impression I had stumbled upon headquarters, the hub of Rumanian military planning. I turned to the second officer.

'Do *you* speak English?'

'*Nix*,' and he shook his head.

'*Sprechen Sie Deutsch?*'

'*Nix, nix.*'
'*Parlez-vous francais?*'
'*Nix.*'

He smiled faintly at my persistence: we were performing a ritual that was meaningless. Eventually the first officer finished taking details of my passport. He handed it back to me.

'*Ambassade,*' he said, '*ambassade.*'

'Yes,' nodded number two, '*ambassade, ambassade.*'

I gathered that a formal complaint was to be made to the British Ambassador. The first officer was still in a rage: possibly because in the new enlightened Rumania he was not allowed to take me straight to prison. Or perhaps his rage stemmed from the fact that I had dared to use the steps of their building. Number two, however, said: 'Photo'–and made a negative sign with head and hands, 'nix.' Then he smiled and indicated that I could leave. He walked with me to the doors and once more shook his head in a negative yet sympathetic way. I crossed the square to see what building I had photographed: the 'museum' turned out to be the Ministry of Economic Planning. The church, of course, was firmly locked.

I continued my walk along a busy main street thronged with people until I came to a charming park laid out in a long avenue with beds of red flowers between lawns and pathways down either side shaded by overhanging trees. It was not unlike a formal English garden. I wanted a photograph but fearful of more military descending upon me I looked surreptitiously to right and left and only when satisfied that no uniform was in sight did I whip out my camera. I took a picture at speed, furtively, like a bad professional spy. Anyone observing me would have decided at once that I was a suspicious character. But nothing happened, I was ignored. I walked through the park and found a café overlooking a lake where, happily and inexpertly, people were enjoying themselves in small rowing boats. I enjoyed a long cold beer.

The train was a holiday special to the Black Sea. I shared a compartment with an old matriarch, two large blond Norwegian girls, a friendly elderly man and a young man who could not take his eyes off the Norwegian girls and fancied himself as something of a Lothario. The Norwegians were not impressed and after a while, angry and humiliated, he went into the corridor for a smoke. The old matriarch eyed us in turn from beneath half-closed lids, a look of deep suspicion furrowing her brows. It was a two-hour run with only a few stops and the train was clean. The countryside remained flat, part of the Great Plain along the north of the Danube.

Cernavodă lies on one bank of the Danube; the railway station is high above the river on the other side, for here the river has ceased to act as the boundary with Bulgaria and a ferry connects station and town. Further downstream the railway crosses the Danube over a dramatic high bridge. Trajan built a line of fortifications from Cernavodă to the Black Sea at Constanţa and traces of these can still be found.

The matriarch also got off at Cernavodă and graciously permitted me to help her with her luggage until a relative came along the track to find her. The passengers trooped down a steep hill to the waiting ferry which was battered and ancient but serviceable. More heavy rain had fallen and when we reached the town side we had to pick our way over an expanse of waterlogged mud to reach drier land. Cernavodă looked dilapidated although on hills above the town were some new high-rise apartment blocks. I went in search of a hotel but found nothing. Eventually I stopped a man to inquire and after some difficulty the word 'hotel' registered. He laughed at this, intrigued, looked me over and then signalled me to follow. He led me to a side street and there, sure enough, was a small crumbling hotel.

A friendly woman in reception greeted me volubly in Rumanian. A single room? Well yes, that could be arranged. She consulted her register, nodded, demanded my passport. Slowly, over 20 minutes, she entered the required details. She became confused: it was a British passport, I was a UK citizen and had been born in England. When at last these details had been set down and digested she made some extraordinary mathematical calculations and came up with the odd figure of 62 lei (£3.60) as the price of my room for the night. Other names in her register had 35 lei (£2.00) against them so I assumed they were sharing. Finally she led me up to my room which turned out to be the best in the hotel. I asked where the toilet was and she went along the corridor well ahead of me to flush it. This was interesting: exciting hope and suspicion at the same time. At least she felt there might be a toilet problem. It turned out to be better than some but she had been right: there was a toilet problem.

It was then about five minutes to eight and I went downstairs in search of food and drink. 'No,' she firmly replied. There was no food and no drink. It was too late. I told her I had seen a café down the road. She shook her head negatively. I insisted I was hungry and with resignation she shrugged–yes, try them if you like, was her attitude, but you will learn. I entered an attractive café, at least the decor was pleasant, where several people were sitting at tables but no food was in sight. I took my place at a table but though my presence was noted no one came to serve me. Three youths then entered to be told the café was closed. I approached the woman who had told the youths to go: food? drink? anything? No! There was no food, no drink, they were closed. There was nowhere else. It was too late! In fact it had just struck eight. Outside it drizzled but I wandered in the muddy streets and through a forlorn little park until the rain increased in intensity and I returned to my hotel. I tried once again to interest the landlady in providing me with food but to no avail. In my room the light was too dim to permit reading without damaging my eyes so I tried to sleep, listening to the cries of children splashing in the mud of the street below my window.

Chapter Twenty Five

To the Black Sea

I knew I would not get any breakfast and despite my landlady's gesture the lavatory was unusable. On the other hand my room had once seen better days and been quite well furnished. Idly in the early hours of the morning, as it became light, I made an inventory of its contents. The carpet was threadbare and holed, vaguely pink and yellow though so faded as to render impossible any deciphering of its original design. A square table covered by white cloth occupied the centre of the room; there was a dirty upright chair beside it whose covered seat was also holed. The bed was comfortable, the linen and blankets an off-colour. There was a large chintz-covered easy chair and a wardrobe of cheap plain wood. The focus of the room, standing floor to ceiling in one corner, was a huge brown-tiled stove. It must have made the room like an oven in winter but may also have been expected to heat half the hotel. The washbasin was filthy; under it a plastic wastepaper basket acted as an overflow, catching more drips than went down the leaking pipe. There was also a little sideboard and a trestle for cases. All this had been available to me at 62 lei (£3.60) for the night.

A train left early for Constanţa. I packed and went down to leave for the first ferry. So far I had not seen another guest. I discovered that the glass door separating the reception hall from the guest rooms was locked, trapping me at the bottom of the stairs. I tapped, I knocked louder, I called. No answer. Perhaps the landlady thought I and all the other guests had already left and had gone out for the day, locking the door behind her for security. It was not secure. I examined it and reckoned I could take out one of the glass panels and open the door within five minutes. I examined the window at the bottom of the stairs: this was small, not designed to open, and would take a little longer. I pondered. I did not want to dismantle her door but nor did I wish to miss the ferry and my train. I was contemplating this curious situation when a couple followed by a

single man came down the stairs. I demonstrated our plight. Each
in turn examined the door and one of the men rattled it a good deal
more fiercely than I had done. We stood jointly bemused, thinking
out the next step when the landlady came in from the street. She
fetched keys from her desk and released us. There followed some
voluble but on the whole good-humoured argument and as far as I
could judge the landlady got the better of it. I left them busy together
and headed for the ferry. It was raining again.

The Danube was churlish and heavy to suit the day. The steady
rain made the water almost black and the rippling waves, slight yet
persistent, gave to this stretch of river a sea-like quality. A short
distance downstream of Cernavodă the Danube swings due north to
run parallel with the Black Sea coast, sometimes in two branches,
until at Galaţi it turns sharply east again before spreading out in its
great delta. The station waiting room was dirty, full of large sluggish
flies. The people looked drab, their dress a replica of a Hollywood
film of a Communist country. At least the train was fast. Constanţa,
which is the Rumanian Blackpool, was a diversion away from the
line of the Danube. In the large railway station I saw overnight trains
arriving from Moscow, East Germany, Prague and elsewhere in
eastern Europe bringing the holidaymakers to town.

Walking along a road high above extensive docks and marshalling
yards I considered that the scene spread out below me did indeed
represent a perfect spy shot for any photographer: a revelation of
the country's industrial activity. The marshalling yards were full,
great trains (one loaded with new tractors, for example) waited to
move out and I determined to take some photographs. I am not
actually a spy but I do like industrial shots. So, mindful of my
encounter with the soldiers in Bucharest, I found a convenient tree
and, putting that between me and the road, I stood somewhat
precariously at the top of a steep, muddy slope–the beginning of
the high embankment down to the railway yards far below–to take
pictures.

I found a *brasserie* with pretensions to style where an old woman
with a trolley was putting bottles of beer, mineral water and wine
into ice buckets beside each table. It was still only half past nine but
there must have been a dozen customers scattered about the large
restaurant. While I ate breakfast the old woman made a new round
of the tables putting chunks of ice into the buckets.

The residential and shopping area of Constanţa is on a cliff well
above the Black Sea. The sea was grey-blue and glassy smooth, the
rain had ceased and a pale sun was peering through high. wispy
clouds. On the horizon ships were silhouetted against a light grey
sky as they waited to come into port.

The day was cool and few people were on the beach beneath the cliffs when I went walking on the sands. Later, at an open-fronted bar facing the sea, I found myself surrounded by holidaymakers from a number of countries, almost all of them in groups on arranged tours. When I changed money Czechs ahead of me were changing a single cheque for 100 lei (£6) each. Such a sum was not going to last them long even if their room and board had been paid in advance. There were some interesting peasant faces, tough and careworn, the faces of workers. Constanţa was clearly for the masses; more elite, expensive holidays had to be taken elsewhere.

As I strolled about the bustling centre of the town looking at shops full of tawdry holiday goods I was approached more than once by moneychangers. They would walk beside me for a few paces mouthing 'money–you want lei–good rates?' They tried German first, then English. I would pretend not to know what they wanted until I got them to talk English. They were fluent in languages, or at least in those phrases necessary to further their occupation. Once, as I waited at a busy crossing, two men appeared on either side of me. 'You wish to change money?' they asked in unison in English. I am not sure whether it was an accident, whether there had been a race to see who could reach me first, or whether one was a moneychanger and the other a secret policeman working in harness to catch Western tourists. I didn't want to change any money.

Constanţa has long been an important port, its mass holiday business is a recent development. Ovid was exiled to Tomiş as Constanta was known in Roman times, and he complained of his life on the frozen banks of the Danube.

From Constanţa I went to Tulcea at the head of the Delta. I was frustrated more than once along the lower Danube when I tried to travel on the river. This in any case is something of a problem as I had discovered when I was a passenger on the barges, for once you are being carried it is impossible to stop when and where you wish. Thus in Austria I had passed Melk and other historic places in the night. I could have travelled from Vienna to Cernavodă on one of the DDGS tourist steamers but that would have defeated my whole purpose. At Cernavodă I discovered I could only travel on the river in one of the tourist buses and decided against it. So, once more, I found myself travelling by train. The nature of the land changes as you approach the Delta. We passed through low hills and long stretches of oak forest, a small variety of the tree for which the region is famous.

The first sight of Tulcea from the train was of an industrial wasteland. A huge aluminium plant belches forth grey-white smoke all day long, often blanketing the town in mist. I booked into the Delta Hotel which I intended to make my base. My tenth-floor balcony looked down on the 'pool' of Tulcea which is the port serving the two southern branches of the Delta–the Sulina and St George. Cargo vessels up to 5,000 tons use it and a short distance below the town Rumania's naval vessels, low-lying sleek grey craft, were moored ready to move out for action in the Black Sea. Everywhere in the Delta one is aware of water. Here it is almost as though the great Danube has become tired of its long journey before finally coming to rest: instead of the huge river single-mindedly forcing its way to the Black Sea it develops a dilettante, lazy character, splitting into three arms and then, even between these, it plays tricks by dividing again, losing itself in a great stretch of lakes and reeds and little channels.

The staff of the hotel must have just completed a course in hotel management. They certainly tried very hard. In the dining room that evening the waiters were all dressed in dark blue suits, white shirts and dark ties, the waitresses looked even more severe in dark blue skirts and tops, black stockings and white oversocks. A young man who appeared to be headwaiter served me. He spoke a little German, but I felt he needed taking in hand: not for his German, which was hardly my province, but because of the way he served. He was in too much of a hurry. He brought me one course before the previous one was finished. On this occasion (for it was a top holiday hotel) I had a salad, a main course and, for once, a sweet. I had just received my small dish of caramel when he brought me the bill. I told him I also wanted coffee, so he took the bill away to bring it back suitably amended with the coffee. I then asked for brandy at which he became flustered, clearly unused to such pressures.

We were serenaded throughout the meal. Two men in national costume, soulful and doleful-looking men with receding hairlines, came among the tables to play to us. The leader was the versatile one. He began playing what looked like a set of Pan pipes, switched to a flute and later to a set of bagpipes. His companion played a sad violin. He played so execrably badly that it took time to work out each new tune for he did produce theoretically recognisable nostalgia such as *Ave Maria*. Usually I had just determined what one piece was meant to be when, with a squeak rather than a flourish, he brought it to a conclusion. I felt that a lifetime of such playing deserved some reward, for they looked exhausted with the sadness of their own performances and this led me to take pity on them at one point during the meal when, rashly, I smiled at them to show how I appreciated their efforts. That was a mistake. In gratitude for a gesture of recognition which, I suspect, was all too rare they came to stand behind me to wail, screech and moan their music into my ears.

175

Chapter Twenty Six

The Delta

Tulcea is another city which, like Rome, claims to have been built on seven hills. It is a pleasant town though the aluminium works seem determined to smoke it out. On my first morning I heard a ship's foghorn and went onto my balcony. Below me, nosing its way out of a thick mist which entirely obscured the opposite river bank, was a large ship heading downstream for the Black Sea. It made a dramatic picture and earned my first photograph of the day. Then, with sudden abruptness, the wind changed direction, the mist disappeared and I realised it was not mist at all but smoke from the great chimneys of the aluminium plant. Rumania needs to become pollution-conscious if it is not to do irreparable damage to the ecology of the Delta.

Tulcea has a long history and some attractive architecture: in the hill streets behind the waterfront an elegant pencil-like minaret, all that remains of the Turkish mosque, marks the beginning of an area of nineteenth-century houses and winding back streets.

The triangle of the Delta between the northern Chilia branch of the river and the southern St George's branch covers about 2,600 square kilometres (1,000 square miles). Most of this area consists of marsh and lakes (Col. pl. 19). The third or middle branch of the Danube, the Sulina, runs in a straight line due east from Tulcea to the Black Sea. Since earliest times there has been argument as to the number of mouths the Delta possesses. Herodotus, writing of Darius' campaign against the Scythians, gives the Delta five arms. Strabon of Pontus, writing in the first century after Christ, gives it seven arms. Pliny the Elder speaks of six arms.

The Danube is an alluvial river and carries an estimated two tons of alluvial deposits per second to the Delta mouth which is currently extended a further 40 metres (130 ft) a year. The Chilia branch of the river with its numerous mouths pours 85 cubic metres (3,000 cubic feet) of sand and mud into the sea every minute.

The Delta's great attraction is its wildlife; it is one of the last remaining wildlife reserves in Europe. The region is a sanctuary for birds, many of which come from outside Europe. About 250 species have been recorded here and the Delta is the natural halting place for migrating birds. The more spectacular birdlife ranges from cormorants, roseate pelicans, herons, storks and spoonbills to ibis, mallard, sheldrake, marsh harriers and isolated sea eagles. The Delta's mammals include wolves and foxes, wild boar, otter, the curious enot dog and wild cat. Carp, pike, tench and bream are abundant throughout the Delta's waters and the common sturgeon is also found.

The Delta is being developed as a tourist area. Rumanians who can afford to do so take their holidays here–my friend Dudu had come with his family the previous year–and it is being opened increasingly to tourists from all over Europe, both east and west.

One trip I made in the Delta was on a small pleasure craft with a number of other tourists and Mr Gigi, a Rumanian teacher who acted as a guide. He had about as much German as I and when this failed sign language supported by his Rumanian and my English sufficed. There was an American couple, something of a tourist rarity, in the group: John and Helen Keene. He was a retired Methodist minister and both were concerned with the peace movement. 'I am not really political,' he told me, 'but everyone has to be against the bomb.' We discussed politics as we chugged through Delta streams or into its lakes, constantly on the lookout for rare birds. We saw herons, ibis and cormorant as well as many seagulls but nothing more exciting.

I learnt a new technique from John Keene who carried a polaroid camera with him. Its value, he claimed, lay in its capacity to win instant friends with the instant pictures he could produce of the people they met. He proved his point on board our craft. He took a picture of Mr Gigi who roared with delight. The captain then appeared and wanted his picture taken. John obliged. A pretty Rumanian mother with two small daughters looked longingly at the camera so John photographed the children–to their excitement and their mother's gratitude. 'You see,' he said turning to me; but he ran out of film during the cruise and in the end had to disappoint others who also wished to have their pictures taken. He said the polaroid had been an infallible aid to them both while travelling in eastern Europe. Once people knew they would have a picture it became easy to get into conversation and make friends.

We took lunch at the riverside hotel at Maliuc and then lost ourselves in the endless stretch of flat marshlike Delta, the green reeds waving elegantly against the wind-disturbed blue waters. At our approach flocks of birds rose with a great rustling and flapping of wings. The Keenes were the personification of genuinely humble Christian people not easy to find. We had supper together on our return that evening and were treated once more to the extraordinary musical performance of the sad duo of players.

Discontent stems from what people do not have. The West is so arrogant about its best attributes–the open nature of its societies for example–that it spoils the effect, while the vulgar flaunting of its material power is one of its least pleasant characteristics. Yet in countries such as Rumania, which by comparison with the West have so little material wealth, the simple delight that John Keene gave by taking his polaroid shots of people brought home the difference between what in the West is taken for granted but elsewhere is a luxury.

On a prominent hill behind Tulcea a tall monument commemorates Rumania's independence. This was gained from Turkey as a result of the Russo-Turkish war of 1876–80. On a clear evening it is possible from this height to see miles down the Sulina branch of the Danube along which oceangoing ships are anchored. Rumania was directly ruled by Turkey until 1821, when the Ottoman Turks permitted the Rumanians to elect their own rulers. In 1866 Prince Charles of Hohenzollern-Sigmaringen (whose castle I had visited a long way back on my Danube journey) was elected ruler and following Rumania's independence in 1880 the country became a kingdom (1881) and Prince Charles its first king.

I spent time exploring the Delta, meandering for two days in a little boat rowed by a vodka-addicted guide whose silences were so stunning I never even learnt his name. That was peace indeed! Then I made a final trip down the Sulina to the port of the same name on the Black Sea. Sulina was a sleepy place although a number of quite large ships were docked along the river front. There were some interesting nineteenth-century buildings with a familiar Rumanian appearance of slightly crumbling decay including a finely decorated church, firmly locked as usual. On a promontory along the north shore of the Sulina by the Black Sea stands a small elegant lighthouse. Men sat along the riverbank fishing and familiar strings of black barges passed hooting out to sea. I sat opposite this little lighthouse and decided that it marked the end of my Danube journey–2,840 kilometres (1,765 miles) from the crystal clear pool in the gardens of the *Schloss* at Donaueschingen.

The sight of a familiar barge nosing its way out of the Sulina into the Black Sea made me wonder, for I had thought they confined themselves to the river: perhaps it meant to hug the shoreline on its way to one of the other Delta ports. As I viewed the elegant little lighthouse Donaueschingen seemed very remote. Since then the Danube had passed through many transformations and I had seen it in a variety of changing moods. The sparkling stream of Baden-Württemburg, whose passage through the gorge at Beuron appeared to have been engineered by a friendly god creating a fault in the rocks for it to pass through, had become the axis of war from Ulm to beautiful ancient Regensburg.

Then, while it acted as a great highway, regulated by locks, argued over by ecologists, sometimes a mile wide, its progress from Regensburg to the sea had the quality of a triumphant military commander advancing unstoppable to his goal. The cities along its banks are famous the world over, their names part of the fabric of European history. Ulm, Ingolstadt, Regensburg or Passau in Germany, Linz and Vienna in Austria, Bratislava, Budapest, Belgrade are not just ancient centres of arts and commerce or famous capitals. They also represent Europe's astonishing mixture of races and cultures. In this respect the Danube ranks with the world's ancient cradles of civilisation: the Nile, the Indus and the Yellow River.

The different moods of the river—fickle and sparkling in the sunshine, grim and surly under dark cloud, roiling and defiant in the rain—are all expressions of an ancient, subtle, arrogant and powerful deity whose passage across Europe from west to east has fashioned half the continent.

In Tulcea I had a final appointment before taking the overnight train to Bucharest. I had asked the guide, Mr Gigi, to have a drink with me. I had got to know him quite well during my stay in Tulcea and we had become friends. Mr Gigi was dressed in a natty suit of chocolate brown; he wore a dark shirt and tie and a white linen cap which was firmly in place on his head at all times. He was a square, thickset man who seemed to know everybody, but since he acted as a Delta guide perhaps that was not surprising. He had helped me book tickets and make other arrangements and accompanied me on my trip with the Keenes.

While waiting for Mr Gigi I visited the hotel's hard currency shop to buy him some cigarettes. By then I was very short of hard currency myself but the shop displayed a brand new Diners Card sign so I offered my card in payment for my purchases. The young shop assistant examined it and told me I was the first person to present one. Would I help him fill in the receipt? I did so. This took some time as we carefully went over each entry together. When at last he was satisfied I signed and took my modest purchases. Mr Gigi arrived punctually at seven and we headed for the bar but the young man from the shop now called to me: Could I help him with one more detail? I did so and he gave me a can of German beer to celebrate his first Diners Club customer.

Mr Gigi and I shared a bottle of red wine and sat on the hotel balcony overlooking the wide Danube 'pool' of Tulcea. According to Mr Gigi we were drinking a wine reserved for tourists: it was certainly very pleasant. We discussed politics. He told me of the restrictions placed upon Rumanians who wish to travel even if they can find the money with which to do so. He described the paucity of goods in the shops and their general shoddiness. I had seen evidence of this at Constanţa which was well stocked for the summer tourists. All the country's best products, he said, its wine and fruit, were exported.

Mr Gigi was a schoolteacher and he taught boxing. He apologised: he would have liked to invite me to his home for supper but his wife had not been expecting anyone. I think he was embarrassed at what he might or might not have to offer me, which was a pity. I asked him about Rumania and the Russians. He laughed and then, slowly in German, trying to translate from memory the English proverb, he said: 'While we choose our friends you are stuck with your brothers–your comrades.' At the addition of comrades he giggled. The wine was taking effect.

We finished our wine and had a glass of cognac. He toasted me in Rumanian: 'Noroc si sanatate.' I gave him the cigarettes I had bought. Finally, as the setting sun turned the belching smoke from the aluminium plant into a brilliant red glow against the evening sky, we shook hands and he weaved his way through the crowded tables to turn at the door and raise his hand in salute before he reeled happily home. 'Noroc si sanatate.'

It was a beautiful evening; before it finally disappeared the sun made the Danube glisten. For my supper I had fish which I shared with a thin voracious little cat which appeared beneath my table, its hunger overcoming its timidity. A pleasantly drunk beggar, the first I had come across in Rumania, approached my table and asked in good German for drinking money. I gave him the price of a beer. In the dark I found my way to the station and settled into the train for Bucharest.